All Geographers Should Be Feminist Geographers

All Geographers Should Be Feminist Geographers

CREATING CARE-FULL ACADEMIC SPACES

LINDSAY NAYLOR
WITH CONTRIBUTIONS FROM
EMERALD L. CHRISTOPHER, EDEN KINKAID,
CAROLINE FARIA, AND LATOYA E. EAVES

THE UNIVERSITY OF GEORGIA PRESS
Athens

Most University of Georgia Press titles are
available from popular e-book vendors.

Printed digitally

EU Authorized Representative
Easy Access System Europe—Mustamäe tee 50, 10621
Tallinn, Estonia, gpsr.requests@easproject.com

Library of Congress Cataloging-in-Publication Data

Names: Naylor, Lindsay author
Title: All geographers should be feminist geographers : creating care-full
    academic spaces / Lindsay Naylor ; with contributions from
Emerald L. Christopher, Eden Kinkaid, Caroline Faria, and Latoya E. Eaves.
Description: Athens : The University of Georgia Press, [2025] |
    Series: Geographies of justice and social transformation |
    Includes bibliographical references and index.
Identifiers: LCCN 2025019875 | ISBN 9780820366289 hardback |
    ISBN 9780820374208 paperback | ISBN 9780820374215 epub |
    ISBN 9780820374222 pdf
Subjects: LCSH: Feminist geography | Geography—
    Study and teaching (Higher)—United States
Classification: LCC HQ1233 .N35 2025
LC record available at https://lccn.loc.gov/2025019875

To all those who are openly defiant against universalizing systems.
For scholars of geography everywhere, an urgent call to be the now.

Look closely at the present you are constructing.
It should look like the future you are dreaming.

ALICE WALKER

CONTENTS

FIGURES

FOREWORD

Feminism of Futures Past

> To be truly visionary we have to root our imagination in our concrete
> reality while simultaneously imagining possibilities beyond that reality.
>
> —*bell hooks* (2000, 110)

During the spring of 2024, I came across a now-deleted viral video on social
media. The user had someone film her doing certain tasks while she listed
reasons why she is not a feminist. The most popular portion of the video is
her statement "I'm not a feminist. I can actually cook" as she slides a plate of
pasta toward the camera. Other social media users stitched this segment to
offer their own response. Those reactions often feature women stating "I'm a
feminist. Now watch me cook" as they show themselves performing their jobs.
Lawyers, doctors, pilots, and countless others used the platform to demonstrate what feminism can look like.

There is a stark contrast between the original post and the responses. While
the original video ridicules feminism through stereotypes, the responses are
powerful in that they do not demean those who choose to be homemakers or
subscribe to perceived "traditional" feminine norms. Rather, the replies reflected a different form of "cooking," and the value women bring regardless of
what they choose to do.

Despite the counterstatements and countervideos, in 2024 stereotypes and
myths of feminism persist. Feminists can cook, have a career, have children,
wear makeup, love men, love women, and so much more. Yet feminism is diluted to tasks and often serves as a political pawn to distract from the actual
implications of feminism.

While it has a variety of definitions, at its core, feminism as a framework
incorporates a range of ideologies that aim to ensure that political, economic,
and social outcomes are not dictated based on one's identity. While all movements for progress may not use the feminist label, the core work of building a
more just society is still the driving factor.

Opposition to the actual work of feminism—whether it is exercising the vote, accessing education, holding a bank account in one's own name, not defining oneself as property, or critiquing gendered divisions of labor and the healthcare system—means that myths and stereotypes of feminism continue to be remanufactured. They are remade under the guise that feminism is about individual mannerisms and behaviors, versus a collective approach in generating possibilities for resistance.

An opposition to feminism is a dissent against a reorganization of society into an equitable and inclusive one. An opposition to feminism attempts to uphold a division in society in which women in particular are relegated to the private sphere. An opposition to feminism upholds restrictive gender ideologies in an attempt to fuel a neoliberal state. It is the structural power of neoliberalism that also fuels a restructuring of feminism from the collective to the individual. That restructuring is exemplified in the individual tasks highlighted in the viral social media post as well as the first-person accounts in the responses.

A neoliberal state results in hierarchies of human value that have material, representational, discursive, and political consequences for marginalized, occupied, and subjugated populations. Examining the ways feminism can be applied to multiple disciplines and areas of life is key to developing strategies to address the failures of neoliberal ideals of freedom, citizenship, belonging, autonomy, property, and land.

Despite my disagreement with feminist opposition and the neoliberal state, I make no claim that the processes and practices of feminism are without critique. While the scholarly fields of women's and gender studies focus on applying a feminist lens to cultural, social, and political issues, oftentimes that "lens" is marred in specificities that have a historical level of exclusion. This is ironic at best given that the most basic understanding of feminism is based on inclusion. However, there has been a history of exclusionary practices within feminism. For instance, while the passage of the Nineteenth Amendment in the United States is heralded as a feminist accomplishment, there continues to be a struggle in acknowledging the historic racism, classism, and homophobia that existed in the women's movement of the time. That specific history is integral to understanding how feminism has been shaped, received, and experienced by people. We should therefore question exclusionary and gatekeeping aspects of feminism, just as we should question the impact neoliberalism has had on feminism.

One such impact is the extent to which feminism is packaged within the neoliberal university, often sited in women's and gender studies departments, if they exist, and seen as a niche politic rather than a visible and expansive politic. It is important that we challenge the notion that efforts to exclude feminism from disciplines are individual anomalies. Instead, we must treat these actions as intentional strategy in addressing representational economies and controlling images that lead to differential suffering.

Feminism of futures past refers to the ways in which the past has shaped the present. Today's pursuits are as much about the future as they are about the past. Feminism of futures past conceptualizes history to open spaces for, and connections to, the generative possibilities for resistance in the present and future. What makes this moment in history different is our capacity to refer to the past and see how feminism changed the sociopolitical landscape. Within those collective movements of change, feminism was challenged and critiqued along the way. Those challenges and critiques did not stymie progress; rather, they broadened the reach and depth of feminism.

To dispute the endemic distortion of our lived realities, histories, and truths, we must name the effects of distortion and see feminism beyond the neoliberal manufactured version. Feminism isn't about one department or division conducting the work, and it isn't about a one-dimensional list of tasks or behaviors. Moreover, a feminist is not a monolith. Feminism of the past, present, and future provides us with a framework for possibility beyond our lived realities.

Emerald L. Christopher

FOREWORD

Transforming Geography

The discipline of geography is in dire need of transformational change. As inheritors and carriers of a colonial, racist, sexist, and queerphobic tradition, we can no longer rely on incremental progress to create the geography we want to see in the world.

Indeed, as I've argued elsewhere, the idea of progress itself is part of what stands in the way of transformational change in geography. Geography's "liberal progress narrative" (Oswin 2020, 11; and quoted in Kinkaid 2024, 193)—the story that geography is getting ever more self-conscious, ever more inclusive, ever more critical, ever more just as a simple function of the passage of time— gets in the way. It flattens the political spaces of our discipline into a nearly forgotten history; it excuses us from action and responsibility. Meanwhile, the discipline's progress appears painfully slow and never quite measures up to justice. How long must we wait for geography to change?

This story of geography leaves us waiting. It leaves some of us—trans, Black, Indigenous, minoritized—waiting for our "time to come," waiting for a space to open up, waiting for an audience for our voices, our struggles, our critical visions. It leaves us waiting for justice, for recognition; it leaves us waiting on and deferring to institutions that are content to reproduce the status quo or, worse yet, plunge us into precarity. It leaves us waiting forever for "an other geography" (Oswin 2020, 14), a living, bold, critical tradition that can keep pace with the ongoing crisis of our world.

What would it take to create this reimagined geography? What would transformational change look like for our discipline? How can we make this change happen, not in some deferred future, but now—in the spaces we work, teach, research, write, and imagine?

Transformational change looks like a wholesale reappraisal, a deep reckoning, a critical reorientation to our discipline, its history, its narratives, its identity, its legacies, its problems, its limitations, its exclusions. It requires that we take stock of our tradition with curiosity and critical clarity and ask how it might better deliver on its imagined intellectual, political, and creative potentials. It requires, in other words, that we care: that we care about the tradition we uphold, that we care what work our knowledge does in the world, that we recognize our responsibility for co-creating what is a staggeringly uneven and unjust world, and that we choose to throw our weight behind a vision and a project of a different world, a different institution, a different geography.

For the feminists among us, we realize that this care is work. To do the work of care requires acts of dismantling as much as acts of nurturance, acts of getting in the way (Ahmed 2023) as much as acts of holding space, acts of disruption as much as acts of reproduction. Indeed, we cannot create the conditions for a caring university, a caring geography, a caring world, without first addressing the systems of power and oppression that make the university so uncaring in the first place—a mirror for, rather than a sanctuary from, the larger world. It means, in other words, dismantling white supremacist cishetero patriarchy as it insinuates itself into our bodies, our spaces, our institutions, our discipline, our world. Caring thus requires that we become activists—maybe even that we become feminists—and activate our principles into a form of praxis to transform geography and its spaces toward a less oppressive, if not more liberatory, project; caring requires that, inspired by the possibilities of this new geography, we commit to the difficult and unending work of trying to build a world in its image.

In the book that follows, Dr. Lindsay Naylor develops the concept of care as an entry point for this critical reappraisal and for a radical reenvisioning of the discipline of geography, a geography that is not isolated from the broader world and its logics. Moving within and across the complex and often inequitable spaces of our universities, research, classrooms, and our broader world, Naylor envisions a feminist ethic of care as a means of reorienting our individual and collective work so that it might deliver on its liberatory aims and potentials.

Within this vision, feminism is not the sole purview of women, nor is it a project based solely on sex and gender-based equality. It is not the feminism of cishetero white women, but a vision moving toward alignment with intersectional and decolonial feminisms. In this vision, feminist geography is not a subfield or special interest group within geography; it is a fundamental challenge to the way we know and practice space, place, belonging, and the discipline of geography; it is a grounding ethical orientation. It is a project to democratize decision-making, share labor, and attend to the tedious and messy work of community, social reproduction, and institutional change. It is a commitment to reckoning with difference and inequality in our own lives, knowledge, and practices; dispensing with privileged ways of knowing and being; and acting in alignment with an ethos of care, reflexivity, and justice.

If this vision sounds unwieldy, multidirectional, and expansive, that is because it is: feminist geography, as Naylor envisions it, is nothing short of a project of world dismantling and world making. But in order to do more ethical, critical, and transformative work as geographers, as "writers of the earth," we must reckon with and resolve the ways systems of oppression shape and delimit our discipline and its imagination.

Where does the work begin? It begins literally anywhere: in the classroom, in the field, in our mentoring relations, in our writing, in our citational practices, in the service we perform to our discipline and institutions, in our imaginations. After reading the pages that follow, you will be equipped with a blueprint: a detailed statement of the problem and many ways that we might do something differently. Then it will be up to you to decide: Are you going to care? Are we going to care?

Eden Kinkaid

PREFACE

As this manuscript went into production in 2024, I planned no preface for it. Yet the first months of 2025 made me think otherwise. COVID-19 has been with us for five years. And in the intervening time we have seen war, genocide, revolution, and eroding democracy on a global scale.

I finished the first full draft of this manuscript at the end of 2023, not six months after the World Health Organization declared the end of the global health emergency brought on by COVID. As you will read further on, the care work and outpouring of demands for radical change to our institutions during the height of the pandemic are the foundations on which this book was built. I wrote to capture the threads of these ideas and to stitch them together, perhaps to make a patchwork quilt of love and care, hopes and dreams, toward a warming feminist geography. A place we could inhabit and grow.

I imagined a postpandemic life and the practices we would nurture. I imagined our collective work. I imagined being energized.

Today, I am exhausted.

This is a book about creating a care-full academy. *And we will need a care-full academy if we are to withstand this particular moment in time as academics.* Since the inauguration of the forty-seventh president in the United States, there have been dozens of executive orders issued and litigation-based responses. Groups of people dehumanized. Science defunded. The environment brutalized. Government hollowed out. It is a chaotic, hateful, and destructive campaign that we may not fully recover from in my lifetime.

But. I see the tiniest sliver of something shining through—in 2020, I wrote that we might not have felt prepared for a pandemic, but that we certainly had the tools to support one another through one if we just worked together.

Today, I see the collectives gathered during a global health emergency being activated once again or otherwise reinforced. What is more, I see refusals, resistance. I see accomplices and allies. I see skill lending and building. I see possibilities.

As a feminist political geographer, I have a lot I might say about the state of things both in the United States and globally. However, in the beginning pages of a book where I suggest that we could become the wildest manifestation of our dreams, I will put it simply: Things are not okay. Let's care for one another.

In solidarity—
February 2025

ACKNOWLEDGMENTS

It was a conversation with Joe Jasper that became the inspiration for this book, when he asked me how the academy would have to change to value all the missed work and undervalued labor we were seeing during shelter-in-place orders as a result of the COVID-19 pandemic. I said, "It would need to be feminist." At the same time, I was inspired by some in my larger academic network who pointed to hardships, demanded support for less secure groups, checked in with one another, and wondered how academia might change for the better when we emerged. Turns out, I was not the only one to find this spark and want to ignite the fire; many academics wrote papers, op-eds, and social media threads that I attempted to bring together in this space. It took me a long time to write this book because of the outpouring of demands for making an academy and a geography that cared—both in the published literature and across our institutions.

←◆→

bell hooks left this world while I was working on this manuscript, and that event was such a devastating loss to the feminist community and to Black intellectual thought more broadly. I could not have even considered such a book as this without the intellectual foundations of her teachings.

I say it took me a long time to write this book, and I repeat it, because along the way it became intensely personal. At some point in the rage I was feeling, I found that instead of using the words "world dismantling" I opted for "world destroying," which I had to go back and edit across many chapters of the manuscript. Some of the anecdotes shared herein come from a deep memory of care and neglect augmented by a present where I found it profoundly difficult to write a book about care in the academy while so much of the carelessness

I am writing against washed over me in wave after wave, some of them quite literally knocking me down. You are reading this because I was able to stand back up again, but only because of the support of others—those whom I attempt to honor herein.

I owe my first and utmost thanks to the Embodiment Lab for a generous read of the front matter of the proposal in late 2020. Georgie Ramsay sent me everything she saw coming out of the woodwork about care as part of her support of this project. I also appreciated evenings in the park and around the fire pit with Georgie and Andrew; I'm glad we're neighbors. The 2022 Embodiment Lab got to see the introduction that I finally dragged out of myself after much reading and rethinking. I absolutely thrived on the energy that came from that conversation, where we were joined by Becca Nixon, who jumped in with both feet (or perhaps headfirst?) to co-facilitate with me while at UD. We are better for the community we build in this collective space, and I hold it sacred. *You all give me life.*

I am grateful for the early and enthusiastic support of Julie Klinger and Nick Bojda. They helped me keep momentum when it was difficult to imagine taking on something that felt so immense in such an uncertain time. I had trouble making new memories in 2020, but I will never forget the two of them masked, winter cloaked, and sitting at our picnic table as we sat on the other side of the window screen, perched on the couch in the living room, and they let me read out the chapters I had planned.

My mom and stepdad were gracious in their support all around in ways I didn't know I needed, and that maybe seemed tangential to the writing of this book, but I am so deeply grateful for their love, understanding, and unwavering faith. A hearty pumpkin-dove salute to them both.

Encouragement from Mick Gusinde-Duffy early on (April 30, 2020, to be exact), when our original email thread had been about checking in and swapping our best stay-at-home beers and baking ideas, and I instead pitched this book, gave me the courage to pursue this idea. He also generously allowed me more time as the project took on a different depth. Thank you, Mick, from the bottom of my heart.

To the anonymous readers of my initial proposal and the first full draft of the book: my enormous thanks for what and where this manuscript might land based on your thoughtful and generous reviews. In a moment of uncertainty, you asked much of me in good faith, and I aspired to deliver. My goodness, I am grateful for you both.

Sofia Zaragocin kindly agreed to read the first draft of the first chapter of this book, the one I kept saying I would never get right, but I had to at least get somewhere. She provided me with such enthusiastic support, I felt like I was actually onto something. Jo Sharp offered initial comments on that chapter as well, buoying my spirits and sense of feminist solidarity in geography with her support.

Didi Martinez sent me photos of braided rivers from her fieldwork within minutes of me asking. She also dropped the concept of anastomosing into my life, and I am here for it! Connections and openings. I hope my river thinking makes her smile. I also hope we keep up our (old-made-new) tradition of kicking ass together!

Sarah Bednarz gave the chapter on reframing the other academic labor we do outside of research and teaching—a read that warmed my heart. And then she asked for other chapters to review because she was interested in what I was getting up to with the book! And gave even more wonderful feedback! I am still stunned and so grateful for the perspective she offered and the gentle nudges to not just write to my geography bubble.

Rebecca Lave took on the research chapter(s) and made me a better geographer with her edits and suggestions. Her encouragement and gratitude for the work we are doing powered me through some of the hardest bits of writing for the final chapters of this book. My goodness, I am glad she took on the ask of running (successfully) for American Association of Geographers (AAG) president.

Dydia DeLyser is someone I will always have stars in my eyes for. As the editor responsible for my first-ever paper, she absolutely ruined me for what it was like to write/edit/revise/publish a manuscript (read: she was generous and amazing). She also read the writing chapter of the manuscript, and, folks, I was grounded by her words and wisdom.

Mike DeVivo, generous as always, gave me comments on two chapters. I also wore my Grand Rapids gear—"nevertheless, she persisted"—more than once while working on this book. I appreciate being seen as an early and mid-career scholar through Mike's efforts with the Visiting Geographical Scientist Program and remain grateful for the mentoring spaces opened up therein.

I am thrilled and grateful that Caroline Faria graciously supported having her beautifully cutting height-of-the-pandemic piece inserted into *All Geographers Should Be Feminist Geographers* as an interlude, and that she showed such lovely excitement for the book!

This work was about half written when we had our first in-person AAG again in Denver in 2023, and I anxiously and excitedly pressed a printed copy of the draft into the hands of LaToya Eaves and asked her to consider writing the afterword. What LaToya has done for geography and geographers should make people stand up and take notice, and I am honored to have her friendship and her contribution to this book.

Eden Kinkaid was most generous with their read of the full manuscript, and I am honored by the creative directions they made me think in, as well as their willingness to write a foreword to the book. I owe them an intellectual debt that I will be paying forward with every day I seek a geography for here and now.

Emerald Christopher is my rock. At every step we held on to each other and the idea that what we believe and how we act matters. I thank her from the care-full place we aspire to inhabit, and also for taking on a feminisms foreword and letting me know I could maybe write across some potential interdisciplinary divides.

Nathan Thayer was reading and writing about care right alongside me the whole time I was drafting the first bits of the book. It was such a delight to have a companion on this intellectual journey. I appreciate the reading and writing time we established once again, and I'm so glad that James Bryan could join us in the middle, all of us working toward a finish line together. I am so deeply proud to have worked with both of them as we all moved through our own spaces of becoming. As my resident "teaching with care" expert, Nathan also took a first look at the introduction and the teaching chapter, and he pushed me on discomfort in ways for which I am most grateful. In addition, he read my self-dubbed "rage chapter" and liked it.

I am most appreciative of my students and mentors, past and present. I hope anyone who ever got an ask for a mentoring moment from me knows how deeply it has enriched my ways of being and knowing in the academy. I thank Shaul Cohen for early recognition and understandings of how I wanted to shape myself in the academy, and for always encouraging me to literally look up and figuratively shed the stars in my eyes; I am forever grateful for time spent in the earliest moments of my academic life.

Some folks don't know it, but conversations I had with them left me buzzing with ideas for these chapters. Tracy DeLiberty, Dana Veron, Fabrice Veron, Pinki Mondal, Chandranath Basak, Jen Biddle, Julie Maresca, Kyle Davis, Ben Stanley, Davy Knittle, Kelli Kerbawy (extra shout-out for all the fiction recommendations and good chats in PR and beyond), Gary Langham, Wendy Jepson (I thank my dear mentor from the bottom of my heart for taking my frantic pandemic calls), Coline Dony, Julaiti Nilupaer, Becca Nixon, Lily Assad, Chad Giusti, Liz Arcta, Vaish Tripuraneni, Kelsey Obringer, Angela Chen, Carrie Chennault, Alec Murphy, Corey Johnson, Derek Alderman, Nusrat Mohana,

Faisal Islam, Nora Lucas, Dharni Grover, Kaanan Thakkar, Emily Popielec, Kevin Oluoch, Naznin Sultana, Mehrnaz Haghdadi, and Manan Sarupria are all deserving of my deepest gratitude. Also, to everyone who wrote about care during the pandemic, I write this in deep appreciation for your ideas and gentle pushes, which I hope I've captured to some degree herein.

I was honored to be named a fellow of the American Association of Geographers—a title I do not take lightly—while writing this book. I hope I continue to advance the state of geography with these words. I am deeply grateful to Becky Mansfield for her support in this regard.

July 2023, as I was beginning to finish the first draft of this manuscript, presented me with enormous challenges that took me away from many of my scholarly commitments. I watched as years of effort by my partner were squandered away by petulant people, and I saw all of the ways they tried to take, take, take from us. The scales tipped in a terrifyingly dramatic and negative way—and then, miraculously, they were somewhat righted as we received overwhelming support from all corners of our world: Russ Yetter, Micha Becker-Klein, Sasha Aber, Craig Wensell, Amish Trivedi, Andrew (Co-mandante) Cabron and Georgie Ramsay, Luc Reilly, Chris Staheli, Kyle Davis and Glen Davis, Bhoktear Khan and Nusrat Mohana—y'all rock. I will never ever forget what you did to help us.

Finally, once again to Joe Jasper, I continue to marvel at the world with you. We don't finish each other's sentences; we add to them and make the narrative richer. I continue to thrive on the interwoven threads of our story.

Where Do We Go from Here?

The Care-Less Academy and State of Geography

> Caring is anxious—to be full of care, to be careful, is to take care of things
> by becoming anxious about their future, where the future is embodied in
> the fragility of an object whose persistence matters.
>
> —*Sara Ahmed* (2010, 186)

I am anxious about the state of geography. As geographers, we stand on a precipice—can we create the "just geographies" Raphael (2022) calls on us to provide in our earth writing, in our community? Will we accept the invitation to craft geography's future by reenvisioning its present (see Kinkaid 2024; Rose-Redwood et al. 2024)? I am anxious, but I am also full of hope and ready to maintain and uplift the work of making a geography of belonging in, around, and outside the academy. Are you hopeful? In this book, I make an offering for the here and now, toward the possibility that, rather than pursue a course that maintains a "care-less," exclusionary academy, we might perhaps look to more hopeful pursuits. I am not suggesting one right way out of here, but encouraging an approach that is multiple. I am hopeful that we will take what we know and work collectively, that we might make visible knowledges as we write the earth, that we might make a "care-full" academic space for geography and geographers.

The Academy Is Care-Less

We all require care.

Feminist scholars (among others) consistently call for attention to care and care ethics within the academy, as well as academic research and writing. Yet, as Lawson notes, even though care is a critical component of human life, it has remained on the margins of theory, heightening unequal relations along gender, race, and class lines (2009, 210). Despite increased attention to care in our research, Lawson's argument remains relevant. Oswin (2020) notes that a significant number of geographers are still othered and remain marginalized in geography, and calls on the discipline to create sites of solidarity in order to create "an other" geography.

Moreover, this marginalization neglects the role of the nonhuman and our earth others in relations of care. Care is brought to our attention by highlighting reproductive labor, such as social reproduction, relations of exchange, and affect. It is an everyday practice that takes place in public, private, and liminal spaces; it can be messy and entangled in power and resistance.

Feminist geographers began to draw attention to an ethic of care as a basis for creating change in all aspects of the academy.[1] This work represents a clarion call to not only examine care relations, but also respond to spaces that, as part of neoliberal shifts and hierarchies within the academy, have become increasingly "care-less" (Lawson 2009). Thus, in this book, I contend that more feminist training is needed for *all geographers* so that we can co-create a care-full geography of belonging. At the start, let us be clear: I am suggesting that in being feminist we will be conducting our earth writing with equity at the mantle.

The neoliberalization of the university has changed relations within higher education. As I have argued before, the university is now largely a site for creating consumers, not informed citizens (Naylor and Veron 2021; Naylor 2023). As I will discuss in more depth in chapter 5, the commodification of higher education stripped the public of any ability to claim a right to education (Connell 2013). Students became customers/debtors, and institutes of higher education became producers (Slaughter and Rhoades 2000). A neoliberal paradigm narrows the focus of higher education to what can be marketed. Indeed, Mountz et al. (2015) argue that success in the academy is now based on efficiency and productivity under a market logic that is damaging to how we produce knowledge as scholars.

In general, neoliberalism is a contemporary form of capitalism that reduces the role of the state and social services in favor of market-led approaches ensconced in the creation of profit and the protection of private property. In a system where what counts has to be quantifiable, many of the everyday workings that make the academy possible do not count and are therefore deprived of their value. The academy as a monolith has always operated to the benefit of some and the exclusion of others; that it has been captured by neoliberal currents reinforces such dynamics. I state this with the understanding that even as there are homogenizing tendencies, the academy at large is not defined by sameness and is actually quite messy.

I should further note, however, that some academic institutions were built out of this exclusionary character (historically Black colleges and universities [HBCUs], Hispanic serving institutions [HSIs], and Tribal colleges, for example). Thus, when I talk about exclusion in the institution in this book, I am largely referring to predominantly white institutions (PWIs) in the United States, such as the one I am based at. Nonetheless, the academy as a whole has been drawn into an (uneven) neoliberal fold.

Academia in the United States and elsewhere continues to be a place rife with uneven power dynamics, hierarchies, and care-less spaces. Narcissism and big egos, extraordinary labor demands and "shadow" service burdens, precarity, mental health issues, impostor syndrome, harassment and sexual assault, exclusion and marginalization, citation politics, and the myth of the autonomous academic exist in large measures today. Scholars and students experience harm and trauma, especially those who are Black, Indigenous and people of color (BIPOC), something that is often rendered invisible as part of what Hamilton (2020) calls the "white unseen." Simultaneously, networks of support, effective mentoring, peer-to-peer exchanges, community, collective action (including unionizing), and other resources are being developed to address some of the toxicity that casts a shadow over academic life. Yet the latter are not part of the metrics for performance, and the time given to the academic categories called "leadership and service" is often overlooked and undervalued as well.

Indeed, we are so often told that to take on leadership and service roles is a sacrifice. This message tells academics that their service is not valued and that they must go it alone, instead of recognizing the group effort that makes service possible, and without which the academy could not function. The same measures of "excellence" in research established in an academic world almost completely dominated by one group (men who are largely white, able bodied, hetero, and cis), is what remains in place today with little exception. This devaluing of other forms of labor is not only tenuous and unacceptable, it ignores the everyday realities of academics, students, and the academy more generally. Furthermore, it undergirds the possibilities for creating, maintaining, and defending care-less spaces by asking those who are not in the dominant group to assimilate.

How, then, do we proceed? There is no space in the academy untouched by one or more of these issues, including geography. Therefore, I take up a question in this book: How do we move toward and strive for a present that includes Lawson's (2009) "caring geography" and Oswin's (2020) "an other" geography, a present where a feminist ethic of care guides our examination of and interaction with the contemporary world?

In this work I am arguing toward a feminist praxis in geography that is both world dismantling and *world making* (see Ahmed 2017). In the following chapter, I take up the discussion of the promise and problematic of feminisms as a way to address the care-less academy and the long-standing violent and exclusionary character of geography. Critical to this discussion is an introduction to the premise that this book is built on: geography is well placed for this introspective moment, as we study and explain difference while "writing the earth."

Very little published starting in 2020–21 will be able to ignore the coronavirus pandemic begun in 2019. During the COVID-19 pandemic, which fundamentally disrupted our lives and laid bare long-standing structural and systemic inequities on the basis of race, class, gender, and access/ability—many of which feminist scholars have been interrogating for years (Bartos 2021)—many academics looked inward to look forward, attempting to imagine a new reality in the academy.[2] Academics were told to take advantage of campus closures and shelter-in-place orders to boost their productivity, and to channel those historical figures who had major breakthroughs in quarantine (e.g., Newton). Those of us who teach were suddenly thrust from the intimacy and interactive space of face-to-face meetings with our students, then forced to take our classes virtual. Labs became inaccessible overnight, and fieldwork plans were canceled until further notice. Conferences and other scholarly activities were put on hold or made virtual, and scholars close to retirement faced uncertainty in their plans.

As institutions closed worldwide, academic parents found themselves not only charged with their regular (if changed) teaching duties, but also with creating a home-school or other caretaking environment for their children. Other academic caregivers were forced to deal with new demands on seriously constrained medical and social services for older adults or their partners. In some cases, these carers were actually shut out of their roles by lockdowns in residential caregiving services. For some academics, these uncaring processes were tied to increased labor burdens grounded themselves in tired, worn gender binary roles. Women academics found themselves not just with the traditionally unjust "double day," but with an added triple burden as it related to attending to their children's care/education during conventional school/work hours (see Faria 2020; this work's interlude).[3]

Yet at the same time, networks of support emerged. These included technical resources for going virtual, teacher training for the online environment, weekly check-ins, telephone trees, spatial-distancing happy hours, "quaranteaming," and online K-12 education and entertainment hosted by family and friends. We also found many resources to provide self-care. Self-care is tricky, as it puts the emphasis on the individual, often through marginalizing practices. However, when done as part of a larger collective or suite of caring acts, it can be rebellious and an act of resistance. So, spaces of care were actively created out of crisis.

For those able to attend to their academic labors, changes in the processes were quick to emerge. Authors began to receive emails or see social media posts about peer-reviewed academic journals "pressing pause," not accepting new submissions, and anticipating major delays for reviewing manuscripts and processing accepted papers (cf. Oswin 2022). Journals halted print production, relying on online publication only. Reviewers for manuscripts, proposals, and tenure dossiers became scarce as labor burdens increased—these most important activities/forms of labor that, pandemic or not, remain undervalued.

And for many, the ability to process this new reality caused a significant drain on productivity and mental health. Six weeks into widespread shelter-in-place orders in the United States, journal editors were reportedly seeing dramatically fewer papers submitted from authors who presented as women—to the tune of a 50 percent reduction (cf. Ribarovska et al. 2021)—while those who presented as men seemed to be submitting more papers. Many universities rushed to support their pretenure faculty by offering a blanket policy of "stopping the clock," and to support tenured faculty on sabbatical by offering them that time back for the 2019–20 school year. Yet in some cases schools simultaneously initiated hiring freezes, pay cuts, staff furloughs, and cutbacks on contracts for adjunct/contingent faculty. Graduate students and postdoctoral scholars were in many cases completely ignored in efforts to maintain the undergraduate tuition base.

These stopgap measures often demonstrated the neoliberal and care-less character of the academy that disrupts the lives and careers of those most vulnerable while also assuming a homogeneity among academics that does not exist. However, academia applauded itself for a swift transition and a minimization of lost revenue and anxiously looked to a pandemic-free future. Many argue that we could not have anticipated this and that we were not prepared.

In this book I make the additional argument that, while forecasting this pandemic and its widespread impact on society might have been impossible, and we might not have been prepared to pivot to a new "virtual reality," we do already have the tools to support one another as a community (in the context of a pandemic and otherwise). In 2018, Dombroski et al. published a paper disrupting the idea of the autonomous academic (something Lawson noted as problematic in 2009), and highlighting the character of the collective care work undertaken in their academic program in the aftermath of disaster. Whether we believe it or not, none of us achieve success in academia without an immense network of support.

All Geographers Should Be Feminist Geographers builds from this foundation, focusing on the possibilities that are opened up when we take on the organizing principles of decolonial, intersectional feminisms (described in detail in chapter 1) and, more specifically, a feminist ethic of care. This work is an examination of what feminist geography is, what it can do, and how we can apply it to make academia a space that lifts people up. Through discussion of care, mentoring, ethics in research, leadership and service, and keeping geography and geographers relevant, I make the case that the basic ideology of decolonial, intersectional feminisms and feminist geographies is necessary to understand the realities of a care-less academia and a possible new present (see Kinkaid 2024). As Oswin offers, "the failure to reimagine and rework, and thus the failure to arrest the continued decline of a system already broken by design," is what is at stake here (2022, 390). Thus, in this book, seeking a feminist way out of here is a politics of hope and possibility.

This book is about feminist praxis. It is about taking action in creating new spaces, not looking only to a long-awaited future, but to care-full geographies, for *now*.

For Another Geography

When I say "all geographers should be feminist geographers," I mean *all* geographers. However, this is not to the exclusion of other approaches. Instead, I follow in the thinking of Ahmed that "feminism needs to be everywhere" (2017, 4), and of hooks that "feminism is for everybody" (2000, xiv). We need a multiplicity of knowledges and methodologies. What I mean to suggest with the title of the book is that we should all receive some training in feminist thinking as part of being broadly trained geographers and members of a wider disciplinary community. That is, feminist training will enrich all of our academic lives and make the work of dismantling oppression less "exhausting" (Ahmed 2017, 32).

However, this is not to suggest an exclusive community of feminist thinkers is the endpoint. Here, I am imagining scholars to understand and employ a feminist ethic of care in their own sites of the discipline. There is nothing mutually exclusive about a feminist approach and biogeography, climatology, geomorphology, or GIScience, for example (as is already well demonstrated by small groups of physical and GIS geographers alike). As feminist political ecologists, feminist political geographers, feminist Marxist geographers, and other feminist theorizations from classical positions in human geography demonstrate, a feminist approach opens up new opportunities in geographic research, writing, and teaching.[4]

Some might find this to be a wild idea; however, it was radically proposed by Monk and Hanson in 1982, when they went to great lengths to point out the sexism, bias, and inability to "see" gender (if in a binary form) in human geography. In considering how feminist thinking, which was proliferating in other humanities and social science disciplines, might be brought into geography, they suggested two paths out of the omission of women in the discipline: "One is to develop a strong feminist strand of research that would become one thread among many in the thick braid of geographic tradition. The second approach, which we favor, is to encourage a feminist perspective within all streams of human geography" (1982, 11). Forty (!) years later, I am suggesting that we "encourage" a feminist perspective within all areas of the discipline of geography.

Geography matters (Massey et al. 1984; see also Murphy 2018). It absolutely does; that is why we are here. But geography also faces a reckoning, as many have suggested (cf. Bruno and Faiver-Serna 2022; Dowler, Cuomo, Dasgupta, et al. 2019; Faria et al. 2019; Hamilton 2020; Kinkaid 2024; Kinkaid and Fritzsche 2022; Kinkaid, Parikh, and Ranjbar 2022; McKittrick and Peake 2005; Oswin 2020; Radcliffe 2022; Rose-Redwood et al. 2024). In writing about the exclusionary character of the discipline, Oswin recalls the universal geophilosophy and geohistories that many of us are taught and carry on / perpetuate through our "classical" training. A passing or deeper glance at the compendia of geography's history (generally self-described as Anglophone) shows a white, masculinist, imperial, deterministic focus—some works unapologetic, some offering critique, and some in newer editions expanding on the so-called canon (cf. Johnston and Sidaway 2016; G. Martin 2015; see also Keighren 2017, 2018, 2020; Keighren et al. 2017).[5]

Wittingly or not, we are taught exclusionary geographies (see Hamilton 2020; Kinkaid and Fritzsche 2022; Oswin 2020) and are expected to disseminate this universalizing geography (Keighren et al. 2017). In writing about graduate education on the history of the field, Kinkaid and Fritzsche (2022) argue that whiteness and the whitening of our academic lineage as geographers limit the potential of the discipline; indeed, Keighren argues that we would have much "to gain from an intersectional approach" in historicizing geography (2017, 643). A review of tomes historicizing geography and geographers often reinforces the little attention that is paid to the heterogeneity of this area of study, and the exclusionary character of what counts as geography.

Keighren argues that "chronicling geography is no harmless hobby" (2017, 644). In the three-part reports typical of *Progress in Human Geography*, Keighren acknowledges the complex character of writing and reading the history and philosophy of geography (note the singular), arguing that those who write geography's history "become the keepers of its memory" (639). A troubling thought, as there are deep silences in the archives that stem from the largely "biographical impulse of its architects" (Keighren 2017, 643). Such an approach reflects the paternal and white cis male character of the discipline and the authors of many of these texts (Rose 1995).[6] Moreover, a biographical approach bestows credit for scholarship on individuals, reinforcing the idea of the autonomous academic. A dearth of "authorial diversity" (Keighren 2020, 165) is visible and recognized, and it contributes to the exclusionary (pre)disposition of the discipline.

Exclusions on the basis of race, gender, sexual identity, and access/ability are rife within these histories. As Kinkaid argues, these institutional histories present barriers to "what constitutes knowledge and who can be a legitimate, institutionally recognized knower" (2019, 1789; see also Kinkaid 2024; Kinkaid and Fritzsche 2022). In reflecting on gender- and race-based exclusions, many scholars will point to numbers. But these numbers reflect what we already know—representation is uneven (Schurr, Müller, and Imhof 2020). While attempts to increase diversity in the discipline show more women and BIPOC scholars in geography programs, these gains are modest, and in many cases they do not reflect a commitment to inclusion, equity, or belonging (cf. Raphael 2023).

Pulido (2002) demanded a cultural shift in the field more than twenty years ago, arguing for the inclusion of more POC scholars to create a sense of belonging for geographers of color. However, there is still an "inhospitable whiteness" in the discipline that pushes BIPOC scholars to the margins (Bruno and Faiver-Serna 2022, 157; see also Mahtani 2002, 2004, 2006, 2014). It is these toxic geographies that Mahtani (2014) identifies (particularly around anti-Blackness) that are still being struggled against.

A secondary site of exclusion works in concert with the foundational one, in that much scholarship that is not quantitative or not published in English is dismissed as unimportant. This is the case despite the cultural and creative turns in geography and its vibrance across the globe.[7] Moreover, we learn next to nothing about non-Western genealogies (cf. Santos [1978] 2021; Sharp 2013). These are compounding exclusions, as much of this work is done by historically underrepresented and excluded groups, such as women, BIPOC, LGBTQIA+, global periphery scholars, and scholars with disabilities. Feminist, antiracist, decolonial, queer, crip, and creative geographies are taken less seriously and undervalued (see also Kinkaid 2019, 2024).

As Hamilton (2020) demonstrates, both the recent reconfiguring of the U.S. National Science Foundation under the Endless Frontier Act and the renaming and restructuring of the Geography and Spatial Sciences (GSS) program into Human-Environment and Geographical Sciences (HEGS) render this work "disposable." Hamilton deftly argues that the change in prioritization for funding "reeks of colonialism wherein marginalized voices are erased and frontiers are expanded for the purpose of profit," where "qualitative, humanistic work is framed as neither 'scientific' nor worthy of advancing the 'health, prosperity, and welfare' of the nation" (2020, 301). This rendering falls cleanly into a discussion in Anglophone geography outside the United States, where Cupples, in dialogue with scholars in Oceania, considers the "geoscientisation" underway in the discipline (2020, 3).

Cupples argues that the grouping of geography with the geosciences privileges STEM approaches, devaluing the social science and humanities work conducted in geography. This grouping also asks critical human geographers to assimilate into STEM priorities in the academy in order to be legible and valued. We are all doing science, but the strictures of physical, or hard, science differ from social science and humanities approaches, leading to epistemic erasure (Cupples 2020). Kinkaid (2019, 2024) makes it clear that to push on the boundaries of what geography is, is to call your scholarship into question.

In the launch of the new journal *Environment and Planning F: Philosophy, Theory, Models, Methods, and Practice*, a special issue entitled "Geographical Research for the 21st Century" is written out of the worn canon of geohistory. Yet it hints at possibilities, as we are asked to think about geoethics and new directions in physical geography, and to reimagine geography's future (Castree et al. 2022). In addition, Ferretti's (2020, 2021, 2022) trio of papers building from the work of Keighren (2017, 2018, 2020) nods toward calls to decolonize geography, which I will discuss more in the final chapter of the book (cf. Daigle and Ramírez 2019; Jazeel 2017; Noxolo 2017; Radcliffe 2022). However, I suggest (in tandem with Kinkaid and Fritzsche 2022; Oswin 2020; and others) that we cannot start from the same tired universalizing narrative. This refusal can be part of the world dismantling and world making we do in "an other" geography. We cannot forget our geohistories, but we need not perpetuate them. We must find new ways to do this storytelling (Keighren

structure | agency

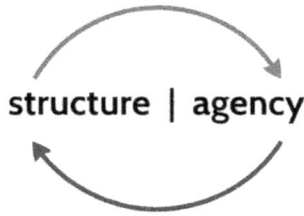

FIGURE 0.1. Structure pushes on agency, and agency pushes on structure.

2017). As Kinkaid (2024) argues, we must stop only looking toward a better future and instead create a new *now*.

By imbuing feminist thinking throughout our geographic training, there is a potential threefold effect. It allows for us to tangle with toxic geohistories and contemporary marginalization, and to build a more inclusive future for the discipline. As Kinkaid and Fritzsche (2022) argue, there is nothing incompatible about teaching antiracism, feminism, and the decolonial in our geography classes, nor any more so with incorporating these concepts into our research, service, and diversity work.[8] Likewise, a feminist approach has long observed structure versus agency as it relates to human-institution relations (particularly around the patriarchy), but as Falconer Al-Hindi (2000) notes, we had not looked inward considering how geography as a structure impedes (in this case) women's agency (see also Schurr, Müller, and Imhof 2020). In examining agency, it is essential that we query the power relations that replicate inequitable structures. We can then see where agency is being pushed on and how it pushes back (see figure 0.1), and we can consider the multidimensional character of power, including "power over, power to, power with, and power within" (see Mathie et al. 2017, 58). The work being done in decolonial geographies, Black geographies, queer and trans geographies, Indigenous geographies, feminist geographies, and more in the intervening time has begun this work. Here, we are reflecting on the white cisgender men's makeup of the discipline, naming the exclusionary practices, and refusing to be neatly folded into the structure of academic geography even as we are pushed to assimilate.

←◆→

Feminisms are a heterogeneous social movement and a core academic and activist space of theory and practice that span differences in training. I pluralize "feminisms" here because there is not and should not be a singular and universalizing feminism that shapes our work (something I discuss in great

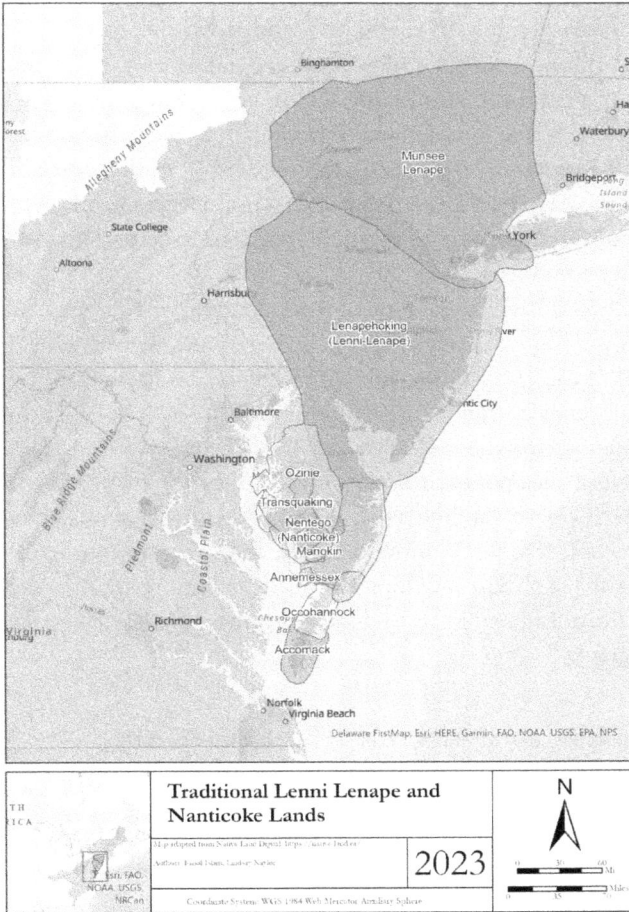

FIGURE 0.2. I am here. *Traditional Lenni Lenape and Nanticoke Lands*, a map created by Faisal Bin Islam (Islam et al. 2024).

depth in chapter 1). A limit of this book and of my training is that because of the Anglocentric character of the academy, the discussion is situated in empire and housed in the neoliberal university. I am writing this book on stolen land surrounded by the legacy of forced work done by stolen people (see figure 0.2).⁹ My call to decolonize feminisms speaks to this shortcoming, but it does not absolve me of having a largely U.S. focus throughout the book. Nor does it absolve me from being a settler-colonial scholar housed at an institution that benefited from the violent displacement of Black and Indigenous peoples. I write with/from that discomfort.

There is a power relation at work here that pushes on me and that I am making attempts to push on as well. In writing this book I am joining a chorus of feminist thinkers within and beyond geography and the United States. It is important that feminist thinking within and outside the United States be incorporated into the foundational thinking around creating a feminist ethic of care in the university—this book cannot do that work alone, nor should it. This work must be done collectively and in multiple contexts, including writing, thinking, and teaching in multiple languages (see Blidon and Zaragocin 2019; Müller 2021).

In this book, I will draw largely from Anglophone feminist thinking to direct a conversation around largely U.S. institutions of higher education. This is not to the exclusion of non-Anglo places and spaces, but it is a limit of my position as a bilingual (English and Spanish) scholar, and it is also a form of linguistic privilege (Müller 2021). Furthermore, calling for geography to remake itself as a nonexclusionary place is a use of the privilege I have (see also Dowler, Cuomo, Ranjbar, et al. 2019). To create decolonial, intersectional feminisms, as I describe in more depth in chapter 1, we must work together and from a space of care and hope. Feminisms plural recognizes the collective work that lies ahead and must be done. Feminisms plural make a space for "an other geography."

Caring Geographies and a Feminist Ethic of Care in the University

A feminist ethic of care is an attempt to democratize decision-making and labor in all its forms, and to distribute responsibility and benefits equitably while simultaneously creating spaces of belonging. A deeper ethic of care is also reflexive, asking who benefits from the established relations of care and what forms of listening, advocating, and allying can happen through the sharing of care practices. Care (in this guise) requires us to do the necessary labor to "survive well" (Gibson-Graham, Cameron, and Healy 2013). This means moving ahead from considerations of caregiving and care receiving, where the care work (such as reproductive labor) that makes all work possible is illuminated (see de la Bellacasa 2017), and thinking about "caring with." As Lawson notes, "Care ethics also move beyond critique to think through how we are implicated in uncaring relations and to engage in radically open, democratic and transformative practices for change" (2009, 212). As noted earlier in this chapter, geographers have indeed incorporated care and a focus on care ethics in their research, but the demands for creating a caring geography are far from met.

In this book I suggest that collective care and a care ethic exist in large measures in academic geography, but they are undervalued, invisibilized, and isolated. And here may be the place where thinking about "an other geography" gets sticky, because if a care ethics is already always existing, whom is it supporting? Therefore, it is also important to consider who benefits from care (see Bartos 2018, 2021; Dowler, Cuomo, Ranjbar, et al. 2019; Thayer 2025), as it is unevenly distributed and can sometimes support uncaring systems.[10] It is abundantly clear that no academic work is independently supported; there is a collective, whether intentional or not, that provisions the possibilities of conducting research, teaching, and service. However, in many cases we look past it or through it, or, as Kaufman states, "keep it private" (2021, 1749). Wood, Swanson, and Colley note that "maintaining, recognizing, and bringing care into systems where care is devalued is itself a radical act" (2020, 426). Lawson (2009) might well agree—but I suggest that instead of being radical, we normalize care in the academy.

There is no entry concerning care or an ethic of care in the *International Encyclopedia of Geography* (Castree et al. 2017). I find that puzzling, as there is a tremendous amount of work on both topics (see Popke 2006) in geography. In fact, feminist geographers have been talking about these subjects for some time. We understand from this large body of literature that care is relational (cf. McEwan and Goodman 2010), unevenly distributed across space (cf. Raghuram 2016), emotional (cf. Askins and Blazek 2017), more than social reproduction (cf. Thompson 2024), and a radical response to neoliberalism in and beyond the academy (cf. McDowell 2004).

Many earlier discussions of care in feminist geography focus on gender and, necessarily, the binary dividing of the care work that makes up social reproduction—the "care-giving/receiving," "caring for," and "caring about" (cf. McDowell 2004; McDowell et al. 2005; Staeheli and Brown 2003). Through reworking and critique, feminist geographers (and other feminist thinkers) also examine "caring-with" as part of considering mutual aid (cf. Askins and Blazek 2017; Lopez and Gillespie 2016); this is consistent with Dombroski et al.'s (2018) move from "I to we." In a caring-with approach lies the opportunity to make care and care ethics visible (Askins and Blazek 2017, 1097). Such visibility disrupts neoliberal notions of public versus private and centers the collective work that makes possible our (academic) lives.

However, much of the work on care comes from a white heterocisnormative feminist space in the global core, which I will address and critique in the chapter that follows (see also Collins 2002; Dowler, Cuomo, Ranjbar, et al. 2019; Dowler and Christian 2019; Kaufman 2021; Narayan 1995; Raghuram 2019). Furthermore, as Thayer, drawing on Narayan and Raghuram notes, "The interdependency and attentiveness to the needs of others that undergirds care can also produce harm, oppression, and systemic violence against 'othered' people (Narayan 1995; Raghuram 2019)" (2023, 6). Narayan (1995, 134) argues that the violent practices of colonization were made "morally palatable by the rhetoric of responsibility and care for enslaved and colonized Others." Similarly, Raghuram (2019, 629) notes that "colonial 'caring' encounters have shaped transnational hierarchies but also ordered postcolonial racialized violence" (Thayer 2023, 5). Turning our attention to care work as scholars, when we call for greater attention to and practices of care, knowing how caring labor tends to be unevenly distributed in the academy, we also get stuck in the question of who does the caring.

As geographers, we must understand that an ethic of care will differ across context and place (see Raghuram 2016; Raghuram, Madge, and Noxolo 2009). For it to be effective, this idea of care must be intersectional and decolonial, and it must include multiple ways of knowing and being. It must involve attentiveness to Indigenous relationality (TallBear 2019 cited in Kaufman 2021), as well as queer, trans, crip, racialized, and otherwise nonuniversalizing lived experiences (cf. Kinkaid 2024). These critiques inform on the decolonial, intersectional approach that I undertake here.

A care ethic in geography is described as embedded, messy, political, situated, relational, and a part of survival. Dowler, Cuomo, Ranjbar, et al. (2019) suggest a radical care praxis that recognizes vulnerability and precarity while putting the support for those groups experiencing intersecting exclusions and oppression first. The collective of care that I discuss here is intended to consider caring-with not just to survive, but to thrive. Because a geography of care can be emplaced and thus can, as Raghuram notes, "respond to the challenges offered by place to care in non-normative ways" and consider the "embodied challenges of care," and through this practice, it can find ways that "care can be better integrated into care ethics" (2016, 515). We must, then, emplace a feminist ethic of care in our academic spaces. To do so can expose the power relations at work in care; create a space to see, support, and value care at the site of the neoliberal university; and begin to disrupt who performs and benefits from it, while also exposing "false care" (Bartos 2021, 313). A care ethic unveils the ways that care can reify the neoliberal tendencies of the university, be exclusionary, or be considered an act of resistance (Bartos 2021, 313). To bring a feminist ethic of care to our academic spaces is not to simply put differently colored lenses in our view; it instead asks us to actively listen and be attentive to those who are systematically harmed and excluded (see Dowler, Cuomo, and Laliberte 2014). It presents the possibility of creating sites of accountability and belonging.

Dowler, Cuomo, Ranjbar, et al. called for a "manifesto of radical care in geography" mere months before the pandemic changed our lives forever (2019, 35). The authors' "Care" demands that "geographers move beyond recognition into action, actively working to infuse radical care into our everyday interpersonal interactions and into our departmental, institutional and disciplinary policies" (35). They further offered concrete practices that could be undertaken toward this end (Dowler, Cuomo, Ranjbar, et al. 2019, 37–38). I have found that practicing care is not a switch to be flipped—nor am I suggesting that the authors are saying that. However, I think we are still having these conversations with ourselves (see also McDowell 2016). It is a worthy pursuit to put these ideas out there in the world and then go away to our various institutions and organizations and try to put them in practice as individuals.[11] Kaufman, while envisioning a "more caring academia inspired by feminist geographers through their advising, teaching, and writing; their caring; their risks," simultaneously notes that care and caring cannot be mandated (2021, 1749). However, we must work collectively within the discipline and with a common vocabulary to do what needs to be done.

This book attends to such matters. While feminist geography has long been a subdiscipline within geography more broadly, here I argue that while it should remain a vibrant space in the field, geographic learning for all should include feminist geographies. A feminist approach to the academy and geography specifically should form the foundation of all the work we do. I join the call for academic geography to look forward, toward creating sites of care across the discipline to assist with securing a strong and ethically responsible future for geography. If we are all trained in feminist thinking, maybe care might not seem so radical or risky. As noted earlier, a number of academic geographers have raised the issues I address in the book, and I write this as part of an imagined collective that has been quietly and loudly demanding that care be visible and valued, and that we should strive for "an other" (Oswin 2022) "caring geography" (Lawson 2009; see also Dowler, Cuomo, Ranjbar, et al. 2019).

This book does not have to be read in any particularly linear way, but I do suggest starting with chapter 1 and then "choosing your own adventure" from there, based on your scholarly curiosity. Chapter 1 provides the theoretical underpinnings for the arguments advanced in the book. Here, I provide a noncomprehensive discussion of feminist thinking and feminist geographies, and make the case against mainstream (read: white) feminism and toward a decolonial, intersectional feminist geography. Chapter 2 starts with a fundamental reframing of how we think about the academic category of service. In this reframing I consider a new vocabulary for talking about this work, and discuss it alongside care work and the revaluation of labor.

Chapter 3 examines a care ethic in research. I suggest a number of sites where an ethic of care can be brought to a research agenda, in our data collection, and how we might assign value to all geographic work. This is a book that was largely written in the aftermath of a global pandemic, and I offer a critique of the care-less academy's response to concerns about productivity in the form of an midbook interlude authored by Caroline Faria in 2020, during the height of the COVID-19 pandemic. Chapter 4 stays with the research but turns our attention to the writing and dissemination of our work.

Chapter 5 brings attention to the classroom and teaching. I discuss the neoliberal character of the university and tuition as exclusion to ground a deeper reflection on approaches to teaching in the pandemic, as well as how to think about creating a care-full classroom and feminist training in geography. Chapter 6 recognizes that the institution is a foundational part of some of the struggles we face as geographers. I provide a deeper look at mentoring and training, as well as diversity, equity, and inclusion as care work, and offer shorter commentaries on pervasive problems in the academy more broadly.

I close the book with an entreaty to geographers, discussing geographic training, and the ways we can move toward a discipline that has a sense of belonging in the now. I discuss the violent and exclusionary character of the academy more broadly and of geography specifically. In addition, I address efforts to create spaces in our professional organizations, and the identity of who does the work of care. Finally, I revel in the possibilities of a care-full geography, arguing that we can cultivate a community of geographers through care-full practices in recruiting, sharing, and supporting geographic knowledges.

It remains a great honor to be in conversation with so many feminist, abolitionist, antiracist, and decolonial thinkers as I wrote these pages. I ask you, dear reader, to join the exchange. Sit with the discomfort, wave the flag for geography, and create a community where *we*, in all of our difference, belong.

CHAPTER 1

Feminisms for the Twenty-First Century

> Feminism is less a fixed platform than a rotating scene of ongoing tensions, debates, and outright conflicts.
>
> —*Kyla Schuller* (2021, 107)

Feminism is messy. It is simultaneously a tool used in the pursuit of creating a more equitable world, and one that can be wielded in a divisive way. I am a feminist political geographer. When I introduce myself with that label, people often assume that I study gender or topics focused on women. I do not. While examining gender is an important component of feminist work within and outside geography, a feminist approach is far greater in scope (cf. Davis 2016). Moreover, while feminist movements are and have long been struggling for and demanding equal rights for cisgender women, how their efforts motivate and inform feminist scholarship requires critical examination. In this chapter, I draw out the context for the decolonial, intersectional feminist approach that undergirds the thinking foundational to the premise of this book—that a feminist ethic of care can fundamentally disrupt exclusionary and oppressive structures and create sites of inclusion and belonging in the discipline of geography.

In this chapter, I offer a brief entry point into feminist thinking, as well as critiques of feminism both as a movement and as critical theory used in geographic thinking. Understanding that feminism is a broader social movement that is not synonymous with feminist theory, but that the two inform each other, I am broadly discussing feminisms and feminist thinking. This approach conflates those topics in some ways; however, attempting to parse them out is counterproductive in a book about praxis. I begin by approaching feminism as plural and examining the foundations and critiques of feminist thinking, focusing in on how we make feminisms plural by addressing intersectional and decolonial approaches to knowledge production. Feminist geographies are built out of these spaces. I follow this discussion with a brief (and nonexhaustive) treatment of feminist thinking and critiques in geography, and the challenges of being a feminist geographer. After these foundational discussions, I delve into intersectional and decolonial feminist geographies to situate the imperative for change in geography. Finally, I close this chapter with a nod toward the praxis required to make (an)other, care-full geography.

The "F Word"

I begin with the considerations of Ware (1970): "Radical feminism is working for the eradication of domination and elitism in all human relationships. This would make self-determination the ultimate good and require the downfall of society as we know it today" (in hooks [1984] 2015, 20). In this book, I discuss feminisms plural. I multiply "feminism," that hefty "*F* word," and take what is a sometimes monster and give it many heads. This study is not about gender, and it is not about women. However, we necessarily must discuss both, because feminisms are rooted in struggles against the patriarchy. Much of the globe is impacted by patriarchal systems and structures that were intentionally built in a myopic way that privileges a particular group. From where I sit in the United States, the systems I inhabit regularly were/are built for white, abled, economically mobile, straight, cisgender men. Seeing and naming this reality is a part of the feminisms discussed in this book.

But that is not the end point. For geography to be feminist and to take up a mantle of care in the academy is not just to have gender parity (which is stuck in a binary), or equal access/standing, as the privileged party currently holds. It is about generating care-full spaces that see, name, and examine difference attentively. Put differently, it is about the concrete practice of including people *without* asking them to reshape themselves into a system that was not built for them, while also building on perspectives and knowledges that stand apart from white, Western ways of knowing the world. We must do this work collectively (cf. Puāwai Collective 2019).

I did not add "feminist" to my geographer title until after I was some months into my tenure-track faculty position, and it certainly was not a word I used in any of my job applications. In the classroom, social circles, and the academy more broadly, feminism can be maligned and derided. People can feel threatened by it, and it is often misunderstood. Moreover, the long history of the U.S. feminist movement's ties to white supremacy has allowed it to be captured by capitalism (see Schuller 2021; Zakaria 2021) and made into a hostile space for those who are Black, Indigenous, and people of color (BIPOC), and for white feminism's "others." I was afraid to openly declare myself a feminist in scholarly spaces without a preamble. However, in writing this book, I want to decry the alienation that feminist thinkers broadly and feminist geographers specifically experience in the academy (see Ahmed 2017; McDowell 1999; Monk and Hanson 1982; Vergès 2021).

In stating that all geographers should be feminist geographers, I am arguing in favor of training in feminist thinking so that the goals of broader movements toward equity, inclusion, and belonging are advanced in and beyond our academic spaces, and so that we can move toward the "caring geography" suggested to us by Lawson (2009). But how to define or make legible this idea of feminism, which can be poorly received and ill-used? I (among others) argue for a feminism that is plural—one that is attentive to intersectionality (see Ahmed 2017; Falconer Al-Hindi and Eaves 2022; Collins and Bilge 2016; Crenshaw 1989; Kendall 2021; Lorde 1984; Zakaria 2021; Zaragocin 2023) and the geopolitics of knowledge production, and that in the process of becoming is simultaneously being decolonized (see Zaragocin 2019, 2023; Zaragocin and Caretta 2021; Zaragocin in Naylor et al. 2018). In my office I have a bumper sticker that reads "feminism is the radical notion that women are people" (attributed to Marie Shear). At this point, I think feminism is more than that. Feminisms are the radical notion that white, cisgender, abled, straight men should not have a concentration of power. Feminisms also hold that multiple ways of knowing and being must be accounted for as we work to create and encourage already existing equitable and care-full spaces—a geography of belonging.

As noted in the introduction, this work must be collective, and the chapters hereafter, while informed by non-U.S. feminisms, are largely focused on the U.S. experience and academy.[1] Conventional and singular (Anglophone) histories of feminism situate it in the United States in historical waves that reverberated from public organizing and into the home, the academy, and the corporate office (to name a few). I have no interest in repeating these historical fictions of the fight for equality, as they are mired in an exclusionary feminism that has at its heart white supremacy. The origin story of the U.S. feminist movement is situated in the fight for women's suffrage to the exclusion of Native American struggles for sovereignty and against genocide, as well as abolitionist and antiracist efforts that were already existing and the result of the very white supremacy that the suffragist movement in large part maintained (see Schuller 2021). This feminism is not only too small for a "world in which many worlds can fit," but it is also violent. If we are to truly gaze at power, then it must be deconstructed; it must be part of the world dismantling we do in geography.

As hooks ([1984] 2015) pointed out early in the period of critiques of mainstream feminism, due to competing ideas, no specific definition of feminism was agreed on. What scholarship across disciplines shows over time, however, is an emphasis on gender and reflexivity, with a particular emphasis on inequality and critical approaches. Even though "feminist" and "feminism" singular are often used to describe broader social movements, social theory, and methodology, I can describe no static universal feminism. However, big ideas remain important within this scope of work: gender has been troubled (Butler 1990), knowledge and position questioned (Haraway 1988), exclusions made visible (hooks [1984] 2015; Moraga and Anzaldúa [1981] 2015), intersecting structural oppressions examined (Combahee River Collective 1986; Crenshaw 1989), class struggle revisited (Gibson-Graham [1996] 2006), and uneven development queried (Mohanty 1984; Spivak 1988). In many cases, this pathbreaking work coincided with critical turns in the social sciences and laid the foundations for much of the scholarship of feminist thinkers today. However, in the parceling out of feminisms much simplifying and mainstreaming is done, which brings us full circle to hooks's critique.

What scholars have more recently described as white feminism is the conventional and normalized feminism that so many of us are taught and many more are alienated by. As Zakaria notes, discussing the historical waves of feminist organizing in the United States is to discuss the history of white feminism (2021, 199). Feminism in this guise is about gender equality and attaining rights. It is an exploitative and singular ideology that both benefits from and feeds into white supremacy and settler-colonial and colonial/neocolonial/imperial practices (hooks [1984] 2015; Phipps 2020; Vergès 2021; Zakaria 2021). This is a feminism that is reliant on cheap labor, a savior and "civilizing" mindset, individualism, essentialism, assimilation, universals, and top-down approaches. To seek equality in white feminism is to require the subjugation of nonwhite and noncisgender women, both in the United States and abroad.

In writing a counterhistory of feminism, Schuller (2021) makes clear the single story of feminism in the United States. Simultaneously in the book, Schuller unearths the white and BIPOC, as well as queer and trans feminisms that historically and contemporarily clash with white feminism to disrupt romanticized accounts of the feminist waves so often used to describe the feminist movement in the United States. From Elizabeth Cady Stanton's equating of whiteness with womanhood to Margaret Sanger's eugenics, Schuller shows the tearing down of women of color that occurred to lift white women up. Schuller additionally centers the stories of Black, Indigenous, and women of color, as well as those of LGBTQ women. These narratives include the interdependent feminism espoused by Frances E. W. Harper, the fight against "Jane Crow" by Pauli Murray, and the demands for bottom-up approaches and accountability from Alexandria Ocasio-Cortez. Similar to arguments made by Kendall (2021), these accounts show that white feminism is boiled down so much that it became devoid of any social justice goals and has no sense of solidarity.

The absence of solidarity among people who identify as feminist is acute, and it was most recently visible during the forty-fifth presidential administration. For example, the #metoo movement ignored founder Tarana Burke in 2017 when it went viral on social media, and the tangible artifacts of the 2017 Women's March came in the form of pink pussy hats. This form of feminism is written, spoken, and enacted as if the experience of white cisgender women is the *only* experience (see also hooks [1984] 2015). Moreover, this feminism is unambitious, tending to primarily seek to have the same power, or to be treated similarly to the dominant group (e.g., white men). As Cooper writes, "White women's feminisms still center around *equality*. . . . Black women's feminisms demand *justice*" (2014, n.p., emphasis in original). Thus we must, as Roy describes in a discussion of white supremacy and the university following the 2016 election, "divest from whiteness" (2016, n.p.).

This Bridge Called My Back, published in the early 1980s, represents a catalytic moment in the struggle by BIPOC women to raise their voices in feminist theory and praxis (Moraga and Anzaldúa [1981] 2015). Indeed, in the early 1980s hooks wrote about the exclusions in feminist discussions, arguing that "women who dominate feminist discourse have made it practically impossible for new and varied theories to emerge" ([1984] 2015, 9). These dismissals also homogenized nonwhite, non-Western women, as Mohanty drew to our attention in 1984 when discussing the construction of the "third world woman." Later, in the context of the war on terrorism, Abu-Lughod (2002) asked, "Do Muslim women really need saving?" (see also Abu-Lughod [2013] 2015). Many other feminisms are being practiced and discussed (historically and contemporarily), if also being pushed to the margins by white feminism. They are grounded in radical, abolitionist, queer and trans, crip, social justice, intersectional, and Black feminist theory. They are the result of more recent critical theorizing and practice, and they are long-standing and threaded through the struggle; they are drawn from both collective and personal experience, they stand alone, and they contain multitudes.

The recognition of multiple layers of oppression by Black abolitionist suffragists (see Schuller 2021) and the theorizing of intersectionality much later by the Combahee River Collective (1986) and Crenshaw (1989) show a thread that is pulled through feminist thinking and practice. White women have historically rejected an intersectional feminism (Schuller 2021). Yet it is still a vibrant area of feminist thinking and doing in the United States. Intersectional feminism has justice at its core. Kendall (2021), in discussing "hood feminism," advocates for a movement that has basic needs (rather than privilege) as a key element, including housing, education, healthcare. Abolitionist feminists show the violence and exclusionary character of mainstream (read: white) feminism, its reliance on bondage and the carceral state, and they call to decenter white voices, as well as recognize systemic, structural racism and the need to divest from the criminal legal system (Davis et al. 2022). These forms of intersectional feminism advocate for social justice and against state violence.

An intersectional feminism is attentive not just to sexism and gender equality, but to equity across difference. As Nash argues, an intersectional approach provides an opportunity to address the legacy of exclusions and center those voices long ignored (2008, 3; see also Collins 2015). Intersectionality is about identity and the layered experiences of exclusion. Claiming an intersectional feminism does not withstand critique, however, as it has been used in dynamic ways (see May 2014), some of which have erased Black women from the discussion (see Alexander-Floyd 2012) and in effect colonized epistemologies (see Mendoza 2015). As I discuss later in this chapter, a decolonial, intersectional feminist geography provides a potential path out of the troubles of feminism and toward feminisms.

Intersectionality, as Thomas argues, *highlights* oppressive epistemic structures created by dominant hegemonic groups (2020, 511, emphasis in original). Collins and Bilge (2016) suggest that an intersectional approach (as an unfinished framework) should address social inequality, intersecting power relations, social context, relationality, social justice, and complexity. To this list I would add that the approach be spatial. An intersectional approach invites us to see difference and to understand that there are multiple ways of knowing and being in the world, a process that requires pluriversal, decolonial, geographic thinking.

However, reading for difference is not enough. We must also fundamentally rethink how we are producing knowledge in ways that are not universalizing (see Naylor 2019). To *Decolonize* (capital *D* decolonizing) is a larger political project focused on "land back" and Indigenous futurity (see Tuck and Yang 2012). What I am discussing here is the *d*ecolonial (lowercase *d* decolonizing), something I will reemphasize throughout the book. Decolonial thinking is part of the work to confront the multiscalar, colonial modern power dynamic at work in the world (see Quijano 1999). It is a recognition that the colonial period did not end with sovereign independence, but continues today as part of the coloniality of power (Quijano 1999, 2008; see also Mignolo and Walsh 2018). This coloniality is pervasive in relations between the white Western and its "others" at all scales, from the global to the embodied.

Decolonial thinking can address the call to "divest from whiteness" made by Roy (2016), as it multiplies knowledges and, similar to intersectionality, centers excluded voices (Naylor and Thayer 2022; Tuhiwai-Smith 1999). This centering includes seeing from the colonial difference (see Mignolo 2002) and disrupting it. As Grosfoguel contends, "The Western/masculinist idea that we can produce knowledges that are unpositioned, unlocated, neutral, and universalistic, is one of the most pervasive mythologies in the modern/colonial world" (2002, 208). It is a universalizing form of knowledge production that sits in the West and is used as a tool of subjugation. Thus, our attentiveness to where and how knowledge is produced is crucial—something that (as I will later discuss) is crucial in our work as geographers.

A decolonial feminism is attuned to the hierarchies of knowledge production across space and embodied (especially gendered) experiences. This approach is also a departure from white feminism, in that it assists with the project of making feminisms plural (see de Jong, Icaza, and Rutazibwa 2019). It is an avenue toward the pluriversal thinking that is demanded by a decolonial approach, and a corrective to the usurping of feminist thought that homogenizes and erases. Decolonial feminism is a form of resistance and a way to address intersecting forms of oppression (Lugones 2010).[2] As Vallega (2020) notes, Lugones's decolonial feminism multiplies the way we think about power, as it demonstrates that race, labor, and gender are enmeshed in the coloniality of power. I would add sexual identity and disability to multiply further as part of this work.

However, in many cases BIPOC authors have been written out of the narratives of decolonial work (cf. Ortega 2017; Pérez 1999). Much of the feminist work that draws on the decolonial comes from women of color—concepts such as border thinking (Anzaldúa 1987), *cuerpo-territorio*/body-territory (Zaracogin 2017, 2018), and the feminist survival tool kit (Matallana-Peláez 2020) come from Latin American and Latinx thinkers (see also Velez and Tuana 2020). Decolonial feminisms bring to the forefront the (embodied) experiences and knowledges of the historically silenced and excluded, recognizing the layers of oppression experienced in systems imbued with the coloniality of power (see Collins 2015).

Thomas, in seeking to reconcile Lugones's decolonial feminism and Crenshaw's intersectionality, draws out the case for their interdependence as feminist praxis:

As an epistemic tool, intersectionality works to find subjects rendered socially invisible by dominant frameworks. These dominant frameworks operate under the guise that identities formed by social categories (such as race and gender) are mutually exclusive. Decolonial theory then operates to deconstruct these logics as being used by colonial regimes to subjugate and dehumanize subjects. At any rate, if our goal is to change or replace these dominant frameworks, the epistemic critique that intersectionality presents is crucial. *It is not enough just to critique the structures; we must develop an imaginative resistance within our epistemology to create new structures.* These structures are infused with the tenet of intersectionality and aim to view subjects as multiple. The combination of decolonial theory and intersectionality allows for the production of a methodology that makes subjects epistemically visible, in addition to critiquing colonial logics. (2020, 518, emphasis mine)

A decolonial, intersectional feminism uplifts voices and creates a site for feminisms. This site is not one where we move on or beyond different strands of feminist thinking. Rather, it is one where the spaces that the knowledges are produced are amplified, and where we walk and shout together, decentering a universalizing voice. It is a dialogic space, one where there can be harmony and dissonance. As Velez and Tuana remind decolonial feminist scholars, we "must remain vigilant to tendencies to reduce complexities and appeals to purity that deploy categorical logics" (2020, 371). Moreover, we must be attentive to whose knowledge counts.

Feminist thinking cuts across many academic disciplines. Here, I turn to feminist geographies to consider the work that has and can be done in writing the earth.

Feminisms in Geography

Along with other critical theory, feminist geographies are relatively new compared with other areas of focus that might be considered better established or more central to geography (see Staeheli and Mitchell 2005). To some degree, feminist geographies and geographers—and from where I sit, feminist political geographers in particular—have fought hard for relevance in the discipline. Peopling geography with women, both as research participants and as researchers, is tied to struggle. To declare oneself a feminist geographer is both bold and risky. Gökariksel et al. express this sentiment beautifully: "Claiming the title of feminist proclaims a willingness to accept or provoke discomfort" (2021, 1). Spaces in the discipline had to be created, structures of support designed, and outlets for dissemination cultivated. Feminist geography was marginalized and belittled in a "white man's discipline" (see Kinkaid, Parikh, and Ranjbar 2022), and it is perceived as remaining at the fringes, even as a new generation of scholars challenges its malignment within geography.

Feminist geographies are a vibrant component of geography. Although, as noted by many, they were introduced later in the game than in cognate disciplines, feminist geographies still provide an important corrective. They draw attention to the scale of the body and the importance of discussing gender and women, both as participants in human-environment relations and as valued members of the field (cf. Nelson and Seager 2005). An important intervention in the discipline more broadly in the United States, feminist geographies grew alongside gender equity movements in the 1970s and 1980s. Early work, although mired in gender binaries, drew attention to the exclusion of women in geography and situated feminist geography as a way to "people" human geography (see Monk and Hanson 1982).[3] At the turn of the twenty-first century, feminist geography was described as being primarily focused on the "social construction of space and place and the ways gender is implicated in those constructions" (Staeheli and Martin 2000, 571). In the intervening time, many feminist geographers have queried (Mollett and Faria 2013; Sharp 2009) or moved beyond gender (Coddington 2015). As part of their training, some (including me) have decentered gender in feminist thinking, considering inequities that are written across difference.

Feminist thinking is vibrant across the discipline, and, as Mohammad (2017) notes, it includes feminisms plural. Feminist geographies challenge the patriarchal character of the discipline (see Falconer Al-Hindi 2000; Moss and Falconer Al-Hindi 2008), as well as masculinist epistemologies put to work in geography (see Domosh 1991; Rose 1993). They have additionally been a place to engage with questions of positionality and reflexivity (England 1994; Gökariksel et al. 2021; Sharp and Dowler 2011), something I will discuss in more depth in chapter 3. And feminist geographies have provisioned new ways to gaze at knowledge production and power (Hiemstra and Billo 2017; Moss 1993; Nast 1994). A central component that I focus on here is the inclusion of an ethic of care in much work in feminist geography.

Care ethics is not part of feminist geography alone and is woven through feminist theorizing more broadly. Yet here I suggest that, as Dowler, Cuomo, and Laliberte (2014) following from Robinson (1999) note, an ethic of care should be informed by understanding difference within power dynamics. Lawson argues that "feminist care ethics assert the absolute centrality of care to our human lives: we are all in need of care and of emotional connection to others" (2009, 210). Although care is still less well represented in geography, and calls to create change (as discussed in the introduction) are still rather recent (cf. Dowler, Cuomo, Ranjbar, et al. 2019), conversations around an ethic of care in geography began in the mid-2000s (cf. Conradson 2003; Lawson 2007; McDowell 2004; Smith 2005), drawing on work in the 1990s by Robinson (1999), Tronto (1993), and others outside the discipline. Here scholars use care as a lens, but they also suggest both centering and troubling care in our work (cf. Kim and Naylor 2022; Naylor, Clarke-Sather, and Weber 2020).

Hanrahan and Smith more recently pushed on the boundaries of care, suggesting a topological approach that multiplies and expands care by suggesting it has neither a beginning nor a "final state" (2020, 232; see also Bartos 2021). Thayer (2025) similarly challenges weak-theory approaches to care, noting that in reading it alongside power and race geographies, care can work in violent and messy ways (see also Bartos 2018, 2019). In advocating for an intersectional approach to care, Raghuram (2019) argues that race shapes care practices. While the lens of care is applied in multiple different case studies, one idea that cuts across most discussions of a feminist ethic of care in geography is a desire to build livable worlds (see Roelvink, St. Martin, and Gibson-Graham 2015). The project that I am suggesting we undertake here must be world dismantling and world making, as I discuss later in this chapter. We can begin building this project by starting with an ethic of care.

All of this discussion is not to overly celebrate feminist geography. As Gökariksel et al. note, "Discomfort haunts feminist scholarship in the discipline" (2021, 7). Thus, we must sit with the discomfort of feminism "in order to question and destabilize the status quo while simultaneously acknowledging that the arrangement of this discomfort is uneven and falls along lines of privilege and power" (Gökariksel 2021, 1; see also Eaves et al. 2023; Thayer 2025). Because feminist geographies have also historically perpetuated exclusions stemming from a whitening or whiteness in the discipline (see Faria and Mollett 2020; Hanrahan, Oberhauser, and Besch 2020; Kobayashi and Peake 1994). The long-standing focus on gender, which often reads as women, which in turn reads as white women and people with vaginas, has made so-called feminist geography a hostile space for many.

There is another crucial point to draw out here while critiquing universalizing forms of feminism. Put plainly, it is the occurrence that not everyone who calls themselves feminist, whether personally, professionally, or both, is actually, well, feminist. They may not practice an ethic of care, or perhaps it is "false care" (Bartos 2021). Alternatively, some self-described feminists may not have considered that the histories of white feminism are tangled up with the racism, cisheteronormativity, and colonialism that must be addressed as part of our praxis, and they may instead perpetuate them. It may also be the case that they equate studying gender with being feminist, believing that there is no other personal or political commitment tied to that role. These self-named feminists are what I call "paper feminists." They are people who in their work or everyday practices do not activate a feminist ethic of care and efforts to build equitable worlds. They may simultaneously maintain and uphold white supremacy, the patriarchy, and cisheteronormativity in ways that both work against the aims of feminisms and are exclusionary and potentially harmful (see Queering Feminist Geography Collective, Kinkaid, Sharp, et al. forthcoming).

However, the work of reimagining feminist geographies (or feminisms in geography) is well underway, as many of us seek approaches that are multiple and that continue to interrogate the patriarchy, while also critiquing heteronormativity, capitalism, ableism, and racism. Here, I weave together feminist geographies' engagement with intersectionality and decolonial feminist geographies to anchor the underpinnings of this book.

As Mollett and Faria state, "Intersectionality is a spatial concept" (2018, 570); this allows scholars to examine intersecting relations of power. Valentine's intervention in 2007 brought a greater (if perhaps rushed) engagement with intersectionality in feminist geographies. It was a call to repoliticize feminist geography, to question structural inequalities and power relations (Valentine 2007, 19). However, intersectionality in feminist geographic thinking has not escaped the problems of whiteness I discuss earlier in this chapter, with gender standing in as difference in many cases, invisibilizing other power dynamics (Gökariksel and Smith 2017; Mollett and Faria 2013).

For too long, we have done a disservice to theorizing intersectional oppression, as Dowler writes, merely paying "lip service to theories of intersectionality" (2021, 291). Eaves names the problem clearly, stating, "Intersectionality has been far more utilized as a way to talk about a reductive category of gender, race, class, or sexuality. . . . The configurations of intersectionality seem to be less concerned with the historical, institutionalized oppressions and their effects on one's identity mediations in society and more about an additive multi-culturalism-style framework that operates to explain differences" (2021b, 258). An "add layers and stir" approach (which Valentine [2007] warned against early on) loses the structure/agency dynamic that I discuss in the previous chapter. However, there is a growing recognition of this issue within the discipline.

Falconer Al-Hindi and Eaves provide an important corrective/directive for intersectional feminist geographies, arguing that they must be grounded in ending oppression and suggesting that this work must be "care-full" (2022, 80). Eaves and Falconer Al-Hindi also argue that intersectional feminist approaches make for better geographical scholarship, as they provide an opportunity for [all] geographers to "include multiple subjectivities" within their methodologies (2020, 133). It is, as Faria and Mollett argue, an approach that "insists that we recognize powers as lived, and where they are disrupted, as lived at-risk" (2020, 25). In this case, it is (and must be) intentional.

Intersectional feminisms do not apply the framework of intersectionality to all, but they are attentive to difference while addressing uneven power relations, exclusions, and structural oppression. However, Falconer Al-Hindi and Eaves note that intersectionality may be "the pre-eminent exemplar of subjugated knowledge that has arisen from lived experience and found its way into the academy" (2022, 70). Thus, an approach that is multiple and that is attentive to pluriversal thinking and the recovery of subjugated knowledge provides a potential productive push for intersectional feminisms in geography. In 2013, Mollett and Faria proposed a postcolonial intersectionality for feminist political ecologies that attended to colonial/imperial hierarchies and categorizations (see also Mollett 2017). Here, in recognition that there is no post, or after, to the colonial period, I take their suggestion to the broader discipline to take up decolonial, intersectional feminisms, building together with their call and that of others seeking to decolonize geography (see Jazeel 2017; Naylor et al. 2018; Noxolo 2017; Radcliffe 2017, 2022).

Decolonial feminist geographies are an emergent part of the discussion on decolonizing the discipline. These discussions build on Lugones's (2007) ideas around the coloniality of gender, which was an important corrective in decolonial theory that demonstrates the imposition of Western gender hierarchies and the dehumanizing that happens through systems of surveillance and control (Radcliffe 2022, 102; see also Wynter 2003). Expanding on this idea, Radcliffe notes that decolonial feminisms in geography start at the "intimate scale of the body," thus "shed[ding] light on coloniality's expression through embodied intersectional relations of power" (2022, 103). Decolonial feminisms reject the heteronormative, imperial, patriarchal, racist, sexist, and ableist dimensions of coloniality as part of this work. Bringing decolonial feminisms to geography allows for identifying and mapping the spatialities of the coloniality of power.

While few scholars identify as decolonial feminist geographers (as an exception, see the work of Zaragocin 2017, 2018, 2019, 2021, 2023), feminist thinkers in geography are having similar discussions around a regenerative feminist praxis. Decolonial feminisms are all at once spatial and intersectional. For example, Zaragocin's work on the countergeographies represented by Abya Yala (living earth) draws on Massey (2012), noting that the "living and multiple process of the experience of decolonization, must take space as a dimension of multiplicity." Therefore, Zaragocin continues, "the multiplicity of various feminist postures, used geopolitically from Abya Yala has to do intrinsically with notions of intersectionality" (2017, 21, my translation from the original Spanish).[4] Likewise, as discussed earlier, intersectionality is now woven through feminist geographies in productive ways. For Mollett and Faria, the refusal to "erase race" from the project of feminist geographies demonstrates efforts to "de-center whiteness and recognize multiple forms of power" (2018, 570). Decolonial feminism's version of intersectionality is expansive, toward justice. Indeed, intersectional feminist geographies might be productively pushed in decolonizing directions.

Cultivating decolonial, intersectional feminisms in geography will be a difficult task, but the work has begun. As a way of approaching research and teaching, any theory or critical theory is part of a process of becoming where we will make mistakes, learn, and adjust. An inward-looking feminist geography is in discussion. For example, in the flagship membership organization the American Association of Geographers, the current Feminist Geographies Specialty Group (of which I am now a member) changed its name from Geographic Perspectives on Women (GPOW) (where I never felt I belonged). The change followed discussion of how the GPOW name was alienating and exclusionary, and how members desired transformative and inclusive spaces (Hanrahan, Oberhauser, and Besch 2020). This move shows reflexive change making and perhaps signals a piece of the sitting with the discomfort that is needed. To fully participate in the feminist praxis that is imperative demands that we apply this thinking throughout our everyday work, not just on paper.

Paper feminism is nonperformative (see Ahmed 2006)—it talks the talk but does not walk the walk. Being feminist in our geography of belonging must be more than just words. We are also called to participate in the unbinding of feminist geography, whereby we work to pull "its borders and boundaries" toward solidarity and community by "directly grappl[ing] with difference, no matter how uncomfortable" (Gökariksel et al. 2021, 5). Here we are pushed to examine the strengths and weaknesses of this approach. As Dowler argues, "To secure an unbounded feminist geography, we must recognize the consequences of nullifying discomfort and instead validate how comfort normalizes our relationships with control, power, and even the status quo" (2021, 291). This undertaking demonstrates that we can and must put justice and care at the center of feminist work.

Toward Decolonial, Intersectional Feminisms in Geography

While this book is a demand for geographers throughout the discipline to undertake feminist thinking so as to create more care-full or, as Lawson asks of readers, "caring geographies" (2009, 210), it additionally serves as a clarion call to decolonize and pluralize feminism in the discipline. Not only am I fiercely advocating for all geographers to be feminist geographers, but I am also suggesting that we must eliminate white feminism as part of the process (world dismantling). This necessarily means tearing down the sibling systems of white supremacy and the patriarchy.

The argument of Kinkaid, Parikh, and Ranjbar (2022) is salient here: this project of breaking down the toxic legacies that still permeate contemporary geographies (including feminist geography) requires a praxis that is not limited to the epistemological, but that extends to the ontological. We cannot theorize our way out of geography's exclusions and oppressions. We must also strive for accountability, as the authors note: "Such a praxis must transform the way we recognize and relate to each other across differences of identities, positionalities, and relations of power" (Kinkaid, Parikh, and Ranjbar 2022, 1560). If we do not dismantle, if we accept the institution for what it is, we become the "master's tool" (Lorde 1984 in Ahmed 2017, 160), and we must be willing to metaphorically burn it to the ground and build (rise) anew. We will be world dismantling and world making (Ahmed 2017; see also Gökariksel et al. 2021).

Feminist thinking should be everywhere in our work; it should not be an afterthought (Ahmed 2017). To be trained as a feminist is to share historical and contemporary trauma, see it, name it, sit with the discomfort of it, and then collectively work against it. As Smythe argues concerning harm and care for Black people "of all genders" and what "kind of academy we might want to move in relation to," "we must fully acknowledge" that "the present academy is causing harm, and that risks are required to produce an otherwise academy in which it is possible to breathe" (2022, 86–87; see also Gumbs 2020 on unbreathing). If we "sit with the trouble" and begin this work from a care-full space, we can recognize that we have to create other ways of being in the world in order to undertake this creative destruction in our discipline and in the academy more broadly. Moreover, we must, as Zaragocin urges, "question where and how feminist geographies travel" as a key component of the decolonizing work that must be done (2021, 238).[5]

A decolonial, intersectional feminism is anticapitalist / alter capitalist / more than capitalist, rejecting the neoliberal university and its strictures. Recognizing this stance is critical to moving beyond a feminism that simply seeks gender parity through the accumulation of wealth and property, and moving toward a practice of equitable relations of belonging that are enmeshed in livable worlds (on livable worlds, see Roelvink, St. Martin, and Gibson-Graham 2015). The decolonial is a trajectory toward feminisms that value interdependence, knowledges, and differences across place. And here is why geographers are so well placed to undertake this work—our discipline is already always invested in understanding and explaining difference. Reflecting on feminist geographies so far in the early 2000s, Nelson and Seager argued that it was an "innately inter-disciplinary sub-field" (2005, 6). I argue that feminist geographies have ceased to be a subdiscipline in the intervening time, and instead should be considered interdisciplinary, period, and thus imbued throughout geographic thinking. Let us undertake this work to embrace the caring, another geography *we deserve*.

CHAPTER 2

Care-Full Geographies of Purposeful Labor

What good is it to be valuable if nobody values you?
—*N. K. Jemisin* (2020, 9)

At a recent national meeting, I found myself with time to pop my head into a session on leadership building for "women in the academy," and I thought it would be incredible to hear from women in geography discussing their experiences across different institutions. I had heard firsthand how women felt sidelined in upper administration and how promotion had been delayed, or how their lack of promotion had turned uphill battles into cliff climbing. I had hoped to hear something different—not about struggles, but successes. And successes outright. Instead, it was a deeply discouraging room to sit in. I heard cautionary tale after cautionary tale: "expect to experience microaggressions," "you will not get what you want, so aim low," and so on. It was preparation for disappointment after disappointment. I heard those women, though; I heard what they had endured and why they believed it was important to be in these roles nonetheless. But I resolved to try to think and do differently, to reframe service and leadership.

In this chapter, I build from my initial resolve to first reframe how we discuss this form of labor in the academy. Drawing on new ideas about how we can make visible and significant the work that falls into this conventional category, I turn to revaluing labor and using a feminist ethic of care to rethink labor that is often dismissed or overlooked. Approaching rethinking service work through a decolonial, intersectional feminist lens here may seem redundant, as it is often clear where this labor work resides—largely with BIPOC individuals and women in academia. However, if we consider the different experiences and needs of the collective community of care that exists in the academy through this work, the need for such an approach is more evident.

Here, I consider gender and racial imbalances in who is assigned and who undertakes care labor, and how those efforts are undervalued by not being counted and compensated as work. I then turn to how we can change the ways we think about care labor in the academy, drawing from ideas around slow scholarship and mentoring as a collective site of care toward building spaces of belonging. Finally, I discuss the importance of valuing geography and providing this labor within our discipline toward a caring geography of belonging.

Disrupting the Vocabulary

In most cases in the U.S. academy, we are all assigned a workload—everyone from graduate students on contract (such as twenty hours per week toward administration, research, or teaching for the department) to upper administrators (who may have 100 percent of their workload coded as service or administrative). Duties for faculty members often involve a three-way split between research, teaching, and service, with teaching and research emphasized most heavily and balanced toward the institution's goals.[1]

For upper administrators in academia, service is generally the bulk of their workload. These positions are titled and generally well compensated, and in many cases the majority of them are populated by cis men. Again, for faculty, service is a percentage of their labor that follows research and teaching (but not always in that order). For those precariously laboring in higher education (postdoctoral scholars, contingent faculty, and graduate students, for example) it is "extra." For many faculty members who have not tipped the scales to have their service percentage outweigh their research and teaching, it is often the smallest percentage of their workload. When not completed under the guise of upper-administrative work (and sometimes when it is), service is undervalued, underappreciated, in many cases unquantifiable (and therefore not counted), and demeaned as lesser work—with research remaining the gold standard. Study after study shows a bleak landscape where this labor occurs (cf. Farris et al. 2021; Hanson 2007; Monk 1999; O'Meara 2016; Pederson and Minnotte 2018; Porter 2007; Pyke 2011; 2014).

Much of the literature on forms of labor framed as service (in the academy) revolves around gendered (binary) divisions of labor. While positing critique of who performs this labor, this scholarship reinforces stereotypes, uses gendered language, and relies on a yes/no dichotomy in describing how we should approach these labor roles. The way we talk about this work must change. It is well known that this area of the academy is a site of inequity. We know that women and BIPOC scholars and staff more often perform this labor, while men are actively shielded from it (O'Meara 2016; Pederson and Minnotte 2018). However, the questions we ask about taking on these roles are not changing, creating a feedback loop into the neoliberal character of higher education. When scholars ask who does this work and why, and the answer is roughly the same and the solutions are too (e.g., protect certain groups, learn to say no), we are missing an opportunity to reframe the discussion.

If we consider the inequitable character of the university at large, it is no surprise that women and BIPOC scholars and staff are often providing this labor. By and large (at predominantly white institutions) the university is a white supremacist, patriarchal institution that excluded these groups from anything but providing service throughout history. The exclusion was so great that new institutions were built to support these groups—women's colleges, HBCUs, HSIs, and Tribal colleges, for example.

Studies purporting that "representation is needed" at PWIs, or that certain groups have a "preference" or "willingness" to perform service, neglect the structures that exist to create such an atmosphere. They further neglect the agency or lack thereof on the part of the laborer (see my comments in the introduction on structure and agency). And saying that the answer is to "protect people" or "say no" while not changing the landscape of the work itself (because saying no doesn't make it go away; see Pyke 2014) reifies the inequities. For example, many early career scholars are intentionally shielded from service. What if we instead mentored people to prioritize time, not protect it? Because shielding scholars from certain types of work (e.g., service, advising) at any stage does them a disservice.

Protecting faculty from these forms of labor means they miss out on opportunities to grow, learn, network, provide, and receive care. It may mean fewer opportunities to meet colleagues in other units or to form a bond with colleagues in their own department. The result is that these faculty do not get noticed or networked on campus for much longer, and very few of their colleagues can say much about them or their work. Those who do not engage in service might not get invited to proposals or symposia, to other writing and reading opportunities, or even to seats on graduate student committees, thus reinforcing hierarchies and problematic power dynamics.

Also, keeping people from providing their labor early on potentially opens the floodgates once those doing the so-called protecting stop shielding these faculty members from service. Alternatively, it may create a mindset for these faculty that they must continue to say no because they need to keep up their research productivity (demands for productivity are an issue I thread through the latter parts of the book).

FIGURE 2.1. Instagram image of "Saying No to Things Punch Card" by @sophiehollandart and @leah_pierson (Gibert and Pierson 2022). It is important to note that these are pitched at saying "no" across the labor spectrum of the academy, not just to "service" alone.

Saying no and encouraging others to say no are hallmarks of the discussion around the gendered inequities in labor distribution in this arena. These actions are sites of solidarity among women and BIPOC scholars in the academy (see figure 2.1), where refusing to undertake this work is rewarded as an act of resistance. They do not suggest another option, though.[2]

Noting that saying no does not make the task go away, Pyke suggests a counterpoint, offering "don't ask" (2011, 2014) as a way forward. This suggestion sheds light on who is being asked to do the work and why, which is important, but it also exposes the problem of a say no / don't ask paradigm. At the end of the day, devalued or not, this labor is necessary and constitutes a form of care.

Saying no to service in the academy is a form of refusal that lacks care for the collective. It is a neoliberal and individualized form of care that is intended to protect the self at the expense of others. Under the current framing of this type of labor, saying no is a means of resistance for those who are regularly imposed on in the inequitable distribution of service work. This circumstance shows the deep need to reframe how we think about this sort of work, who does it, and when. The vocabulary around service must be disrupted and imbued with a feminist ethic of care. This ethic must support the collective and see these forms of labor differently so as to make them activities that are valued and taken up by everyone.

Taking to social media to disrupt the idea of saying no, Mayes declared, "When minoritized folk talk about invisible labor, the solution isn't for us to learn how to say no. It's to understand that this labor is for love, resistance & survival for ourselves and other minoritized faculty & students" (2022, n.p.).

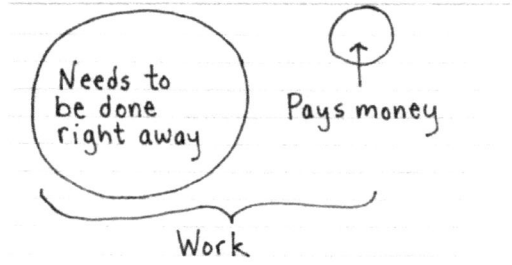

FIGURE 2.2. "Caretaking of everyone and everything, for example." On the website where it appears, this image is categorized under the keyword "stress" (Hagy 2022).

This rejection of the neoliberal narrative demonstrates that the labor provided can be caring for, caring with, caring about. That it is valuable. Moreover, this rejection shows that it is possible to attach a new vocabulary to the work we do. The vocabulary can change because, as I discuss subsequently, this form of labor is threaded throughout academic undertakings and cannot be parsed out from research and teaching (Hanson 2007). Indeed, they are braided, which I will explain in more detail. Put differently, they are interconnected in myriad ways.

It is clear why this work needs to be reframed, revalued, and reworded. When we say "service," the associated words that come to mind are "load," "burden," "sacrifice," "unpaid work" (see figure 2.2), "academic housework," and "mothering" (some of this language alone shows how this work is problematically gendered). We must decolonize the production of knowledge around what this labor is, who does it, when it is taken up (or put down), and why and we must not limit our understandings to the same tired answers.

Service as a workload category captures a wide range of activities, ranging from official, formal administrative posts (such as provost or dean) to a variety of committee work, or shared governance, or collective bargaining. Beyond the language and types of service, we also say "leadership and leaders" in reference to administrative roles, which can tend toward the patriarchal and masculinist—leaders require "followers" (Titus and Sanaghan 2021), which again invisibilizes the collective and reifies academic hierarchies. Indeed, the language around leadership is so steeped in neoliberal underpinnings that it actively distances people and sets them apart. It is these negative words that shape how we produce knowledge about what "service" work is.

Clearly, we need to radically rethink how we frame service in the academy and in geography—because we do service to/for the institution, and we do service to/for the discipline. However, not only is this type of labor often coded invaluable while being gendered and belittled, but the very vocabulary we use to discuss this labor is also violent. Hanson draws feminist geographers' attention to the etymology of the term "service," pointing out that it is derived from the Latin *servus* (slave) and *servitium* (slavery) (2007, 33).[3] Such terminology should be refused. And so a decolonial, intersectional feminist approach suggests that we reject this violent vocabulary and the geopolitics of knowledge production that effectively demonizes these forms of labor, and begin the work of reframing that is fundamentally needed.

A Reframing for Purpose and Care

I once attended a symposium at my current university that was focused on prioritizing Black health. One of the speakers was a master's candidate at a nearby university at the time, and he discussed the difficulties of navigating the academy as a Black man. He invited us to shut our eyes and raise our hands above our heads. We did. The auditorium was filled with upper administrators and senior and early career faculty, all surrounded by support staff. I squinted for a glimpse of the audience's participation and saw hands raised. And we sat with our hands raised and received no further instruction. And we sat with our hands raised. And we sat, and my arms started to get tired.

I am not a competitive person, which lends a particular bias to the perspective I bring in this chapter and the book overall. However, I was determined to keep my hands in the air until further instruction was given. I do yoga, and I convinced myself that I could keep this pose. And I did, though many others did not. I cannot tell you the exact instruction or revelation we received as the tingling feeling of my regular blood circulation flowed through my hands, but the point, the main takeaway that this scholar left us with, was thus: Was that difficult? Yes. Did you see or sense others around you struggling? Yes. Did you struggle to keep your hands raised for that amount of time? Sure, but . . . why did you not hold the hand of the person next to you? Why not share the burden?

I have always considered geography and the academy a place for community. But this exercise exposes that the academy in many ways asks us to go it alone, or makes us think that is how it is done. It is not. Even for those who think they are "self-made." Many times, there is a visible or invisible network of support that makes possible academic life. Sometimes it is formalized, other times ad hoc, much of it a shadow of the person it ultimately is supporting, but it is there.

Having now rejected the existing vocabulary of and bound to "service," let us instead start from a premise raised by Mountz et al.—this form of labor is care work that is "radical and necessary" (2015, 1238) and thus is in need of a new vocabulary. This work is foundational in keeping the academy moving, and its framing as unimportant drudgery stops here. Indeed, the fact that pretenure faculty are often shielded or protected from this work makes it sound all the more ominous. However, all academic service, no matter the percentage of workload, no matter the audience served, is both important/essential and enriching for individuals and the collective, no matter the stage of their career.[4] How, then, can we produce knowledge about this labor that is imbued with an ethic of care? That is, in what ways does a decolonial, intersectional feminist approach disrupt how we produce knowledge about academic labor?

Starting with care signals a recognition that caring forms of labor are foundational and fundamental to the academy and to everyday life. To reframe academic care work through a decolonial, intersectional feminist lens is to expand on the who of care (including our nonhuman others, which may include machinery, animals, bacteria, etc.). It is also to recognize that this labor in academia is not and cannot be individual (or neoliberal)—just consider the role or work of masks in the classroom during the COVID-19 pandemic as a way to reframe here.

Dombroski, Healy, and McKinnon (2019) point to the multiple and joint effort of care that encompasses many beings and nonliving things as a collective of care. As Dombroski asserts, "Care is the work that makes all work possible" (2020, 154). Starks (2022) reenvisions "service" as "purpose." Purposeful work is care-full work. Reimagining this form of academic labor as care creates sites for inclusivity and belonging. It gives all of us purpose and possibility for full participation in academic life. As Dombroski (writing about a diverse economies approach to labor) further notes, "Diverse economies scholars include consideration of care labour as part of a more general consideration of diverse forms of labour including labour compensated for by wages and salary (paid labour), labour only partially compensated by wages and salary (alternative paid labour), and labour that is compensated completely outside of a system of payments or not at all (unpaid labour)" (2020, 155). However, this approach is simultaneously expansive and limiting when thinking about care labor as a site of interdependence and collective work threaded throughout the academy. In that we are able to examine how care labor is valued, this approach is expansive. Yet it is limiting here, as a compensation lens does not easily allow for incorporation of the nonhuman others enrolled in care work or the fact that this work is done in collaboration, and as something that cannot be neatly parsed out and allotted compensation. As a result, focusing less on the compensation component and privileging the formations of collective care is an important corollary exercise.

Reframing our academic labor as care work is not without its own problematics. As Fisher and Tronto note, caring "*includes everything that we do to maintain, continue, and repair our 'world' so that we can live in it as well as possible*" (1991, 40, emphasis in original). Bartos reads this framing through the university, stating that universities have foundational caring practices that do this work for students, staff, and alums; however, this contention raises questions about whose worlds are maintained, continued, and repaired and whether that happens at the expense of others (2021, 313). This question is further complicated by the neoliberal character that universities are taking on as systems of support fade into memory—and these institutions are being revealed as uncaring spaces (Lawson 2007).

Nonetheless, as the COVID-19 pandemic showed, collective practices of care remain (and I will discuss some specific efforts in the final section of this chapter). Although this collective care is important and imbued throughout the academy, Bartos (2021) argues that while it maintains or continues (in some cases merely allowing us to survive), it may not do the necessary work of repair in the uncaring academy. Care comes out of different efforts and at different scales. It may start with an individual member of the community, or be a grassroots effort led by a group across a campus, or be an institutionalized program or activity. It could be formal or informal. It may be reparative and restorative, or it may be "false" (Bartos 2021).

In many cases, we may find that we actively pursue or construct purposeful work for ourselves through the provision of care. Most universities abound with student-run organizations, which are often organized around a collective interest. However, it is clear that having a shared interest in something such as sustainability and starting a group (protecting the environment), is very different from establishing a lavender group (protecting yourself).[5]

This point became heartbreakingly evident to me when I was a pretenure faculty member working with a group of students on a diversity initiative. A student leader in an undergraduate organization supporting our Latinx students talked about how their group was large and well established enough to warrant an office space in the student center. That was the one space they believed they could be their true selves on campus, and where our Latinx students felt safe. They finished these remarks with a resigned sigh, saying, "Sometimes I wish I could just be a student." The need for these spaces and places of collective support is not new, and, as Bartos notes, it demonstrates how "false or mythical care" can play out in the academy (2021, 316). Universities can provide spaces and funding for such groups without ever having to address the underlying roots of the structural oppressions and violence that make them necessary.[6]

Moreover, in the neoliberal university we are more often provided with resources for "self-care" that are individualized, not collective—we are expected to support, maintain, and repair ourselves. At one point during the pandemic, I received an email from our health and well-being center encouraging me to practice hygge (read: Danish coziness) as self-care. All of this is not to deny that strategies for self-care are important; in fact, I work on them with my mentees and in each of my classrooms. What it is to say is that individualized modes of care are but one approach in a suite that should be made possible in the academy if we are to be care-full. Moreover, we must recognize that a universal approach to care will not work because of the differentiated experiences of people across our demographics. Even self-care must reflect the collective care needed. As Dufty-Jones and Gibson (2022) note, working together takes the "I" out of self-care.

Bartos calls for a "care revolution" to "boldly change the oppressive systems of non-care within the university" (2021, 318). The care-full approach needed must be intentional, and it must be attentive to the geopolitics of knowledge production at work (decolonial). It must be aware of difference and allow for sitting with the discomfort of privilege (intersectional), and it must be humanizing and practiced alongside our earth others (feminist). Above all, it must be multiple and collective.

Unraveling the Thread of the Autonomous Academic (Revealing the Braid)

> Research teaching service.
> The mantra of academic life.
> Drilled into academics from the very beginning.
> Especially into budding academics at the very beginning.
> Research teaching service.
> Always in that order.
> Intentionally in that order.
> Research teaching service.
> As if they are separate.
> As if they are separable. (Hanson 2007, 29)

In 2008, during the first quarter of my PhD program at the University of Oregon, I was ushered into an unlit room with my graduate cohort. It was the gathering space for the department, the community area. It had a sink and a fridge and a massive round table made by an alum, and for me that table channeled a fictional King Arthur vibe. We were there for a candlelit induction ceremony led by Dr. Susan Hardwick, then the graduate program director.[7] What, you may ask, were we being inducted into? Gamma Theta Upsilon (GTU), the geography honor society.

Susan not only made make us think this ceremony was a critically important part of taking our place in a geography program, but she also made it wonderfully weird. I will never forget the serious candor with which she entered that room wearing full academic regalia and a globe on her head (I am not exaggerating in the slightest; it was a department fixture I came to know—the world with the bottom cut out to fit on a human head). She came to light our candles and to induct us into an honor society in candlelight and to make us feel like we were doing something powerful, important . . . mysterious.

Gamma Theta Upsilon is an international geographical honor society that stakes a claim to "recognizing geography's next generation of leaders"; "the goals of Gamma Theta Upsilon are directed toward furthering the discipline of Geography, geographic excellence, and service" (Gamma Theta Upsilon, n.d.). In this moment, my fellow graduate students and I were joining the ranks. We were writing the earth in community. We were becoming a collective that inspired excellence—and that excellence said nothing about research or teaching, but instead was about *service*. The pledge by initiates for induction into GTU is as follows: "I do hereby pledge myself . . . *to service in Geography* . . . throughout my lifetime . . . in whatever capacity I may find . . . and to use Geography . . . to the service of humanity" (Gamma Theta Upsilon, n.d., emphasis mine).We talk about excellence a lot in the academy. At my institution, our documents for promotion and tenure say that we must "demonstrate excellence." As you can imagine, most machinations of this quality are tied to research and teaching. Yet as early as 1928 (when Dr. Robert G. Buzzard established the first GTU chapter), geographers suggested that to be excellent was to further geographic knowledge through labor that was not singled out as research or teaching. This act speaks to the necessarily interwoven character of the work we do in the academy.

Academic labor by its very character is not autonomous (as in individual) or singular; it is a multifaceted braid (as in collective). As Araujo notes, if "'we' becomes the basic unit of labor the construction of the individual . . . falls apart" (2018, 216). It is time we disrupted the geopolitics of knowledge production that reinforces a hierarchy that can only exist through the subordination of purposeful (care) work. It is not individual or singular; it is multiple. It is not universal; it is pluriversal. It is interconnected (see McKinnon 2020,

FIGURE 2.3. A braided stream as academic labor collective. Photo credit: Dr. Adriana Martinez.

126). If we take a decolonial, intersectional feminist approach, we render the collective and the many threads that make up the braid visible and deconstruct the hierarchy of what labor is valued in the academy.

To conjure this amalgamation of labor is to see the collectivity and to suggest that each part is irreducible. Jackson, in examining glaciers as multiple, invites readers to consider that the "parts within the whole are not fixed nor stable—rather all parts are fluid based on how they continually relate and re-relate to each other within a greater constellation of the whole" (2019, 99). Addressing academic labor as collective and relational is disruptive; it challenges the power dynamic that renders purposeful work as unimportant. A feminist perspective assists with naming power and identifying sites of inequity, and so we can think of our academic labors as always already collective. In so doing, we can also participate in a world-dismantling and world-making activity. Seeing the "socio-spatial ordering" (Kinkaid 2020, 459) of academic life reifies existing power dynamics that are gendered, racialized, and otherwise marginalized and dehumanized. It simultaneously opens up the plasticity of structure-agency relations I described in the introduction, where power relations are multiple. It invites us instead to imagine three interlocking components of academic labor and our endeavors within our institutions as meshed, as braided (see, for example, figure 2.3).

If we think about the fluvial geomorphology of a braided stream, we can consider multithreaded channels that meet and diverge to create an interlocking pattern. These channels are dynamic and multiple. They are interspersed with bars that are created, dispersed, and re-formed over space, time, and continuum. Sometimes these bars are made stable and full of life, and then they become anastomosing, maintaining connections and openings.[8] Academic work is part of an ontological and epistemological collective that requires care. The channels that give life and animate our work are all important. We cannot teach geography without curriculum, we cannot conduct research without being mentored, and one person a committee does not make.

Thus, we create mentoring relationships, collectives of experience, communities of support. We mentor across the academy. There is experienced, trained, and formal mentoring alongside experiential and informal mentoring. We mentor students, we mentor early career academics, and we do peer mentoring. It is a part of all of our work, and I will not be able to contain the discussion of mentoring to the chapter of this book concerning purposeful care labor. Indeed, Falconer Al-Hindi notes that "mentoring has long been at the heart of feminist geographers' engagement with one another" (2019, 1658), and therefore it sits firmly as something imbued throughout our academic careers and across our work.

The language around mentoring is an additional site to examine and decolonize, as it can be described in hierarchical and patriarchal ways. In a tribute chapter in a volume honoring Jan Monk, Solem and Foote note that mentors are described as "advisors, sponsors, coaches, or guides," but the authors choose the language of "caring friend" to explain Monk's approach (2022, 112). It is a listening, querying, and interpreting role. The university is an intentionally divisive and opaque space for those not already familiar with what is ofttimes called the "unwritten rules" or "hidden curriculum." To some degree mentoring flattens the hill for those who are made to climb it. Care-full mentoring makes a difference.

How, then, do we build mentoring spaces that are care-full? Much of the early mentoring I received shaped and bent me into a structure that was not built for me. Some of this assimilation was by my own hand as I worked to understand the academy as an outsider. Some of it was through the absolutist teachings of how to be in and know the academy, stemming from beliefs that can be summarized as "this is the way things work," or "that's just how it is." Such standpoints are deeply enmeshed in the patriarchal and neoliberal character of higher education.

That there is one right way to approach academic work was drilled into me even as I tried to rebel against the notion. As a first-generation academic and, later, a social scientist in a college focused on physical science, I thought I had "no alternative" to doing things the "right way." This meant that I believed I had to struggle and to work three times as hard as everyone around me to be successful/valued. So, to some degree, I see this book as a rebel act finally able to be shouted out. As part of the decolonial, intersectional feminist work to create a care-full academy, I suggest we be attentive to how we mentor the students and other early career scholars who come from a range of backgrounds and experiences. To do this, we can peel back the layers of the academy, exposing the toxicity rendered through their exclusionary character, but also through disrupting them.

The education system in the United States puts Black people, Indigenous people, and people of color into what Love names "perpetual survival mode" (2019, 39). The academy and sites of higher education are institutions imbued with power and privilege. The character of success at the university is presented as benign meritocracy, yet in practice, women and members of the BIPOC community often find their work overlooked. There is a long history of exclusion and lack of support for these groups, and those who do have a measure of success in the academy are often forced to adapt or assimilate to a structure that was created to uphold white supremacy and the patriarchy. Moreover, graduate students and early career scholars at predominantly white institutions may have difficulty finding a mentor whom they see themselves represented in. The exclusion and underrepresentation of BIPOC faculty remains pervasive (Bernard and Cooperdock 2018; Gutiérrez y Muhs et al. 2012; Reyes 2022).

This situation creates a twofold problem: first, scholars may not establish a strong mentoring relationship that allows them to feel integrated into their units (see McCallum 2020; Posselt 2020); and second, they may end up merely surviving their program, rather than thriving. In a keynote talk at the American Geophysical Union's Justice in Geoscience conference in 2022, Tiara Moore, cofounder of Black in Marine Science, made the following claim: "I was constantly touted as a success story for my department, but I barely survived my PhD program." How are we to do good work if people are barely holding on?

There are greater structural issues that must be addressed at all levels of the university, and multiple approaches will be necessary, especially those that are anti-assimilationist (see Naylor 2021). One approach that can be put into practice immediately is considering how we mentor scholars who are from groups that have been continuously excluded and are underrepresented in our discipline. We can approach these mentoring relations from a feminist ethic of care that allows for breaking out of the assimilationist model imposed by the university, thus permitting scholars to be their full selves. The goal here is to think beyond diversity and toward equitable inclusion and belonging, something I will discuss more in chapter 6. Diversity and inclusion without attention to equity and justice are models for assimilation and adaptation. Without belonging, we reinforce the myth of the autonomous academic and obscure the communities of care that are necessary in our (academic) lives.

No academic is autonomous. No academic work is singular.[9] Perhaps if we were trained to see that instead of otherwise, we might see the value, see the braid I described earlier in this section. Perhaps if we thread feminist thinking through our programs and training as geographers, the collective care of purposeful work will be immediately apparent and valued. What if we build and maintain feminist collectives (see Mountz et al. 2015)?

If we look to the feminist coven peer-mentoring model suggested by Smyth, Linz, and Hudson (2020), we can capture a glimpse of the world making that can be done in this regard. These authors state, "The feminist coven is a pack, a band, a swarm: something admittedly imperfect itself, which carves spaces out of larger structures for alternative conventions to incubate. . . . We are conjuring the caring and threatening energy of witches" (Smyth, Linz, and Hudson 2020, 855–56). Built out of feminist foundations and "fierce care," this dynamic collective emerged out of the precarity of graduate student existence in the hostile spaces of the uncaring neoliberal academy (Smyth, Linz, and Hudson 2020, 856). What started as a response, though, became a space of not just resistance but hope. Much like the collective and caring responses that were created during the height of the pandemic, the authors found that they could not just imagine a different world, but see the scaffolding for it and to act within that possible now. The feminist coven is a rejection and a refusal, and, as the authors note, it is demanding. However, it is also the embodiment of putting care into practice to survive the academy (see also Embodiment Lab et al. 2025). What I suggest we do now is to make our collectives (whatever we may call them) a space to thrive.

←◆→

Now more than ever, our work as geographers is necessary and relevant. That includes purposeful work for geography. It means providing our labor for our flagship organization and honor society, and it means making geography matter not just to our students, but to our institutions as well. In the United States, we have the American Geographical Society (AGS) and the American Association of Geographers (AAG, formerly the Association of American Geographers). I participate in both—though more so with the AAG.[10]

The AAG is staffed, but the myriad things the organization undertakes at regional, national, and global scales are also powered by membership. And members offer assistance not by our fees alone, but through our purposeful work toward supporting geography and geographers. Dozens of standing committees, specialty groups across the span of the discipline, and task forces are all made up of members who contribute their ideas and time, their care and purpose. I am extremely active in these spaces and find them enriching, but I find that many people use the annual meeting as a proxy for what our core supporting institution does. Thus, the AAG is reduced to a place where we disseminate our research, and all else is rendered invisible.

However, when I think about the impact of feminist geography and geographers in the discipline, the AAG is a place where I see feminist praxis at work. Childcare and gender-neutral bathroom options at meetings, the antiharassment initiative and an ombuds position for registering complaint, women presidents during my lifetime, specialty group support . . . and these exist because of our purposeful work. Our labor and organizing around equity and justice, belonging and care.

I repeat a portion of the epigraph to the previous section:

> Research teaching service.
> As if they are separate.
> As if they are separable. (Hanson 2007, 29)

I have made the case that these activities and our relations within them are braided. If we want to maintain a geography that matters, we have to be supportive of it, not just in our research, not just in our teaching, but in our everyday acts of labor as scholars and geographers. These places we create, these ways we write the earth have meaning and importance. In discussions about care work, scholars often ask, "Who does the caring?" Imbuing our training with decolonial, intersectional feminist thinking obviates that question. We *all* need to care for geography and geographers.

CHAPTER 3

Feminist Care Ethics in Geographic Research

> We should nurture—in ourselves and others—the courage and wisdom
> to introduce a wider concern with ethics into "our" discourses of philoso-
> phies, theories, models, methods and practices, even where the dominant
> discourses of science, economics and politics seek to ridicule, humiliate or
> dismiss knowledges rooted in diverse other traditions.
>
> —*Richard Howitt* (2022, 90)

It is entirely possible that some readers will have turned to this chapter first, because of the deeply ingrained feeling that research is the most important part of our work as geographers. We have ahead of us a long process of unlearning and beginning the work of training the incoming generations of scholars not only with a feminist ethic of care, but also in decolonial, intersectional feminist thinking. This will be necessary to untie the knots that bind us to what Hersey (2022) refers to as "the grind," something I will address more specifically in chapter 6 and the final chapter of the book. It is the "get more research fund-ing," "publish more papers," "graduate students in shorter amounts of time" mentality that nips at our heels with every step we take in the academy. It is unsustainable and unhealthy. In fact, it may lead us to produce lower-quality scholarship if we continue to give in to what Dufty-Jones and Gibson call the "escalating demands and 'metric dogma' pursued by university managers" (2022, 339), not to mention force us out of the academy or into severe burnout.

When I first started my tenure-track position at a top-tier research uni-versity, a senior faculty member told me that I should publish three papers per year, and that writing a book was a bad strategy because it was only "one more line" on my CV. I relayed this advice to a mentor outside my department and they laughed—"Do they want your papers to be good?"[1] This form of "counting culture" feeds the grind and fast-paced character of the neoliberal academy, where we are carved into metrics that tell us how we are valued (or not) (Mountz et al. 2015, 1242). Thus, in this chapter I consider our research practices, with specific attention to data collection and analysis. The chapter that follows (chapter 4) is concerned with the sharing back of that data and our geographic thinking through our writing.

The benchmarks for excellence in research in the academy have moved rapidly because of this "grind culture," resulting in fundamentally uncaring training where we are pushed to jump higher and higher. Because that is how we were trained, we pass this culture along through our own performance or mentoring (I will discuss mentoring as a practice in depth in chapter 6). That it is normalized across the academy makes this uncaring practice less visible, something that Mountz et al. (2015) and others have pointed to in calls for "slow scholarship." In this chapter, I repeat this call, albeit somewhat differently. I consider how bringing an ethic of care into our research practices at whatever pace (see Embodiment Lab et al. 2025) might bring us a step closer to "an other geography," for it is argued that *all geographers* need an ethic in their research (cf. Sharp et al. 2022, 68; see also Liboiron 2021a; Tuhiwai-Smith 1999; Watts 2013). Indeed, I argue that a feminist geographic approach to research creates opportunities to do our work in/on place better. This approach also assists with assigning value to the broader array of geographic work across the sciences, social sciences, and humanities.

However, what does it mean to do research undergirded by a feminist ethic of care? Or, rather, what does it mean to be a decolonial, intersectional feminist doing research starting from the site of the neoliberal university? To start, it means bringing "care out of hiding" (Mountz et al. 2015, 1247). Feminist thinking has long been a site of resistance to the grind culture that we experience in the academy—especially for those who are navigating it from a space of precarity (Caretta and Faria 2020). As scholars, we are meant to contribute to the body of knowledge and to ask important questions. We are intended to be curious (even if research ultimately is not part of our assigned workload), to attempt to understand and explain difference across space (and time); but to do this work well, to make it meaningful, it must come from a foundation of an ethic of care. In this chapter, I first discuss feminist methodological approaches and break down the idea of objectivity in the conduct of research. I then expand on the idea of bringing an ethic of care to our work by focusing in on the mundane of the where, what, who, how, and when of geographic research.[2]

Concerning the Conduct of Geographic Research

There is a long history of scientists' claims to "truths" (King and Tadaki 2018, 69). King and Tadaki further note that "science refers to the organized generation of reproducible knowledge of the natural world. By testing scientific theories against observations and consistencies of logic, it is widely understood that science 'progresses' towards providing more accurate understandings of the natural world over time (Sismondo 2010, 6). In this way of thinking, scientists are understood to be authoritative representatives of the natural world, with a responsibility to produce and to test scientific claims rigorously against the collective reasoning of the scientific community as well as reproducible forms of evidence from the biophysical world" (2018, 69). This apolitical and objective approach to scientific research suggests that our work is completed in a vacuum that is free from a myriad of influences.

In geography, this line of reasoning is most closely associated with positivism and the quantitative revolution of the 1950s and 1960s. According to this way of thinking, data are empirical, repeatable, guided by technical laws/universals, and providing knowledge/truth. Yet geographers questioned such conceptions of knowledge that made "assumptions of self-evident universality" (Agnew 2007). They instead began to encourage more critical analytical inquiry across our earth writing.

Positivist approaches assert a hegemony over knowledge production that reproduces colonial/imperial relations (cf. Liboiron 2021a). Agnew attempts to disrupt universals in political geography, specifically suggesting that scholars have in large part projected single experiences of place onto the "world at large" (2007, 142). Arguing that "knowledge is inherently plural," Agnew suggests that we should thus rethink our geographies of knowledge production (2007, 142). As critical geographers (from across the discipline) contend, our research is imbued with influences from start to finish. The ways in which we conduct our research practice, whether as GIScientists, physical geographers, or human geographers, are necessarily subjective.

In writing on lab-based work, Liboiron poses fundamental questions that are an invitation to consider how influences on research may take shape: "Every morning when I put on my lab coat, I have decisions to make. How will we do science today? How will we work against scientific premises that separate humans from Nature, that envision natural relations as universal, and that assume access to Indigenous Land, especially when so much of our scientific training has primed us to reproduce these things?" (2021a, 113). Feminist and decolonial thinking assists with understanding why it is crucial that we abandon the idea that we are uncovering truths objectively, and instead consider multiple forms of situated knowledges.

In discussing feminist methodologies in geography, Hiemstra and Billo note, feminist scholars acknowledge that "there is no one, absolute truth" that we expose through our scholarship (2017, 285). Moreover, we dispute the idea that there is any such thing as objective research. Put differently, all research is subjective, no matter the method you use, the methodology you espouse, or the training you received. Indeed, it is in part because of our training in methods and methodologies that there is no way we could ever be objective. Where you were trained, what you were trained in, who trained you, how you were trained, and when your training took place all contribute to this factor (I will discuss researcher positionality in more depth later in this chapter). These things are true across the academy, and it is no different for geography or geographers.

When we do research, we make choices. For example, we choose what literature to be in conversation with, what methods we will use, and how we will use them. We decide where we will go to conduct our work and what will be the most impactful research questions to ask. This practice requires an ethic of care. As Howitt notes, "Acknowledging ethics as first method deeply challenges claims of abstract and disconnected, disembodied, dis-placed and universalized expert knowledge" (2022, 86). This is where considering a decolonial and intersectional approach to a feminist ethic of care lines up in a wider kaleidoscopic research agenda. As scholars in a continuous process of becoming, doing this work with an ethic of care at the forefront is one step toward making a contribution that is *unique to our way of thinking about the world* and our position in it.[3]

We all bring our own position to the table (as it were) to contribute with our research. I co-facilitate a research, teaching, and professional development lab with other human geographers in my department. At least once a year, whenever students doubt that they are making a contribution with their research, I draw on inspiration from creative writers to assuage their concerns. This sharing is part of trying to make the space care-full. For example, I share the enthusiasm that fiction writers thread through their creative advice. This advice unequivocally states that "your voice is unique, and you bring your perspective in ways others cannot," and that "you just have to start with one thing and then the next." But it also urges you to worry less about "the prescriptive advice," and to know with conviction that what you are doing has value. This type of enthusiasm for the possibilities of our work sheds light on us as scholars, and as part of our intermixing as humans.

How could we even pretend to be objective? We are not. There is recognition in feminist thinking that "knowledge is partial" (Hiemstra and Billo 2017, 285) and in decolonial thinking that knowledge is multiple. Looking to a who-what-when-where-how thematic, I find that if we are to consider an ethic of care across all of our research stemming from a decolonial, intersectional feminist foundation, we need to parse out some of the stickier issues that arise when considering research in our broader agendas/programs. These include the question of how we train and mentor on the conduct of geographic research. Returning to the epigraph that leads this chapter, we must also reconsider what research is valued in geography and which research "counts" (Howitt 2022; see also Hiemstra and Billo 2017; Monk and Hanson 1982; Nast 1994).

As a graduate student I was never funded as a research assistant, and so I never got to see what it was like to do fieldwork or participate in the building of a research project or program by someone more experienced than I was. This is not to say that I did not receive any mentoring on research. Rather, the depth of my training was perhaps different from other students'. There were times when I was in the field and felt absolutely lost and totally disconnected from my mentors, who were thousands of miles and a time zone away. Not everyone does fieldwork to gain access to data and research participants, but there is value in training all geographers about data collection beyond their own methods. I see this mentoring as part of a decolonial, intersectional feminist approach that recognizes that we are an interdisciplinary space, and that the work that human geographers do varies from that of physical geographers, and varies still from that of GIScientists. Of course, some geographers are not neatly siloed into one of these categories, and that makes for an even richer mix.

I distinctly remember one postseminar meetup at Pegasus Pizza in Eugene, Oregon—where you would often find a dozen or so of us every Thursday afternoon—talking about the different experiences we had doing data collection. The physical geographers (predominantly fluvial geomorphologists working in riverine landscapes) thought they had it bad. They talked about bugs and wearing waders and having to camp at their field sites. The few human geographers at the table laughed; we had all just returned from monthslong field campaigns in Sub-Saharan Africa and Latin America (respectively). We told stories about loss of access to our research sites, life-threatening transportation experiences, and catastrophes that had befallen the communities we work with. One of the GIS students gave us all a baffled look. And that was that.

I relate this story for two reasons: First, our experiences are different. Second, I have consistently disagreed with colleagues who are and are not trained as geographers about the length of time it takes to gather/produce data and gain degrees of trust with human participants—particularly as regards the length of time a PhD should take. Our mentoring thus must be expansive and consider these differences and make them visible. You do not, for example, have to build trust with satellites to gain access to their data. While sharing a beer and telling tales from the field is no bad thing, having better knowledge of different research approaches through our training and mentoring would make such experiences more valued/valuable.

We must first acknowledge that we are producing knowledge when we conduct research, and that this production of knowledge is geopolitical from the scale of the globe to the scale of the body. Much past and present geographical research is problematic, as it relates to universalizing tendencies, a white gaze, and groundings in imperialism, militarism, and coloniality (cf. Faria and Mollett 2016; Koopman 2016; Smyth 2023). As Howitt notes, there is a colonial-imperial character to geographic research and a boyish explorer persona to the geographer as "the collector of places, the collector of facts and figures and the writer of worlds for colonial masters" (2022, 87). Smyth reminds us that researchers are bound to structures that are "entrapped in coloniality," making the work of decolonizing knowledge production that much more difficult (2023, 281). Making our scholarship decolonial, intersectional, and feminist means not only wading through this quagmire, but also reconfiguring our training and practice to be care-full and collective. In addition, it means putting an ethic of care "first" as the foundation of our research methodologies and methods (Howitt 2022, 86).

Where?

The "why of where" (which, through my personal geography education, I attribute to Alec Murphy, who often stated, "Geography is the study of why things are the way they are because of where they are") is perhaps the most fundamental part of geographic inquiry. As scholars in the process of becoming, to think about where we start from as researchers feels among the most fundamental of the choices we make—and so here I will focus the most on the foundational elements of an ethic of care in research.

Where we conduct our research from is important. However, the academy has given more meaning to some places—such as the institution of the researcher—at the expense of others. For example, community colleges and the geographers who teach and conduct research at these sites are often overlooked in favor of liberal arts colleges. Both community colleges and liberal arts colleges are overshadowed by the large research universities, institutes, and national labs. However, university-level geography programs would not be nearly so robust without community college programs, which are the most significant area of impact in recruiting students into geography as a discipline (Housel, Shabram, and Wald 2022).

Moreover, the character of two-year degree programs demonstrates that they serve an increasingly diverse population—one that four-year and graduate programs continue to lack (Housel, Shabram, and Wald 2022), and that predominantly white institutions (PWIs) are largely underprepared to serve. Thus, rather than ignoring the work of our colleagues at associate of arts and other similar two-year programs, we should be finding ways to support and recognize their efforts and the knowledges produced therefrom. At the same time, we should look inward to see where our institutions may be falling short.

As I discuss in the introduction to the book, in the United States, many of us are working and writing at institutions built on stolen land. It is important to acknowledge that fact as we situate our work and consider whether it reinforces colonizing/extractive tendencies. The situation and scale of our work factor into the power geometries that shape all places (Massey 1994), whether they are mired in the colonial/imperial or not. As Smyth (2023) argues, we have a responsibility to the peoples and places where we conduct our research—whether in/on a river, on the ice, in the lab, in the city, on a farm, in an archive, at the museum, in a book, on a computer, and so on. For many of us, the institutions that we operate out of are always already structured to privilege positivist thinking and knowledge extraction, so I suggest that we need to consider thinking about where we do our work and how it is situated in its messy multiplicity. The where of research may conjure very specific spaces or places for scholars. These stem from our training and experience, yet they are also prefigured in the grind culture of the neoliberal university, where we are pushed to keep late or long hours in our offices . . . and, in the imaginaries of many, our research labs.

In this discussion of some of the "why of where" of our research, I start with breaking down the hard science lab (especially as a stand-in for scientific inquiry across research programs). In so doing, I address the problems and promises of the legibility of lab spaces, and how they are and can be transformed through a decolonial, intersectional feminist approach. When imagining where we conduct research, many may also immediately think about the field, which is where I next focus. I draw attention to the "otherwheres" of geographic inquiry to suggest why we should take on a feminist ethic of care no matter why we are conducting research where we are.

Much of where science is conducted brings to mind institutionally bound research labs and teams of researchers working on a common project or problem.[4] These visions of labs conjure imagery of discoveries being made and experiments tested, and perhaps of white lab coats and test tubes. However, as a social scientist receiving very different training to conduct my own ethnographically focused research project (all of my methods training was in anthropology) distinct from my adviser's own work, the lab was not how I envisioned data collection playing out. Although I shared ideas with and received feedback from my colleagues, my data collection found me as the "sole researcher." Thus it was not done as part of a team that looked like researchers in a science lab would (despite collective support from colleagues and participants). We are all trained in different spaces, but we are not always helped to understand how our training across the discipline differs. Perhaps lab spaces remain illegible to me in the same ways that advising five or six separate student research projects raises questions for my colleagues. What this difference suggests is that the where of our research imaginaries could stand to be more expansive.

I arrived at the University of Delaware in 2015 as one of a very small number of human geographers. Once there, I wanted to recreate the supportive research environment I and others who were non-lab-based scientists at the University of Oregon had built in the form of reading and writing groups. My new colleagues and I created a weekly meeting of the human geography faculty and graduate students that we somewhat uncreatively called "the Human Geography Roundtable." It was intended to be a space for encouraging professional development, providing mentoring, sharing our writing, developing our research, and creating opportunities for mutual aid. It was hard to explain to our colleagues, though. Pressured to be legible in a largely hard/natural science college (and much like the experiences described by Caretta and Faria 2020), we scrapped the roundtable after a few years and recast it as the Embodiment Lab (2018) (see also Embodiment Lab et al. 2025).

In this space, we are a collective and have worked to push back against the neoliberal character of university lab imaginaries. Our lab does not necessarily emulate a natural science lab, with the characteristic (though not universal) one principal investigator PI and several other scholars ranging from postdocs to undergraduate research assistants. Although we publish together and collaborate on individual research projects, we are all in the space to support one another in our own work. I am struck by Caretta and Faria's recognition that "adopting a 'lab model' reinforces exactly the kinds of knowledge, research practices, and outputs that get to be valued in today's academy" (2020, 181). This also suggests that there are not feminist decolonial labs otherwise in existence, which we know is not the case—lab practices vary greatly among scientists, including ones grounded in the approaches

I suggest here, and they span a wide variety of research environments, no matter the research foci. Where the struggle sits, then, is in the neoliberal university and academy more broadly (particularly at PWIs and top-tier research universities).

So, for Caretta and Faria (2020), bringing their feminist methodologies and mentoring strategies into the space of a "lab" is certainly a refusal of the patriarchal, white privileged leanings of many of the institutions we inhabit. The authors' approach shows the survival strategies we have had to undertake to care in the academy and to be valued. I am grateful for their work and suggest here that rather than think about the lab as where we do research and of ourselves as trying to mimic a seemingly universal hard science model, and instead of leaning into the grind culture of an imagined research lab, we work toward bringing an ethic of care to where we research. Being decolonial, intersectional, and feminist in our approach requires that. This approach suggests that research labs could be embraced and welcomed as spaces where scholars gather in our multiplicity—that they might be built not just out of the research programs of a PI, but out of an ethic of care.[5]

All research spaces, no matter where they sit, have the opportunity to have at their foundation an inward reflection that asks *how they provide equitable opportunities for making decisions and providing labor, how the benefits and responsibilities are distributed, and whether the spaces create a site of belonging.* Wherever our data collection and analysis take place—whether it is between four walls or elsewhere—can be care-full spaces where mentoring, support, professional development, safety training, and transparent and accountable practices all take place. These practices contribute to the world-making project I am suggesting in this book, but they also can simultaneously be part of the world dismantling that is necessary in a decolonial and intersectional approach.

It is important to reiterate, as I note in the introduction to the book, that these spaces already exist throughout the academy. What is needed is for them to be seen and valued, and to become sites of demonstrated praxis that can be adopted/adapted widely across the neoliberal university toward its unmaking. There are the intangible parts of the where, but this process of cultivating an ethic of care and creating sites of equity and belonging can also be tangible, considering what is in the space—what is hanging on the walls, what materials are available, whether the site of data collection is accessible or what accommodations are required, whether an all-gender bathroom is available, and so on.[6] This practice will undeniably force us to slow down, or to make our pace appropriate to the task, to embody the slower scholarship and slower mentoring that feminist praxis demands (Caretta and Faria 2020; Embodiment Lab et al. 2025; Mountz et al. 2015), to be attentive at a different pace.

Our institutions and lab structures notwithstanding, the interdisciplinary character of geographic research allows us to have much difference in the whys of where we collect data. Data can be obtained from the archives, from satellite datasets, through lab experimentation, or in the natural or built environment, which researchers call "the field." Where we go into the field is also of import. Both the living communities that we engage and the built environment that surrounds us form a crucial part of this where. Many of us are conducting our work from settler-colonial institutions. We may also be settler colonials (like I am), or we may not. Our ability to go to the field is a privilege. For some of us who do work outside our country of citizenship, the power of our passports (e.g., having a U.S. passport) opens up many areas of the globe. For others, such work is tied up in a bureaucratic and expensive process of formal travel visa applications. While in the field, we may be working with vulnerable communities (natural and human), and our presence may even exacerbate these vulnerabilities. In addition, we may hold significant privilege based on our own positionality vis-à-vis our research constituents (cf. Naylor 2019).

As I discuss in detail in chapter 1, decolonizing is twofold: Capital *D* decolonizing is about repatriation of land and Indigenous futurity. Lowercase *d* decolonizing is about multiplying and recovering subjugated knowledges. In writing about anticolonial approaches, Liboiron considers the "colonial entitlement" to accessing "Land" to conduct research (2021a, 15). In a separate paper, Liboiron argues that this attitude "leads to scientists sailing around the world to gather water samples, professors picking up rocks on hikes for pedagogical show and tell, and scientists crunching numbers in datasets that seem landless, so they deem no permissions necessary" (2021b, 876). I would add that colonial entitlement can lead scholars working with human participants to demand and extract knowledge, wittingly or not. And so our relations to the field and to data collection more broadly are ripe for change. The relation to the where of our research, and the why of that where, may need to be part of dismantling a prevailing sense of entitlement to these environments and knowledges.

Simultaneously, some researchers, rather than exhibiting a sense of entitlement, risk becoming vulnerable as part of their presence in the communities they are working with. This heightened vulnerability can be based on any number of factors, including those that are visibly written on our bodies (cf. Demery and Pipkin 2021; Dowtin and Levia 2018). However, other sites of vulnerability for researchers that may be less visible or invisible are still important factors to consider when conducting fieldwork. Here, I want to draw attention specifically to the experience of LGBTQIA+ scholars. These individuals may find their very existence perilous, as their sexual and gender identities are not protected by law or in some cases are actively persecuted (Mendos et al. 2020).

The lack of protections or even larger conversations around the experiences of these researchers means that many are confronting multiple overlapping risks from academic institutions to international fieldwork. These risks sometimes compel researchers to conceal their identities or opt out of certain types of research—especially data collection in the field (Zebracki and Greatrick 2022). There is a deep need to claim/reclaim fieldwork through making it more inclusive and accessible, and by putting plans for safe conduct of fieldwork in place, whether in a basement archive, an urban forest, or many additional "otherwheres."[7]

With very little exception, if we are to put into practice decolonial, intersectional feminisms, we have to first recognize the differences in the experience of the "where" across researchers and research participants. Second, we must understand the role of colonialism, imperialism, the patriarchy, sexism, racism, ableism, and other forms of hatred and bias in access to the field or other sites of data collection and our scientific endeavors, and then work actively against it. We must be intentional in crafting safe working environments that are attentive to the different positionalities of the researchers and participants involved. Conducting research with the safety of all in mind cannot be reduced to checking a box for a large funding organization or for the institutional review board (IRB). To care-fully consider research is to do the work of decolonizing and making intersectional our feminist approach to an ethic of care.

What?

If geographers are concerned with understanding difference across space, the what of our research seems boundless. I remember, back at the start of my PhD program, being asked to write my very first elevator definition of geography by then department chair Andrew Marcus. I came up with something that began with "geography is everything." Wide-eyed, yes, but earth writing in all of its possibilities does give us a lot of potential latitude to determine what our areas of inquiry will be.[8] These possibilities are not static, as I discuss subsequently, but the whats of our research do matter.

What we do as our research practice is also measured by an invisible yardstick where some topics, places, or peoples are considered more timely, important, and valuable than others. I once had a grant proposal rejected with a question: "Hasn't Chiapas already been done?" Also, I was publicly ridiculed by a colleague during a faculty meeting for the "uselessness" of my work on access to human milk. By and large, what we conduct research on is a choice—and that choice can be shaped by any number of variables, including funding structures (see Hamilton 2020), lab configuration, collaboration opportunities, research assistantships or postdoctoral positions, recruitment practices, life, and so on. What we research may also be shaped by personal or institutional interests, or our training and skill sets. Sometimes the "what" that is chosen and how it is valued become inflected with race, gender, disability, and sexuality and are assumed to be a "personal project" on the researcher's own community (cf. Pryal 2017). These geographic whats are then sometimes sidelined as niche or particular and not replicable or generalizable, and therefore not important. At the extreme, some areas of research are not even considered legitimate areas of inquiry (for example, the long struggle by feminist and LGBTQ geographers to set an agenda that includes gender and sexuality studies).

No matter what we research, there is an assumption that as scholars we have a "right to research" (Howitt 2022; Liboiron 2021a; 2021b) and ask questions. And so I urge that we care-fully consider the what in our research practice as it extends out from us in multiscalar ways. Moreover, we must also consider what research questions we even have the right to ask, and whether our research is exploitative or extractive (Hiemstra and Billo 2017).

As geographers, we write the earth—we study the "why of where" with a focus on human-environment interactions. As I noted earlier, such a framing gives us seemingly endless topics of research. However, the value we place on certain research topics varies. In some cases, this is because of historical events that redirected our attention (e.g., the end of the Cold War, or the start of a global pandemic), turns within the discipline (e.g., quantitative, postmodern), priorities within the academy (e.g., science, technology, engineering, and math—STEM education), and political arguments (such as those ongoing in the United States right now on critical race theory, something I will discuss in chapter 5). There is what we value as researchers, and there is what is valued by funding agencies.

In this regard, Hamilton (2020) lays out a critique of the U.S. National Science Foundation and what it prioritizes under a neoliberal umbrella (which I discuss briefly in chapter 1).[9] The scholars more firmly situated in the social sciences and humanities in geography are effectively being told that our work is not valuable. In 2019, in a personal conversation with a program officer regarding my high rankings and noncompetitive CAREER proposal, I was told my work was "too postmodern" to be funded with national taxpayer moneys. What counts as geography is certainly at stake, as funding opportunities slowly disappear under the guise of what is valued as science, and as the already few opportunities to receive funding as a social scientist or in the humanities are defunded (for example, the recent loss of the Social Science Research Foundation, International Dissertation Research Fellowship).

I simultaneously recognize that all data collection and funding needs across the discipline are different. The purchase of needed lab or field equipment and datasets or computing time is not the same as the purchase of a plane ticket or compensation for research participants. What I am suggesting is that we have serious introspection into what work we value and how we place value on it, no matter the price tag or budget needed. Indeed, if we were to have a reflexive praxis in our areas of geographic inquiry, we might move away from the zero-sum game of competitive funding.

How?

How we conduct research, though, should be at the heart of any discussion on an ethic of care. Recently, after reading about an academic misconduct case in a physical science lab, I wondered why it is it that only research with human and animal subjects is reviewed by the institutional review board (IRB), and why it is that the ethics training (that I must renew every few years) is not required for all researchers at their institutions. Where is the ethics training for machine learning? Dendrochronology? Ice coring? Perhaps it exists in some classrooms and labs, but it certainly is not institutionalized. Even the established ethics that some of us are beholden to are insufficient (see Howitt 2022; King 2023). As King (2023) notes (writing in the context of U.K. ethics boards), these standards are not based in an ethic of care. Rather, they are a tool used to document risk and provide legal remedy for the institution.

Some physical scientists are starting to look to ethics in research, and to building out/away from the more entrenched form of ethical review and considering training that exceeds institutional mandates. Wilmer et al. suggest starting from the basis of social science ethics but having more expansive training so that natural scientists can "work in equitable and collaborative partnerships" (2021, 454). The authors indicate that "researchers must expand our collective ethical understandings and practices" (454). In addition, Wilmer and coauthors offer the following points for guidance in expanding ethics to our research practice: "Representation: mindfulness of how we represent other people and communities as well as non-human elements in our research. Self-determination: respect for inherent power and self-determination, as well as respect of Indigenous data sovereignty (IDSov). Reciprocity: maximizing benefits for collaborators and participants. Deference: respect for other knowledges and epistemologies, including those of our societal partners and collaborators from other disciplines, and thinking not only about human actors but also non-human actors in research training across the natural sciences" (Wilmer et al. 2021, 454). Recognizing that existing ethics mandates are rarely required or taken up by physical scientists, and that existing board-mandated research ethics have limits, this group of scholars is pushing on scientists generally to take up research ethics in their work and training.

I suggest that this uptake by physical scientists is a world-making practice, and this move could be attentive to an ethic of care in research. An ethic of care *should* be attentive to humans *and* our earth others, including more than human beings (Gibson, Rose, and Fincher 2015). How are we caring for this earth we are writing? How are we caring for ourselves?

Whether we conduct research in our offices, outside our offices, or in a lab space, safety is paramount. As I discuss in the subsequent section, we should never be willing or encouraged to compromise our personal safety or that of others when gathering data. As Nelson (2013) notes, while the "allure" of danger in collecting and reporting on our data is perilous, it also misses out on mundane and everyday practices that are important to our work, and to building enriching research practices and relationships with research partners and participants. Safely conducting our research means bodily autonomy, mental well-being, appropriate expectations, accommodations, and personal protective equipment, as well as transparency and accountability.

Instituting safety measures where people have received appropriate training and the research team has institutional support in this work is not just good care-full research practice that will likely lead to better scholarship. It is a way to maintain and increase diversity and inclusion in our field, as the vast majority of those who feel unsafe or as though they do not belong are from historically underrepresented and excluded groups (cf. Coon et al. 2023; Demery and Pipkin 2021). Thus, we must think about creating sites of belonging in our research practice and throughout our academic work. This is something I will discuss around the care-full practice of diversity, equity, inclusion, and belonging in the final chapter of the book.

Putting safety measures in place for the researcher or the research team is often the onus of the same. Recognizing that this approach has led to decades of harassment, assault, accidents, gatekeeping, and other abuses and dangers in the lab and the field, the U.S. National Science Foundation (2023)—one of the primary external funding organizations that supports scholarly work in the United States—announced, effective 2023, that all proposals were required to have a certified plan for a "safe and inclusive working environment" as part of their submission. Thus, ethics in research is extending across our institutions and disciplinary boundaries. However, I caution here that such plans should not be reduced to the IRB or to certified templates caught up in the strictures of the neoliberal institutions that many of us conduct our research out of.

Indeed, Howitt cautions that having a stamp of approval for ethical research does not necessarily result in an ethic of care in our work: "It risks opening a slippery slope towards mistaking institutional ethical approval as the foundation for research ethics—mistaking the procedural issues for the substantive issues. Ethics is thus reduced to a problem—a momentary hurdle which, once overcome, can be put aside as the research gets underway, and returned to only to complete progress reports for institutional and legal requirements" (2022, 85). What Howitt (2022) suggests is that we imbue an ethic of care within and throughout our research as a means of doing work that is attentive to privilege and power. Instead of considering research objects or subjects, Howitt argues, we should be thinking about participants and earth others.

This approach further requires that we resist universals and the myth of the autonomous academic in favor of cooperation and the act of "being in common" (see Nancy 1991; see also Gibson-Graham 2006). This very act would recast our research as a space of care, of interdependence, and always automatically of ethical decision-making (Naylor 2019). Thus, being in common resists extractive research and requires us to care about the who, what, when, where, and how of our research practices. A feminist ethic of care in how we do our research is also seeking balance between what diverse economies scholars call paranoia and possibility (see Naylor and Thayer 2022). It means "welcoming surprise" (Gibson-Graham 2008, 619) and finding "flexibility and fluidity" with our approaches (McArdle 2022, 620), while also recognizing the power dynamics and privileges therein.

Who?

Who is conducting the research is also crucial, and so reflexivity and positionality are threaded through a feminist approach. We consider limits and situated knowledges. Increased attention to the who in our work is crucial to instituting this praxis; in this section I draw on the ideas of reflexivity and positionality as important tools for doing so. As Coddington discusses, we have to reflect on our decision-making before, during, and after conducting our work and sit in "methodologically complex places" (2015, 318). Because of the development of ideas around reflexivity, feminist researchers have the scaffolding to strike this balance.

Reflexivity is a long-standing practice of feminist geographers looking inward and considering the myriad influences (including who we are) on our research and research practice (see England 1994; Katz 1994; Kobayashi 1994; Rose 1997). We also recognize that reflexivity does not absolve us of the issues of power and privilege in research, and we continue to thoughtfully engage the way we do this work (see Kobayashi 2009; Moss, Al-Hindi, and Kawabata 2002; Naylor 2019; Rose 1997). Therefore, we must practice critical reflexivity so as to not fall into the trap of expecting that in being reflexive, we are then forgiven for the unequal power dynamics produced (Rose 1997; see also Naylor 2019; Noxolo 2009).

However, when we do *not* undertake this practice, we run the risk of our personal experiences and biases unduly influencing our work, and we ignore ourselves as part of our projects (an act of uncaring). When we are not reflexive, it also creates possibilities for harm. For example, not recognizing the power and privilege that many of us hold (tenured faculty, upper administrators, white scholars, researchers who are cishetero men, to name a few) can produce toxic environments for those who do not share that power or who are actively beholden to it.

Critical reflexivity means sitting with the discomfort and decision-making in our research and seeing the process by which research participants give consent (in the case of human subjects, seeing that work as "ongoing and relational" [Smyth 2023, 274]). This process is something that is continuously reflected on, not just something laid down at the start of the project and then set aside once institutionally approved or after participants have consented. This approach makes a space for the research to be dialogic. Here, I ask that scholars who do not work with human participants find that decolonial approach (discussed in depth in the introduction and chapter 1) that reads for difference and consider how their work could be in dialogue with others, including our earth others.

Decolonizing knowledge production renders it multiple, and being in relation to nonhuman and earth others is a component of that. For example, Wölfle Hazard (2022) invites us to consider our research sites as multispecies commons and to think alongside salmon and beavers about riverine ecology; similarly, Gumbs (2020) puts us in conversation with marine mammals to be responsive to our kin within our work. Jadallah (2025) argues for relationality with place and interconnectedness with the land. Finally, Kimmerer (2015) demonstrates reenvisioning what scientific knowledge is, and how we can be reflexive as part of data collection practices by exchanging with our earth others rather than extracting from them. Thus, looking to queer and Indigenous ways of knowing and seeing the world is one way to multiply our knowledge and be reflexive in our approach, and to consider our relations with *all* the participants in our research.

Simultaneously, and in tandem with critical reflexivity, it is crucial to consider positionality. Positionality is another piece of the puzzle of why we can never be objective in our work—because our ontologies (ways of being) influence our epistemologies (ways of knowing) and vice versa. Put differently, the way we experience the world, that embodied everyday lived experience, maps onto how we think about the world and how we build knowledge about it. As Kinkaid, Parikh, and Ranjbar, drawing on Rose 1997, note, "This stance holds that our positions in relation to various social structures necessarily informs the knowledge we produce about our shared worlds. Positionalities are not static, nor are they total" (2022, 1159). We know that knowledge "sits in places." Where we are coming from—our worldviews, race, gender, sexual identity, and (dis)ability—all impact how we produce that knowledge. Where we are coming from also influences what and whose knowledge we value as part of these practices of reflexivity and thinking through positionality. Thinking about these tools, and about how we represent them in our research, train researchers, and engage with our research communities, is vital to this practice.

Here is an additional critical reason why the feminisms that all geographers practice should be grounded in the decolonial and intersectional: the so-called canon is very Western, very white, and very cishetero male. Thus, privilege and whiteness are increasingly being called into question. Drawing on Kobayashi's (1994) early call to "color the field," Faria and Mollett (2016) discuss the lack of interrogation around whiteness and power in international fieldwork—particularly in the global periphery (formerly colonized states still experiencing colonial-imperial relations). They point to the ways that universalizing tendencies in research always automatically "whiten" the field, thus rendering whiteness invisible (Faria and Mollett 2016, 81).

By learning and practicing critical reflexivity and assessing positionality, we can break down universals, disrupt the idea that there is objective knowledge, and decenter hegemonic ways of knowing and being in the world. Simultaneously, we can recognize the ways in which whiteness, for example, is at work when we conduct research. As discussed at length in chapter 1, feminism is messy. Early on in considering feminism as a method, Moss suggested that the "liberation of subjugated knowledge is a political aim of feminism" (1993, 49), but that work still has a long way to go.

When?

We are facing so many challenges and possibilities in the when that we are inhabiting. We are situated in a time period that has by and large been given the title Anthropocene. Debates took place over this epoch within and outside the geosciences. Whether we agree or not, one thing we can oft point to is the impact of humans on the planet and the realities that we are facing in a climate-changed/climate-changing world. However, although I have written about the Anthropocene in the context of the neoliberal university and talking to students about climate change (Naylor and Veron 2021), I now join the call to push on this idea of "Anthro," because it implicates humanity as a whole (Whyte 2017; Yusoff 2018).

In taking a decolonial approach to when, this consideration necessarily changes the way we think about the time period we are in and how that impacts our research. We know that the impacts of climate change are being distributed unevenly, much like who, what, and where benefits from capitalism, colonialism, and imperialism are distributed inequitably. An impending climate apocalypse is layered onto an already existing apocalypse for groups that experience subjugation—such as the five-hundred-year war being endured by Indigenous peoples in the Americas (see Islam et al. 2024). Understanding and explaining difference across place cannot ignore that we are doing this work in this very particular moment.

The practical when of doing our research changes how we collect data and who we are as researchers. The stage we are in our career matters, as does how developed our ideas and our research programs are. We are all scholars undertaking a process of becoming—we learn from all that we do, and from our interactions with one another and with our data and/or research participants.

However, the when we are at in our research programs impacts that progression. Research done as part of a master's degree is often confined between academic terms and is very fast paced. Data collected or models run during a sabbatical leave take on a different character when there are (in many cases) fewer demands on us. Pretenure research may feel like a race to a very specific and daunting finish line. What and how much funding and student or postdoctoral support we have at the time also matter, as do sea changes or theoretical shifts underway in the discipline at the time (e.g., the cultural turn). What caregiving demands exist in all facets of our lives must be considered as well, along with which ones are happening alongside our research. Life happens. We must take into account the time of year when we are able to do the work. What datasets are available or affordable, or what computing power exists. Whether there is conflict, natural disaster, regime change, or, say, a global pandemic . . .

As someone who considers herself to be a predominantly international researcher, I watched the injustice around the distribution of the COVID-19 vaccines and wondered when I could ever in good conscience return to the field to work with farming communities. I also struggled hearing reports out of Chiapas (where I conducted fieldwork and return visits between 2010 and 2019) about the violence and death being wreaked by paramilitary groups capitalizing on pandemic panic. I had no idea what would happen to my research program. In addition, I looked around me and saw people closed out of their laboratories, sabbaticals and postdoctoral positions that melted away, and early career researchers unable to conduct data collection and on a very different timeline than I now was (my tenure file was under review in 2020–21). I saw people lose opportunities to conduct research. We all were experiencing the pandemic and setbacks, but the impacts on our data and data collection varied wildly. What I experienced and witnessed became part of the motivation to write about creating a care-full academy. Like all research, it got emotional (see coda).

However, I return to the idea above, something I say to students with stunning frequency: life happens. I do not mean to suggest that the intervention of personal life events, which disrupt us at any given time from fully pursuing our scholarly work, is the same as the impact of a global pandemic. Instead, in much the same way many institutions are now asking faculty members to provide COVID impact statements as part of merit and tenure and promotion reviews, I contend that we could extend this grace and care to the when of our processes of becoming as well. We have an opportunity not to make up for so-called lost time, but to resist the grind culture that suggests that the when of our work be always and now and more.

←◆→

During the pandemic, the emotional stakes increased while also making visible the very real existence of emotions in our research practice (Ugarte 2020). The who, what, when, where, and how all involve some degree of feeling (which is again subjective and based in our positionality). But whether we are experiencing a pandemic or not, research is emotional. Emotions are a long-standing area of study in geography, where geographers document, per

Pile (2010), "anger, anxiety, caring, desire, envy, fear, grief, happiness, injustice, love, pride, or worry" (in Rodó-Zárate 2023, 676). But in our research, we very rarely confront our own emotions and how they intersect with the power geometries at work (Rodó-Zárate 2023, 676). As I discuss in earlier chapters, there is much discomfort that we must sit with in order to come to a place where we are actively involved in a decolonial, intersectional feminist praxis (see also Eaves et al. 2023; Gökariksel et al. 2021).

Many of us experience profound grief as we watch the fast or slow violences happening where we conduct research—this emotional response ties back to the when of our work facing a climate-changed and unjust world. Dying species facing extinction, melting glaciers, rising temperatures, racist police violence, hateful anti-LGBTQIA+ and anti-immigrant legislation, paramilitary activity, war, and genocide. Wölfle Hazard (2022) writes about the grief of natural scientists facing species extinction, as well as the urge to and practice of suppressing that emotion, which is viewed as "unscientific." These scientists are actively trained out of having any feeling about their research participants (2022, 154, 164). Yet in writing about this topic, Wölfle Hazard simultaneously finds that individual grief is "unbearable" and the act of collective emotional expression is necessary (2022, 155). Collective emotional care is required in our world making.

Beyond what emotions come of working with a specific group of people, in a particular place, on a sensitive topic or existing dataset, or in the archives, feelings are not left behind. As a result, when we conduct research, we must find ways to care for ourselves as researchers. We need plans for support as well as collective and self-care. Even if we feel completely detached from the work, there are still things about data collection that we need to consider if we are to be care-full with ourselves. Again, this speaks to the grind culture that relentlessly scrutinizes the pace of our research and pushes us to do more, more, more.

As we break away from this insidious pressure, we must put measures in place to not be overwhelmed by the space its absence creates. We must make other worlds for ourselves to fill the void of endless academic work. At one point after I turned in my first book manuscript, I did have a moment where I did not know what to do with myself. I was not teaching, and I was not in the field. I had other writing projects, but they were out of my hands all in the same moment. I did not have to or want to work, but I did not have the energy to do or take up something else. So, have a plan. A gift to ourselves. A space of care, whether we are doing scholarly research or *doing life*.

We also need distance from our data (and writing). Putting something down and coming back to it after a few days, a few weeks, or even a few months brings new perspectives that inspire. It is very easy to get too close to your data. In the race to finish my dissertation, I remember presenting a chapter to my informal dissertation writing group, which consisted of four of us finishing up and Skyping (it was 2013) across multiple time zones and providing feedback. I was analyzing data while writing because of an unexpected and accelerated schedule to finish. One of my colleagues suggested that I was not explaining things in a way that could be widely understood because I was too deeply immersed in my data. So, I came back to it later and took a new perspective. I will not suggest that this happened because I was taking on the care ethic I urge in this book, but that experience certainly informs on what I am writing and how I conduct research today.

I reiterate my claim from chapter 2 that we are not autonomous as scholars, and that we are all receiving various forms of support in all the work we do, whether we see it and acknowledge it or not. In the case of research there is an added dimension, as much work happens in lab-based environments with teams of researchers or is a collaborative effort across departments and institutions. Geography is interdisciplinary, and so there is already always an expectation that there will be possibilities for collaboration. However, for these to develop into rich experiences, we may need to reconsider what we value in geography and extend, create, and celebrate sites of inclusion.

Feminist approaches to knowledge production as a core component of our work as scholars require that we start from a space of care, that we be reflexive, that we consider our positionality, and that we acknowledge our earth others. We should be creative and open to surprise (Gibson-Graham 2008; Hiemstra and Billo 2017). We should be dialogic and participatory while also being flexible in our methods (Farrow, Moss, and Shaw 1995; Moss 1993). In addition, we should care for those we do our research with (and with balance): students, collaborators, participants, software, hardware, archival materials, flora and fauna, water in all its forms, and so on. As part of this approach, we must deeply consider how and where we share what we find, something I turn to in the following chapter.

"Call for Papers"

Reproduced in full from its original: Faria, Caroline Veronica. 2020. "Call for Papers." *ACME: An International Journal for Critical Geographies* 19, no. 2 (September): 413–23.

Abstract
Somewhere deep in the heart of Texas a pandemic settles in, a son finally takes his nap, and a feminist geographer receives a call for papers.

Keywords
Care; COVID-19; feminist geography; social reproduction; mental health

Dear Editor,
Thank you for this call for papers on the economic geographies of COVID-19. What a great idea. Research articles, not opinions, up to 8000 words by April 19th? Three weeks from now? No problem! As you note, the AAGs are cancelled, so we'll have plenty of time to devote to this. I'm raring to go.

You didn't list this as a possible line of inquiry, but I have a brilliant piece in mind on how the virus will deepen entrenched gendered, racialized and ableist inequalities via caring labor, its devaluation and invisibilization.

Small ask: to meet that deadline, could you download all twelve seasons of Paw Patrol and ship me your laptop? I'll text you the address. It's $21.99 a season, sound OK? While we wait on that, and so our teacher keeps getting paid, could you log into the three daily Facebook events she offers? You should mute the video though; my son won't actually participate. He'll be building his den empire. There'll be at least ten different versions. Can you assist with, say, eight? Please note that YOU HAVE TO USE ALL THE PILLOWS and you can't tell him what to do, even if in your boredom, you get into the architectural audacity of your own den plans. No sneakily checking emails on your phone, which anyway will need charging. Instead, you must LOOK AT HIS EYES ALL THE TIME! while he tries and fails, with piercingly loud frustration, to balance the blanket on the sofa cushion on the armrest cushion on the bed you just made for the fourth time this morning. Oh, and it's 6am. It's demanding, but he's so fun. You'll love him! And that will make up for it.

Now you've carved out some time for me . . . let's see. I'll begin with a discussion of the gendered labor of care. Start classic, why not. I'll aim to reach all those "parenting through the crisis," assuming a straight, white, middle-class but nonetheless frazzled audience of geographer mums. I'll try to appeal to the geographer dads out there as well. I know, I know it's hard on you too. I'll be drawing here on some of my favorite Marxist feminists, those who've worked tirelessly to document women's "second shift" and how their male colleagues benefit while they keep up the appearances of Doing It All! COVID will be my dramatic entre here. Cue those worried Chronicle op eds, the working-mum stock photo, and those scatterplots of stalled careers. Of course, this is age-old, extensively documented, and feminists have been talking (amongst themselves?) about it for ages. It should go quick.

On reflection (wow, all of this new space to think!) I must also attend to the intergenerational caring labor of COVID. Sandwiches, yes. I'll go transnational and dip into De Silva's recent bit on elder care, being sure to pay homage to the older feminist work on ageing (haha, new found wit). While I parse out those thoughtful, so resonant lines, could you check in on my mum? She's 73 (but looks a decade younger!) and needs help figuring out how to get her newspaper delivered. She's in another time zone, and wants to "do it on her own." Which means you'll need to call her, then set her up online, then teach her how to move the mouse over the icon with the arrow, no not that one, does that look like an arrow? The one on the left, on the left mum! Thanks for that. You'll sign up for the wrong Telegraph because guess what, there's one called The Daily Telegraph in Australia, and turns out they take my credit card, and then you'll sign up for the wrong kind of delivery ("not online darling, to my door!"). But you'll clear that up. Best thing to do then is just wait for 9am U.K time (that's 3am here but you'll be up with my son building dens so no worries) to find and call a local newsagent in her village and offer to send a check. Now I'm not sure where my checkbook is, but after 2 hours of frantic searching you'll realize, of course, that American checks are of no use anyway to a rural British newsagent. It's OK you have a lot on your mind. You left the fresh milk in with the coffee mugs by the way. In any case, can you give my brother in England a quick call and ask him if he wouldn't mind, given he's the favourite child and let's face it the only one in the family with cash, sending a cheque on my behalf? You'll need first to talk through the last row we had (I was right) and make sure he feels heard, but that should do it. I so appreciate your work to keep my mum from "just nipping to the shops!" Now the paper's secured, she'll be sending crossword puzzle clues daily. "Sweetheart can you help?" She'll say. "5 across. Atomic number 31. Seven letters. Blank, blank, L. Blank, blank . . . blank M. Got it?" Pandemic, what pandemic? Since I'm so engrossed in my work, could I ask you to respond? Ideally with a newsy update and some vague but hopeful note about when I'll start trying for my second. Clock's ticking you know and she worries. You'll get the hang in no time.

Of course, any discussion of caring labor must recognize the intersectionalities of power that operate, in part, through the very mechanisms of care itself. No economic geographer of COVID worth his salt would ever forget that! So, while I open by recognizing the differentiated burdens of care for "men" and "women," I must turn to postcolonial feminism to complicate these reductive subjectivities and attend instead to the always-interlocking structures of racial, gendered and classed power. I'll of course draw on Crenshaw here, then take up some of the classic, still urgent work on immigrant nannying in geography from England and Pratt, Lowe and Gregson, Raghuram, Yeoh and Huang. Linda McDowell's lovely and frankly still-pissed-off commentary in EPA from a few years ago will be vital, as will Brennan's work on sex tourism in the Caribbean and Mollett's on the colonial residues of other kinds of caring labor in Central America. Hmm this is complex work, I'll need some time . . . Sigh. By now you've perfected the three-minute shower, the Ender Pearl teleportation and the art of the toddler deal, but of course you must get back to your own editorial things. I do understand the pressures you're under. You've got that production line to maintain, referees to find (good luck), junior faculty to shepherd to tenure, and those pesky impact factor goals to meet. And of course, the moral epistemological drive to produce Knowledge. An enticing CFP like this checks many boxes. But one last ask before I lose you:

Could you find me a nanny?

You could try the provider my university contracts with, but let me text you the URL. Their business name evokes a sunrise serenity but you won't want to google it unless you're ready to reconcile your need for care with their exploitative, anti-union practices, their corporatization of childcare via neoliberal universities keen to look feminist while they conveniently contract out parenting, and their colonial spread across the global south via the allure of western (that is, white) charter-based model of education. There'll be some guilt, but it will pass quickly enough, and the distraction of registering on your phone (because, you know, the kid has the Paw Patrol going on the computer) will counter the brief moral hit to your gut. It will need charging. Actually, they'll want social security numbers and you'll struggle to find, ahem, a good nanny right now. Few will show up now that we're stuck with this do-your-bit-and-stay-at-home nonsense. Instead, could you spend a few hours texting friends and friends of friends and hitting up the academic momma sites for this area to find a precariously employed, ideally undocumented, women of color who will forfeit care of her own baby to come and take mine off your hands for a bit? She's more of a domestic really. You can ask her to do a little light cleaning on the side, which will be good for her anyway since the 2-happy-birthdays-handwash is an aspiration rather than a reality for my grubby son. She does live with and care for her diabetic grandma but she'll need the money and, anyway, it's allowed. We're "surging" but not surging enough to be in lockdown silly. Thank goodness our Governor runs a "Right to Work" state. You'll disapprove of the fact she has to take two busses and a Lyft to get here, her failure to social distance is just making it worse for the rest of us after all. But you'll tell yourself doing so enables me to work, and my work matters. You're not being racist, sexist or classist because, you know, the work. Funny thing, it will take you a couple of hours to locate and coordinate your nanny, and you'll need a nanny to give you that time to do that. A Mobius strip of impossibility and possibility. Hmm, perhaps my piece should bring in some of Secor or Nast's fabulous feminist psychoanalysis. . . .

Which reminds me to say, if you're feeling anxious, don't worry! Try obsessively googling "COVID-19 U.K." and desperately searching in the first, say, 15 pages for hopeful headlines: "U.K. rolls out 100,000 tests a day!," "pandemic over just in time for the cricket!" or, less likely I know, "Boris recovers, emerges competent!" No hits yet but have a go. It will either resuscitate or more likely, deeply mess with, your sanity. While you're at it, I'll certainly be attending to the emotional geographies of COVID in my fifth paragraph. I'll use therapeutic feminist methods to think through the ways that LGBTQ students stuck at home re-navigate their homophobic parents, and how DACA students deal with the deft political use of the pandemic to deepen xenophobic sentiment against them. I'll take on, at once, both the huge rise in student anxiety, depression, obsessive behavior, and suicide, and our universities' feigning narrative of care as we "move online." My anchor will be the feminist crip work out there on ableism, mental health, and this nation's shameful disavowal of universal health care, which I'll beautifully dovetail with something good on the digital neoliberalization of academia. My solution? I'll draw from one of my fave feminist geography collectives to call for "slow scholarship" in the time of COVID-19.

My sister will probably call while I'm digging in here, could you take that? She's trying to cram twelve years of professional training on neuro-atypical therapies in by the end of the week now that her son is cut off from the specialist school he waited four years to get into. You won't be on the phone long (she's apparently "busy" and it will die) but you'll still need a drink afterwards. God she's exhausting. But by then it will be noon and it's fine, there's plenty of memes promoting day drinking right now. In fact, it's a perfect time to nip that desperate two-decade quest for sobriety in the bud. I've ordered you a case of Chilensis and a bottle of Scotch. It'll be on your doorstep within the hour, did you know they're delivering now? Wow, look at that . . . Seems I've blown through mine. Again. Thank goodness alcohol is an Essential Service!

Speaking of self-care, I'll definitely include a section on its importance. It's a feminist imperative. While I write that bit, could you google highly rated meditation apps or YouTube yoga channels, something free ideally? Personally, I've got quite into yoga you can do in four minutes while your kid turns on all the lights, blows out your candles and sits on your back. It's a thing. But wait, silly me! You won't have time for that. Instead you can just imagine doing it in the time after my son finally passes out (945pm) and just before you do (18 minutes later). While you sleep, I'll note the word count for my piece is getting up there. I'll never meet it if I go into the self-care stuff. Contra good feminist praxis, you can't do it all! I'll be scrapping that from my searing analysis but you're still welcome to that whisky shot (or three). You'll need it!

Back to work. McKittrick's Plantation Futures and Katz's Countertopographies will push me at this point to think about the grounded connections across place and time that position people in linked but asymmetric relationships to colonial, racial, gendered, classed, heteropatriarchal power. Daley, Noxolo, Mullings, Mollett and Kinyanjui—they'll be useful here too. I'll look to them all for a postcolonial analysis that links imperial 18th and 19th century exploitation to its 20th century counterpart: the neoliberal restructuring and brutal IMF debt payments that have devastated global south healthcare systems, leaving them faced with a pandemic they have so few resources to respond to. We think it's bad here! I'll throw something in from Nixon about "slow violence" and then, to cut through all the doom and gloom, I'll write some inspiring prose about "resilience" and post-COVID feminist futures.

Goodness, I am moving myself to tears. This deserves my devoted time.

Could I ask you to read and respond to the four WhatsApp requests on my phone from my colleagues in Uganda? It will need charging. Their government responded early, and they're closely following lockdown rules unlike our spring breakers, bless them. But they have families and communities to support and, can you imagine, they don't get paid if they don't work. Could you figure out my Wells Fargo password, it ends either with two !!s or 1$, and look at my bank account, and my upcoming bills, and see how much I can send each one? Remember my mum is going to need the internet access, I have our whisky and the childcare to budget for, oh and the mortgage. Don't count on any of those puny merit raises, or the "diversity" ones that earnest faculty group wasted all their time fighting so hard for. They've both been frozen as our university "tightens its belt." After all, we must share the burden. Together. All of a sudden. While you're at it, for some reason, there's a bunch of new money sending apps out there, so I'd appreciate you taking just a moment to do some research on the least scammy ones. And make sure they have an office within, let's say, 10km of where my friends in Kampala live. They'll be on foot. Not a priority though, focus on those dens. They'll figure it out. They always do.

We're economic geographers, so it's essential I weave these embodied experiences of "caring amidst COVID" (there's the title!) into the wider structures of society. Pratt and Rosner's elegant conceptualization of "the global intimate" will be vital here. It's my go-to. I'll sit with Gilmore and Ramírez, Roberts, Wright and Reese, Torres and Mollett, Cowen and Roy and their wider community of vibrant minor Marxist, antiracist, and decolonial feminist geography to better understand our military-inspired and failing supply chains, the pernicious privatization of the NHS, corporate profiteering on the backs of overcrowded imprisoned labor, South African slum evictions, stock buy-outs and too big to fail airlines, and generally how these settler-colonial presents reek of past capitalist appropriations and aggressions. I'll insist we reckon with the medical ships and luxury hotels that lie empty while the unhoused and sick die in alleyways and hospital corridors. And I'll puzzle over why such an "equal opportunity" virus seems so to love destroying Black, Brown and Indigenous bodies, the poor, the incarcerated, and the detained. Are we really all "in this together"? I'll muse.

I'll need to find space in my schedule for this, groundbreaking, section. Could you find and send my other sister and her NHS nursing team some face masks and rubber gloves? They've got some, but they're a few miles down the road in some warehouse waiting for "management" to decide who gets what. They're just district nurses seeing palliative and suspected-but-never-to-be-tested-COVID patients that the hospitals can't accommodate so they're technically "frontline" but somehow not "essential." Still her whining is distracting, and it would clear my mind for my very important intervention if I knew that was taken care of. Having trouble sourcing masks on Amazon? What are all those factory workers in Wuhan, the so-called "surgical mask capital of the world", doing with their time?! As my mum says, if you want something done, do it yourself. Obviously, I'm busy being brilliant, so could you search the web for how to craft surgical masks and 3-D printed eye shields? Then make them and then ship them to my sister for me? She did need ten sets (they can reuse them, you're busy!) but now four of her team are off "sick" with dry coughs and temperatures, so I guess six will do. Clearly taking advantage of the situation. I did hear there's a wider shortage, even if lots of nurses are pulling sickies, so while you're at it could you print another, say, 4 million? We could do with a few more nurses too. God knows why no one wants to sign up when you get to serve your nation for an average of £22 grand (£8 grand more if you stick at it for 35 years!) Anyway, who needs a "living" wage when you get that nationwide round of applause every day? And during prime telly time! So, could you train a few up while you're at it? If they ask about inflation, that tiny and diminishing fuel subsidy, or those stolen pensions just hush them soothingly and remind them—they're our heroes. Little joke there, training nurses is the work of the government, formal work. Don't bother your pretty head about that. But I will weave that bit into my own structural critique of British austerity. I like it.

Now while I'm doing the real work, and once you've finished those masks, could you master VimeoPanoptoYuJaSnagitCamtasiaProctorio or whichever self-cast-student-monitoring-suite feels most "You" to pre-record my 14 remaining lectures and "retool" my class exams? So many tech solutions emerging from this pandemic. Silver linings all around! Just be sure to find a way to mute out the sound of a child screaming for their fifth HOT PEANUT BUTTER TOAST! of the day while keeping your own voice very calm, clear and audible. And don't fret if this brave new world of teaching makes you nervous, it doesn't really matter how the lecture goes. Half the students will be so numbed by their new 18 hour days of screen time they won't be paying attention, and the other half won't even show up. Too busy helping their parents "pay rent" or something. Always with the excuses. Oh and while you're online, could you take on a few of my Zoom meetings? I've taken to calling them "Zootings," it's bound to go viral (can we say that yet?): There's one on how to use Zoom, how to prevent Zoom bombing, how to "flip" my class for a pandemic pedagogy, how most effectively to gaslight yourself into forfeiting, to Zoom, the remaining vestiges of your privacy, and of course, how to grade in a crisis (no giving all As, we have standards!) Duo's Multi-Factor

Authentication will weevil its way into your now-regular nightmares, but still, my Provost's keeping track of how many we host, so that would be super helpful. Tenure review is coming! If you sub a few of those for me, I'll have time to write my devastating conclusion. If you mute the audio and video no one will know you're making dens. They don't need your self-righteous opinions anyway. Just to know that they organized a meeting and you "came."

I like to close with acknowledgments, it's good practice. I'll be brief, I know I kept you busy caring for me and my loved ones so I could write my article. Thank you. Just to be clear, I won't actually acknowledge you in writing. There's no academic convention for that. Instead I'll keep it simple and do the usual thank you to "three anonymous reviewers," by which statistically we mean at least two more women doing unpaid and unrecognized labor. But I don't have time to go there, and that fact is thankfully hidden by their "anonymity." I'll modestly assert that all errors are my own.

For a moment, I'll wonder what my job is, as an economic geographer in these dark days of crisis. Certainly, we must understand what went wrong, who suffered more. We must contemplate the devastating cumulative and now immediate effects of industrialized agriculture and its novel zoonotic leaps. Of global austerity and its devastating capacity to create, from those incipient viral moves, a monstrous pandemic. Of how a disaster capitalism, a disaster colonialism, was mobilized yet again. Beckoned this time by a predictable, indeed predicted, outbreak of disease, rather than some other not-so-natural natural catastrophe. We must ask "who is accountable?" Because, certainly, someone, something is.

Those analyses are vital. But do we need that call for papers right now? Just as we meet that not-at-all-flattened peak of "the curve"? That is, the moment when we start to learn of friends and students who have lost loved ones, and then that moment when we start to lose loved ones ourselves? Perhaps, I think, we do need economic geographies right now. But we won't hear the ones I want to tell, and those of so many others, if we don't make space for the work of care that makes them possible, and with which they're always bound. We cannot escape the profound geographies of care even if we refuse to see their labors. After all, on whose stolen backs are the seeds of that toxic industrial agriculture planted? What demands of body work, of social reproduction, of love do these newer vagabond capitalisms make? Who will mind the baby so careers, economies, and bodies can be resuscitated? What failures of feminism surface when our angst begins and ends only with ourselves? And what new transformative solidarities might form: feminist, crip, queer, antiracist, from these times—if only we care, we protest, enough? Perhaps, I'll think, this call for papers will pass me by because this must be, instead, a time for care. For caring for our students, our loved ones, ourselves, and for those directly affected by and protecting us in the face of this pandemic: cleaners, truckers, grocery store reshelvers, virologists, teachers, surgical mask makers and nurses like my sister. They might be longing for days like mine, holed up at home with infuriating, adored loved ones. Grappling only with unfinished things, not unfinished lives.

But I won't write that, gawd no. I have so much to say, and you are doing such a good job with that den. I have a few other jobs that need doing. But that should carve out just enough time to put this together for April 19. No problem.

After all, the AAGs are cancelled.

Acknowledgments

I recognize the irony of writing and publishing this piece and creating caring labor for others to do so. Thank you to my editors Jack Gieseking and JP Catungal for their openness to the form, and forgiveness for my unfair reliance on their role as a foil for far more complex, structural things. Four reviewers, Ann Bartos, Sarah de Leeuw, Kate Derickson and Jenna Loyd, along with several colleagues and friends in the UT Feminist Geography Collective and beyond provided solidarity and a push to just-get-on-with-it via their rigorous, critical engagement. I play with foundational feminist book and article titles throughout without citation. I hope this will be understood as fitting with the letter premise, and a practice of appreciation not appropriation. All authors are cited below. Anton Dochtermann, Destinee Wilson and Minecraft PE gave me space to write, Jamaica Kincaid and Binyavanga Wainaina, the satiric aspiration. Last, thank you to my funny family for reading so many versions, and with generosity. Can someone please tell dad to change his Facebook post? It's coming out in ACME that's an m, not an n? It's the leading international journal for . . . Oh forget it. I love you all. P.S. The answer is GALLIUM and, yes mum, I googled it.

References I Would Have Cited

Adeniyi Ogunyankin, Grace. 2019. "The city of our dream": *Owambe* urbanism and low-income women's resistance in Ibadan, Nigeria." *International Journal of Urban and Regional Research* 43(3): 423–441. https://doi.org/10.1111/1468-2427.12732.

Bondi, Liz. 2005. Making connections and thinking through emotions: between geography and psychotherapy. *Transactions of the Institute of British Geographers* 30(4): 433–448. https://doi.org/10.1111/j.1475-5661.2005.00183.x.

Bonilla, Yarimar. 2020. The coloniality of disaster: Race, empire, and the temporal logics of emergency in Puerto Rico, USA. *Political Geography*, 102181. https://doi.org/10.1016/j.polgeo.2020.102181.

Bonilla, Yarimar. 2020. The swarm of disaster. *Political Geography*, 102182. https://doi.org/10.1016/j.polgeo.2020.102182.

Brennan, Denise E. 2004. Women work, men sponge, and everyone gossips: Macho men and stigmatized/ing Women in a sex tourist town. *Anthropological Quarterly* 77(4), 705–733.

Caretta, Martina and Faria, Caroline. 2020. Time and care in the "lab" and the "field": Slow mentoring and feminist research in Geography, *Geographical Review*. Early view. DOI: 10.1111/gere.12369.

Christian, Jenna Marie and Lorraine Dowler. 2019. Slow and fast violence. ACME: *An International Journal for Critical Geographies* 18(5), 1066–1075. https://acme-journal.org/index.php/acme/article/view/1692.

Cowen, Deborah. 2014. *The deadly life of logistics: Mapping violence in global trade.* U of Minnesota Press.

Crenshaw, Kimberlé. 1990. Mapping the margins: Intersectionality, identity politics, and violence against women of color. *Stanford Law Review* 43, 1241–1299 https://www.jstor.org/stable/1229039?seq=1.

Daigle, Michelle. 2018. Embodying Relational Accountability in Settler Colonial Contexts. In, Lindsay Naylor, Michelle Daigle, Sofia Zaragocin, Margaret Marietta Ramírez, & Mary Gilmartin. Interventions: Bringing the decolonial to political geography. *Political Geography* 66, 199–209. https://doi.org/10.1016/j.polgeo.2017.11.002.

Daley, Patricia. Rescuing African bodies: celebrities, consumerism and neoliberal humanitarianism. *Review of African Political Economy* 40, no. 137 (2013): 375–393. https://doi.org/10.1080/03056244.2013.816944.

De Silva, Menusha. 2018. Making the emotional connection: transnational eldercare circulation within Sri Lankan–Australian Transnational Families. *Gender, Place & Culture*, 25(1): 88–103. https://doi.org/10.1080/0966369X.2017.1339018.

Desai, Jigna. 2016. *Contesting Neural Citizenship: Feminist Crip of Color Neuroculture.* Paper presented at the University of Texas at Austin, March.

Domosh, Mona & Joni Seager. 2001. *Putting Women in Place: Feminist Geographers Make Sense of the World.* New York, USA: Guilford Press.

Enloe, Cynthia. 2004. 'Gender' is not enough: the need for a feminist consciousness. *International Affairs*, 80(1), 95–97. https://doi.org/10.1111/j.1468-2346.2004.00370.x

England, Kim (ed). 2005. *Who will mind the baby?: Geographies of childcare and working mothers.* Routledge.

Elledge, Annie, Faria, Caroline, Whitesell, Dominica.—Building a fun, feminist and forward space together: Our research and mentoring collective. In Banu Gökarıksel, Michael Hawkins, Christopher Neubert & Sara Smith. *Feminist Geography Unbound: Intimacy, Territory and Embodied Power.* West Virginia Press. [In Press]

Falola, Bisola. 2016. *Imagining adulthood from the CC terraces.* PhD diss.

Faria, Caroline & Sharlene Mollett. 2020. "We didn't have time to sit still and be scared": The postcolonial intersectionalities of critical geography." *Dialogues in Human Geography.* 10(1) 23–29. https://doi.org/10.1177/2043820619898895.

Gilmore, Ruth Wilson. 2020. COVID-19: Decarceration and abolition. An evening with Ruth Wilson Gilmore. Hosted by Naomi Murakawa. Haymarket Books. April 16.

Gregson, Nicky, and Michelle Lowe. 2005. *Servicing the middle classes: class, gender and waged domestic work in contemporary Britain.* Routledge.

Hallman, Bonnie C. 1999. The Transition into Eldercare: An Uncelebrated Passage. In, Elizabeth Kenworthy Teather (eds.) *Embodied Geographies: Space, Bodies and Rites of Passage.* Routledge, London, pp. 208–23.

Hanson, Susan & Geraldine Pratt. 1995. *Gender, Work, and Space.* London; New York: Routledge.

Hopkins, Peter. 2004. Young Muslim men in Scotland: Inclusions and exclusions, *Children's Geographies,* 2(2): 257–272. https://doi.org/10.1080/14733280410001720548.

Hopkins, Peter. 2020. Social geography III: Committing to social justice. *Progress in Human Geography.* 0309132520913612. https://doi.org/10.1177/0309132520913612.

Jabbar, Huriya. 2018. Charter schools' 'Uberization' of teaching profession hurts kids too. *The Hill.* October 17.

Kafer, Alison. 2013. *Feminist, queer, crip.* Indiana University Press.

Katz, Cindi. 2001. Vagabond capitalism and the necessity of social reproduction. *Antipode.* 33(4), 709–728. https://doi.org/10.1111/1467-8330.00207.

Katz, Cindi. 2001. On the grounds of globalization: A topography for feminist political engagement. *Signs: Journal of women in culture and society.* 26(4): 1213–1234. https://www.jstor.org/stable/3175362.

Kinyanjui, Mary N. 2014. *Women and the informal economy in urban Africa: From the margins to the centre.* Zed Books Ltd.

Kirk, Gwyn. & Margo Okazawa-Rey. 2020. *Gendered Lives: Intersectional Perspectives.* (7th Edition). Oxford UK / New York: Oxford University Press.

Lawson, Victoria. 2010. Reshaping economic geography? Producing spaces of inclusive development. *Economic Geography.* 86(4): 351–360. https://doi.org/10.1111/j.1944-8287.2010.001092.x

Lowe, Michelle & Nicky Gregson. 1989. Nannies, cooks, cleaners, au pairs . . . New issues for feminist geography? *Area* 21(4): 414–417.

MacLeavy, Julie, Susan Roberts, & Kendra Strauss. 2016. Feminist inclusions in economic geography: What difference does difference make? *Environment and Planning A: Economy and Space,* 48(10): 2067–2071. https://doi.org/10.1177/0308518X16659669.

Massey, Doreen. 1994. *Space, Place, and Gender.* University of Minnesota Press: Minneapolis MC.

McDowell, Linda. 1991. Life without father and Ford: The new gender order of

Post-Fordism. *Transactions of the Institute of British Geographers.* 16(4): 400–419. https://doi.org/10.2307/623027.

McDowell, Linda. 2015. Roepke lecture in economic geography—the lives of others: body work, the production of difference, and labor geographies. *Economic Geography*, 91(1): 1–23. https://doi.org/10.1111/ecge.12070.

McDowell, Linda. 2016. Reflections on feminist economic geography: Talking to ourselves? *Environment and Planning A: Economy and Space* 48(10), 2093–2099. https://doi.org/10.1177/0308518X16659482.

McKittrick, Katherine. 2013. Plantation futures. *Small Axe: A Caribbean Journal of Criticism* 17(3(42), 1–15. https://doi.org/10.1215/07990537-2378892.

Mollett, Sharlene. 2014. A modern paradise: Garifuna land, labor, and displacement-in-place. *Latin American Perspectives*, 41(6): 27–45. https://doi.org/10.1177/0094582X13518756.

Mollett, Sharlene. 2015. "Displaced Futures": indigeneity, land struggle, and mothering in Honduras. *Politics, Groups, and Identities*, 3(4): 678–683. https://doi.org/10.1080/21565503.2015.1080620.

Mollett, Sharlene. 2019. The making Of residential tourism space: Land, servitude and embodied histories in Panama. Social & Cultural Geography Plenary. AAG meetings, Washington D.C., April.

Moore, Leonard. 2020. Lecture 1: Freedom? (July 6) History of the Black experience: For University of Texas faculty and staff. https://diversity.utexas.edu/2020/06/29/history-of-the-black-experience/ [Accessed July 6.]

Moraga, Cherríe & Gloria Anzaldúa, eds. 1981. *This Bridge Called My Back: Writings by Radical Women of Color.* Persephone Press.

Morrison, Carey-Ann, Esther Woodbury, Lynda Johnston, and Robyn Longhurst. 2020. Disabled People's embodied and emotional Geographies of (not) belonging in Aotearoa New Zealand. *Health & Place*, 62, 102283. https://doi.org/10.1016/j.healthplace.2020.102283.

Mountz, Alison, Anne Bonds, Becky Mansfield, Jenna Loyd, Jennifer Hyndman, Margaret Walton-Roberts, Ranu Basu, Rita Whitson et al. 2015. For slow scholarship: A feminist Politics of resistance through collective action in the neoliberal university. *ACME: An International Journal for Critical Geographies* 14(4): 1235–1259. https://www.acme-journal.org/index.php/acme/article/view/1058.

Mullings, Beverley. 2005. Women Rule? Globalization and the feminization of managerial and professional workspaces in the Caribbean. *Gender Place and Culture.* 12(1): 1–27. https://doi.org/10.1080/09663690500082745.

Nagar, Richa, Victoria Lawson, Linda McDowell & Susan Hanson. 2002. Locating globalization: feminist (re) readings of the subjects and spaces of globalization. *Economic Geography*, 78(3): 257–284. https://doi.org/10.2307/4140810.

Nast, Heidi. J. 2015. The Machine-Phallus: Psychoanalyzing the geopolitical economy of masculinity and race. *Psychoanalytic Inquiry* 35(8), 766–785. https://doi.org/10.1080/07351690.2015.1087283.

Oswin, Natalie. 2020. An other geography. *Dialogues in Human Geography.* 10(1), 9–18. https://doi.org/10.1177/2043820619890433.

Pratt, Geraldine. 1999. From registered nurse to registered nanny: Discursive geographies of Filipina domestic workers in Vancouver, BC. *Economic Geography* 75(3), 215–236. https://doi.org/10.2307/144575.

Raghuram, Parvati. 2019. Race and feminist care ethics: intersectionality as method. *Gender, Place & Culture* 26(5), 613–637. https://doi.org/10.1080/0966369X.2019.1567471

Raghuram, Parvati, Clare Madge & Pat Noxolo. 2009. Rethinking responsibility and care for a postcolonial world. *Geoforum* 40(1), 5–13. https://doi.org/10.1016/j.geoforum.2008.07.007.

Ramírez, Maggie M. 2018. Reckoning with decolonial praxis. In, Lindsay Naylor, Michelle Daigle, Sofia Zaragocin, Margaret Marietta Ramírez, & Mary Gilmartin. Interventions: bringing the decolonial to Political Geography. *Political Geography* 66, 199–209.

Reese, Ashanté M. 2018 "We will not perish; we're going to keep flourishing": Race, food access, and geographies of self-reliance. *Antipode* 50(2), 407–424. https://doi.org/10.1111/anti.12359.

Roberts, Susan M. 2014. Containers. In, Nigel Thrift, Adam Tickell, and Steve Woolgar (eds.) *Globalization in Practice*. pp. 84–88. Oxford: Oxford University Press.

Roberts, Susan M. 2015. Book Review Symposium: David Harvey's Seventeen contradictions and the end of Capitalism. *Human Geography*. 8(2), 86–92.

Roberts, Susan M. 2018. In Honor of Doreen Massey. Memorial lecture presented at the Annual American Association of Geography meetings, Boston, April 8.

Roy, Ananya. 2011. Slumdog cities: Rethinking subaltern urbanism. *International journal of urban and regional research*, 35(2): 223–238. https://doi.org/10.1111/j.1468-2427.2011.01051.x

Scheba, Suraya. 2020. Covid-19 and the virulence of global capitalism—the poor are on the frontline. *Maverick*, March 30. https://www.dailymaverick.co.za/article/2020-03-30-covid-19-and-the-virulence-of-global-capitalism-the-poor-are-on-the-frontline/ [Accessed April 12].

Schurr, Carolin, Martin Müller & Nadja Imhof. 2020. Who Makes Geographical Knowledge? The Gender of Geography's Gatekeepers. *The Professional Geographer*, 1–15. https://doi.org/10.1080/00330124.2020.1744169.

Secor, Anna. 2013. Urban geography plenary lecture topological city. *Urban Geography*, 34(4): 430–444. https://doi.org/10.1080/02723638.2013.778698.

Sudbury, Julia. & Margo Okazawa-Rey. 2009. *Activist scholarship: Antiracism, feminism, and social change*. Boulder: Paradigm Publishers.

Smith, Christen A. 2016. *Afro-paradise: blackness, violence, and performance in Brazil*. University of Illinois Press.

Torres, Rebecca. 2018. A crisis of rights and responsibility: feminist geopolitical perspectives on Latin American refugees and migrants. *Gender, Place & Culture*, 25(1): 13–36. https://doi.org/10.1080/0966369X.2017.1414036.

Williams, Allison. 2002. Changing geographies of care: employing the concept of therapeutic landscapes as a framework in examining home space. *Social science & medicine*, 55(1): 141–154. https://doi.org/10.1016/S0277-9536(01)00209-X.

Williams, Jill M. "COVID-related impacts on STEM." In process research. University of Arizona. https://wise.arizona.edu/research.

Wright, M. (2006) *Disposable Women and Other Myths of Global Capitalism*. Routledge.

Yeoh, Brenda S. A & Shirlena Huang. 2014. Cosmopolitan beginnings? Transnational healthcare workers and the politics of carework in ohttps://doi.org/10.1111/geoj.12084.

CHAPTER 4

Writing the Earth with Care

> By deliberately drawing ourselves to our writing, we can open a sustainable and sustaining romance between writing and writer, creating an enduring care-full practice of love.
>
> —*Dydia DeLyser* (2022, 410)

Writing is an important part of our academic practice. We author papers, books, reports, policy documents, grant proposals, letters of support, reviews, poems, podcasts, lectures, and other talks. We tell stories. We engage with literatures and weave narratives about people, places, and our earth others. We write to share out data, to move the dial on our epistemologies, methodologies, and techniques. We write to be changemakers. Also, we write because we must. In the academy, writing for publication is effectively required, and the way it is required differs across institutions and disciplines as well as within geography. In this chapter, I focus on two forms of academic writing to think through an ethic of care, publishing and presenting our work at conferences. I take a deep look at writing for publication. No matter where you sit in the discipline, we are exposed to geographic research primarily through these venues, which speaks to the neoliberal character of the university.

I lead the chapter in thinking through writing as a care-full practice. Then I talk about writing and publishing processes and the ways we might bring a decolonial, intersectional feminist approach to weaving an ethic of care through the fabric of our work. I discuss some of the major issues in publishing in a neoliberal, patriarchal system, which is largely (but certainly not exclusively) focused on publishing in peer-reviewed for-profit journals (at the expense of other outlets that are not considered metric worthy). Here, I start by considering exclusions and bias and think about how we might write more care-fully and collectively. Finally, I examine how our writing allows us to dialogue about our work and the promises and problematics of the academic conference as a space for sharing our earth writing, with specific attention to the Annual Meeting of the American Association of Geographers.

On Writing the Earth as a Care-Full Practice

In saying that "we write because we must," I argue that this circumstance is twofold. First, we must because as curious scholars in the process of becoming, writing and sharing our ideas and knowledges is part of that process. However, for many of us, we must write because our research programs require it. And the demands on us to publish more and faster as part of the neoliberal grind of the university continue to grow (see Dufty-Jones and Gibson 2022; Mountz et al. 2015). Being guided by this premise and having publishers and editors as the arbiters of our publications (to some degree) can take the joy out of writing.

Because of the mill-like demands of peer-reviewed academic publishing, there exist multiple strategies for how to get words on the page—writing for fifteen minutes each day, the pomodoro method, "boot camps," accountability groups, "write-on-site," writing retreats, and so on. Some of these strategies promote communities of care and assist with the sharing of data, which is a crucial aspect of what we are all about. What I want to suggest here, following DeLyser (2022) and DeLyser and Hawkins (2014), is that we also be more care-full with ourselves as writers. The practice of writing and sharing our ideas can be an inhospitable one (and this very much includes the peer-review process, which I will discuss more in the subsequent section). DeLyser suggests that, for "academics laboring within and in resistance to the neoliberal university and the increasing precarity of academic work, to craft positive, long-term re-lationships with our writing entails negotiating the intimacy of writing in our lives, and purposely directing our writing practice from aversion and anxiety to attraction, care and devotion" (2022, 406). We need to maintain our ethic of care throughout each part of our research practice—thus creating caring relations with ourselves and others in our writing practice.

In thinking about being care-full in our writing practice, we can think about whom we write with and who/what/where is included as author and producer of knowledge. This reasoning is part of what is needed to reckon with the exclusions in geography and bring a decolonial, intersectional fem-inist approach so that we can write in conversation with one another. It is, as McKittrick suggests, a possibility to "forge relational knowledges" and "work out how different voices *relate to each other* and open up unexpected and sur-prising ways to think about liberation, knowledge, justice, history, race, gen-der, narrative, and [B]lackness" (2016, 5, emphasis in original; see also Mott and Cockayne [2017], who draw on these ideas). In this way our academic writing can be both world dismantling and world making.

This practice is less common in geography but certainly not new, as scholars find creative and inclusive ways to resist the grind culture of publishing. Having a single authorial presence but two embodied experiences allowed J. K. Gibson-Graham to challenge the rigid structures of academic writing and carry forth the ideas and spirit developed in this persona ([1996] 2006, 2006, and, for example, 2011). Early on, Cook et al. (2005) provided an absolute disruption of the myth of the autonomous academic, questioning whether individuals writing ostensibly on their own can actually claim sole authorship for any research artifact. The Puāwai Collective (2019) demonstrates that in working together collectively from a space of care we can be 'disruptive' to the neoliberal university.

Moreover, scholars are unsettling the notion that authorship is dislocated from place (geography matters!) or our earth others. Bawaka Country et al. (2016) suggest that the land where research is performed collaborates ontologically and epistemologically. Salmond, Brierly, and Hikuroa (2019) seek to decenter human researchers in discussing rivers with legal personhood in Aotearoa–New Zealand and provide opportunities to bring in our more-than-human collaborators.

Thus, we must consider what collaborative writing means—not coauthorship, in the neoliberal pecking order or even the newer CRediT system found in some journal guidelines.[1] We must think about students (at all levels), colleagues, interlocutors, research participants. To bring an ethic of care to our work is to disrupt not only the "god eye trick" (see Haraway 1988) of supposed objectivity in data collection and dissemination, but also the universalizing and singular voice of a solo author. Bringing our research participants into a different conversation and "decentering" (see Cook et al. 2005) our voices are parts of decolonial praxis (de Leeuw and Hunt 2018; see also Liboiron 2021a). These acts are a refusal of universals, and they pluralize what is valued as expertise; they also in some cases address or at least illuminate the exclusion of BIPOC voices that is a long-standing issue in geographic research (as I discuss in the introduction and chapter 3 more deeply).

Other forms of writing together as collectives (cf. Puāwai Collective 2019; Storying Geographies Collective et al. 2023), covens, (Smyth, Linz, and Hudson 2020) or labs (Embodiment Lab et al. 2025) are world making. Moreover, as Dufty-Jones and Gibson note, "such collaborations challenge the (neoliberalized) notion that success in research writing is the product of autonomous individual efforts" (2022, 342). Working together, acknowledging contributors, stepping off the pedestal we are effectively made to stand on—these are some of the multiple ways we can create care and make slow and steady progress as part of being in common (see chapter 3).

One of the core ways that we reproduce hierarchies and power dynamics in our earth writing is through the merit- and metric-based attribution of research through tired and worn conventions around authorship of our published work. With respect to the ideas introduced in the preceding paragraphs, it may perhaps be easiest on those of us who are considered human geographers and qualitative researchers to reflect on the power over authorship and invite potential coauthors (such as key figures who are participants in our research). However, I invite physical geographers and GIScientists to critically reflect on how they might flatten the hierarchies in place with those human, nonhuman, and earth others fully participating in our work.

Cook et al. (2005) suggest that considering the "situated knowledges" (see Haraway 1991) produced through our work is not only about our position as researcher, but also about the role played by place, land, recording devices, passports, and visas, for instance. How can we decolonize what Watts (2013) suggests is a divide between ontology and epistemology that is grounded in Eurocentric thinking? How can we instead "embrace" "the contributions of the non-human world" while still being attentive to structure and agency as part of that discussion (Watts 2013, 28)? Indeed, as noted in the previous chapter, Wölfle Hazard (2022) draws our attention to thinking with salmon, for example, as something that can be part of our research practice in aquatic environments. Sharp et al. (2022) call on physical geographers to adopt a "geoethics" in their work that attends to the "more than human."

Where, then, do rivers, deserts, cloud formations, storms, climate models, programming languages, or satellites feature? Is there a future in which we acknowledge collaboration in different ways, one that is both attentive to the very ability for us to do our work and be care-full about who/what/where made it possible? Does the authorship attribution "Landsat 9 et al." mean any less if the work is carried out well, is rigorous, and is thoughtfully (care-fully) peer-reviewed?

The neoliberal structure for publishing creates distance and trends toward otherizing and competition rather than recognition and collaboration. Bringing in the more than human and our earth others is not only a way to practice an ethic of care in our research. It also stands to *bring us closer to place*—which, as geographers, we may consider an obvious undertaking on its face. In addition, this practice may be a way for us to challenge the institutional strictures around publishing by actively and loudly decentering ourselves.

On the Sharing of Our Earth Writing

There is no doubt that at its center, academic publishing is a fucked-up place.[2] Here, I am explicitly focusing on the neoliberal for-profit peer-reviewed journal realm, which is filled with gatekeepers, page or processing charges, paywalls, and unpaid labor, all serving a multibillion-dollar industry that effectively turns academics into "value-generating labor" (Dufty-Jones and Gibson 2022, 340; see also DeLyser 2022; Eaves 2021c; Müller 2021; *as an exception*, see ACME Editorial Collective 2023a, 2023b).[3] As scholars in the process of becoming, we are told that we must publish in these venues—but I will not repeat that tired trope (you know which one).[4]

This idea is baked into our training while we are early career researchers, and it permeates much of what we do / work toward as aspiring academics. In some graduate programs, having one or more publications is a requirement for graduation. For some, this demand can turn writing into a chore or even a nightmarish hellscape when confronted with a blank page. It also diminishes our ability to care in our broader communities and engage more fully with our research participants if the so-called gold standard for reporting it is, in large measure, for most in the academy, in paywalled and cost-prohibitive publishing outlets.

The process of publishing in these journals exposes the Anglocentric, neoliberal, and political atmosphere in which we are expected to write. It pushes us to only see metrics. However, I *am not* my h-index.[5] I hold with Gumbs that we do not have to be "measurable" (2020, 92); my value is not quantifiable.[6] Yet here we are. There are very stark reasons for how we come to find ourselves in this place, which I discuss in specific detail in subsequent sections on citation and moving toward an ethic of care in our publishing.

However, before turning to some of these most common pitfalls in how we share our writing, I want to remind readers that finding that embodied practice highlighted by DeLyser (2022) and working toward feeling the joy in sharing our work (instead of the burden) are exercises we can all feel invited to. Moreover, I also want to caution that doing so not be premised as an individual act. It must be collective—we must work together as authors, reviewers, editors, and the larger "us" of research.

The care-less character of formal publishing maintains long-standing exclusionary practices and in many cases upholds the myth of the autonomous academic. The competitive character (and in the last forty-plus years, this is tinged with the neoliberal) of gaining status through our published work acts against or constrains calls to foreground our scholarship with decolonial, intersectional, and feminist thinking and an ethic of care. The colonial/imperial, white, and patriarchal character of whose knowledge counts in geography faces long-standing challenges and powerful resistance. But, as with many disciplines, the structures in which the norms of the academy sit have exclusionary practices as the very scaffolding and foundations for where we are meant to develop our work. However, cracks in the edifice exist and become more visible as universals are challenged.

As I discuss in the introduction, during the challenges produced by a global pandemic, publishing in academic journals *changed*. Whether with intention or by default, some journals stopped, some slowed down, and, even still, some attempted to seize the moment with calls for papers and invitations for just-in-time commentary. At the same time, finding reviewers reportedly became a thankless task. In particular, women with caregiving responsibilities were disproportionately closed out of opportunities to publish (Faria's 2020 commentary, included as an interlude here, is an incisive critique). Statistics on authors who were coded as women (in gender binary terms) publishing in early pandemic times showed a significant slowdown compared with those who were coded as men (Viglione 2020). In some cases, there was up to a 50 percent reduction overall in who was submitting papers (Kitchener 2020, n.p.).

Again, we might not have anticipated what a global pandemic can do to our writing practice, but we absolutely can emerge into a different writings-cape (cf. Oswin 2022). Taking a decolonial, intersectional feminist approach in our writing holds the possibility for cultivating a care-full and inclusive praxis in our work. It also provides a way to break down barriers in academic publishing by actively working to make knowledge multiple, and by valuing those knowledges and with whom, what, and where they sit. In this moment, such an approach stands to challenge the everyday acceptance of mainstream publishing and academic grind culture.

The Coloniality of Citations

Similar to the who and the where of data collection I discuss in chapter 3, who is writing and from where about the theory/data are crucial aspects of academic publishing, and of the uneven power relations present in the current curation of our academic lives. For scholars who are writing in their capacity as multilingual, editors and reviewers can be more stringent gatekeepers vis-à-vis English-language use (cf. Müller 2021). There is the additional issue of whiteness in much of the writing in the discipline—that is, the problem of data being presented "through western, white eyes" and thus reproducing exclusions in the larger body of geographic work (Kobayashi and Peake 2000, 2008; Peake and Kobayashi 2002 in Hiemstra and Billo 2017; Gieseking 2020; see also Mott and Cockayne 2017; Noxolo 2009; Oswin 2020; Pulido 2002). Not unlike earlier discussions around what constitutes "the canon" in geography (which I cover at greater length in the introduction), citation rates within academic geography show similar universalizing tendencies—a white, Western, Anglophone, cisheteronormative body of knowledge (Kinkaid, Parikh, and Ranjbar 2022; see also Garcia-Ramon 2003; Kinkaid 2024; McKittrick 2006; Oswin 2022; Pulido 2002).

To be able to discuss the coloniality of citations and the problematic biases and exclusions in academic publishing, it is important to first discuss the peer review that is a relatively standard (and therefore widely accepted) part of the formal publishing process. Depending on a number of different factors, submissions to peer-reviewed journals may, in general, be subject to one of the following: an anonymous review process where the reviewers and author(s) are known only to the editors; a semi-anonymous review process where the author(s) are known to both the editor and the reviewers; or an editorial review where the peer reviewers are members of the editorial team, or of the editorial board, or both.

Reviews can be affirming, they can be painful (whether intended or not), and they can be a mix of unhelpful and helpful—which is where an editor becomes a most important mentor. However, after many years of reviewing and being reviewed, I am convinced that some academics use the anonymous peer-review system as a low-key form of academic hazing, where they can hide behind their anonymity with a degree of impunity.[7] I will not dig into this particular culture in any great depth because if we are to build a care-full academic geography I would suggest that it has no place, but also that to radically change the structures of peer review will take time.[8] The formal reviewers and the reviews help shape what will eventually be accepted or rejected by the editor(s) who curate the reviews and make the final decisions on all submissions. Therefore, it remains important to think about review as a site of care.

I see the review process, both informal and formal, as dialogic and as a way to expand my thinking and writing. Thus I have never thought of writing as an individual practice, even though I am certainly the only named author on many of my earlier papers.[9] Informal review groups when I was a graduate student and faculty member, pre-pandemic, were restorative and generative spaces for me as a writer. The loss of those spaces at the start of COVID-19 and the continued stresses on my would-be collective are gutting. Because writing is a social practice—whether we seek out informal review or rely solely on formal peer review. I am a better writer for being reviewed and for reviewing. I invite those at every stage of the processes of becoming to demonstrate care as reviewers, especially since in many cases our reviews will be available to the other anonymous reviewers in formal review settings, and therefore urge setting an example—and making change by emulating what you want to see in the academic review process. Please note that I am not suggesting we abandon critique and just be "nice" to one another; what I am attempting to get across is that there is nothing about being kind and care-full that is inconsistent with academic rigor.

The review process is a gatekeeping element in publishing. However, an imaginary is attached to what it looks like to push open those gates, move on to the realm of page proofs, and then finally see your paper in its final formatting for the journal, ready to be read and cited. Yet what then? The exclusionary, power-laden tendencies in publishing are expounded by how we are able to gain access to the final product—publications—as paywalls, language barriers, and search algorithms maintain the structures they were built out of. Gieseking reminds scholars that the internet and citation searches are not innocent, remarking, "Citations are also shaped by algorithms that reproduce the racism, sexism, heteronormativity, ableism, and colonialism the Others seek to fight against" (2020, 42). Even as historically excluded scholars may find a bubble in which they and their work are recognized, Gieseking urges us to question whether we really believe in an internet that is inclusive and belonging (2020, 42).

As a helpful reminder, it is not that work published outside "the canon"— this very narrow group of scholars—does not exist (cf. Kwan 2004). It is more often simply undervalued, sidelined, and ignored (a practice that is not limited to the authors themselves, but in which editors and reviewers are also complicit). As Mott and Cockayne observe,

> Citation counts have at least two interrelated aspects: (1) who is citing whom—citation as an acknowledgment of the scholarship your research builds upon, and (2) how many times articles or other works are being cited—citation as an academic performance metric. The former relates to the citations within an individual article, the latter refers to how many times an article is cited by others. Both dimensions have a complex politics, and are interrelated insofar as we often cite important or authoritative sources to show that we know the "right" people to refer to, sometimes without having thoroughly read their work, thus boosting the performance metrics of already widely cited individuals. (2017, 961)

Bias plays a role in these citation politics.[10] Moreover, the assumption of who is producing valuable scholarship, which often replicates that bias, privileges an image or idea of a scholar that most do not feel seen in (see Neuhaus 2022). This practice has a ripple effect on what scholarship counts and who is counted.

As Davies et al. argue, "Citation metrics, which have been widely used across most research areas due to their quantitative nature and easy estimation, influence career advancement at all levels including graduate opportunities, funding success, career positions, awards, distinctions, and tenure and promotion" (2021, 3). These metrics are mired in exclusion and bias that perpetuate the historical marginalization of underrepresented groups in the academy and influence recruitment, matriculation, retention, and career prospects (Davies et al. 2021). Bias in citation rates by gender binary and race is well documented in the natural sciences (cf. Bendels et al. 2018; Lerback, Hanson, and Wooden 2020). Metrics again play a role here, and Gieseking (2020) argues against our unquestioned use of the h-index. Google Scholar promotes the h-index as a measure of authorial productivity and citation impact, which is then picked up by corporate sites such as Scopus and Web of Science, and is deeply biased toward "first page results" and false objectivity in search results (Giesking 2020, 43). Thus, systems built in neoliberal, white supremacist, and patriarchal institutions such as the PWI university (discussed in more depth in the introduction) are reified in our conventional publishing and citation practices through and through.

Speaking specifically to gender identity, there are also many times assumptions of he/him/his for authorship. I have what is considered a name that could be assigned to any gender. In many cases, scholars who neither know me nor take the time to look at my work more deeply will often refer to me as "he" when restating my arguments in their own papers—even as I often write about my positionality in my publications. This act of assuming gender and defaulting to he/him/his is a broader problem in society as a whole. However, for our purposes here, I would argue that it signals a rapid-fire and shallow approach to reading the literature, not the deep engagement that makes our scholarly work richer. It suggests a distancing and the use of citation as a means to an end, both of which reflect the grind culture of publishing, where keeping apace with publishing "norms" means surface glances at the work we are drawing on or critiquing.

What if we looked to Mott and Cockayne's (2017) "conscientious engagement" instead of citation metrics? An engaged reading and citation practice that is intentional interaction with scholarly work that is, at its basis, feminist and antiracist and attentive to inclusion/exclusion—something that allows for

a measure of resistance to the grind culture of the academy (Mott and Cocka-
nye 2017, 964; see also Gieseking 2020, 43, which draws on Mott and Cockayne
2017). A care-full practice of writing might then include a deeper look at the
scholarship of the academics we are citing, engaging more care-fully/carefully
with the scholarship and our searches for it.

What if we, as Davies et al. (2021) suggest, multiplied our view of what is
a scientific intellectual contribution?[11] For example, we could acknowledge
community-engaged data discussions, policy and industry influencing, and
the dozens of other ways that some scholars do, and most scholars could,
translate their research that are not limited to where the highest impact factor
can be found. What if we trained ourselves out of the grind culture of publishing in neoliberal outlets? We could take more time to go beyond the "first
google scholar page" (Gieseking 2020) and the dominant so-called canon
(Staeheli and Mitchell 2005), moving toward what the ACME Editorial Collective recently described as a "commitment to care and liberatory praxis" in
how we write about "space and place" (2023b, 752). Please note that I am not
suggesting that not submitting work to peer-reviewed for-profit journals is
a panacea. I instead propose that we consider an approach that is multiple
and care-full when we share our writing, that we ponder the question of who
benefits from our writing.

Another point of contention with publishing our work is the lack of dialogue beyond the period of review.[12] Yes, we are putting our work out into our
academic circles, but what is the afterlife of our writing? Is anyone listening
(see Howitt 2022)? Is our work considered relevant and important (see Kobayashi 1994; Monk and Hanson 1982; Monk 2012; Staeheli and Mitchell 2005)
for, as Staeheli and Mitchell ask, "whose geography?" (2005, 360). Indeed, they
found that what was considered "relevant" in geography and to geographers
was rather narrow (Staeheli and Mitchell 2005, 368). Finally, what are our responsibilities as writers (cf. Noxolo 2009)?

In the introduction and first chapter of this book, I attempt to clearly point
out the exclusionary tendencies of geography, but our writing and citation
practices are among the most recent areas of examination. Mott and Cockayne
build on the introspective character of much of this work in the discipline
to turn our attention to the broader impacts of eliding or excusing citation
politics: "In addition to publication, citation is taken as an assumed proxy for
measuring impact, relevance, and importance, with implications not only for
hiring, promotion, tenure, and other aspects of performance evaluation, but
also for how certain voices are represented and included over others in intellectual conversations. Careful and conscientious citation is important because

the choices we make about whom to cite—and who is then left out of the conversation—directly impact the cultivation of a rich and diverse discipline, and the reproduction of geographical knowledge itself" (2017, 956). Let us ignore the neoliberal thoughts about h-indexes and impact factor and metrics for promotion and tenure that may arise from these knowns. Let us instead focus on multiplicity. Consider what is missed when the canon is universalizing and for-profit journals are at the center of how we write the earth. Geographers study difference, so let us challenge ourselves to emulate that difference and work from a space of care. We all study the "why of where." In this work, seeking an intersectional approach that is attentive to power dynamics and difference across space is a key practice that can be incorporated day by day into our processes of becoming. Piece by piece, it can help dismantle the colonial/imperial character of sharing our earth writing.

Toward an Ethic of Care

As I noted earlier, geographic publishing circles exhibited explicit attentiveness to the stressors of the pandemic, and editorial teams were the ones to step forward and extend care and grace (cf. ACME Editorial Collective 2023b; Bailey et al. 2023; Castree et al. 2020; Derickson 2022; Grove et al. 2021; Hall 2021; Oswin 2022). The official 2020 state of emergency ended in the United States on April 10, 2023. Around this same time, the ACME Editorial Collective (2023b) reflected on its approach to publishing and considered resisting a return to "business as usual," arguing that it was "impossible and unwarranted and that it recreates the injustices we seek to fight." The collective instead offers a framework where we "step forward slowly and carefully or, at times . . . remain in place instead of always pushing forward" (2023b, 750–51). However, the pauses and frustrations shared by journal editors in geography and beyond are not relegated to the pandemic. Finding reviewers and encouraging geographers to publish in our flagship journals are tasks tied to neoliberal demands in publishing that have been decades in the making.

Indeed, even before the pandemic, there was a slowing trend in physical geographers' submissions of papers to geography journals. At one of the last in-person conferences I attended pre-pandemic, one of my physical geography colleagues suggested that the pace of review in geography was too slow for the natural science standard they were being held to. Whither physical geography, indeed (Rhoads 2004, 2022; D. Thomas 2022). The grind culture of publishing has bifurcated our discipline and shown its unsustainable character. What is our body of earth writing without geomorphology, climatology, or biogeography? How can we revive the interdisciplinary character of our earth writing through care-full writing practices?

Despite (in spite of) the pandemic, much of what I am discussing here is part of a much larger conversation about the demanding character of the academy. Indeed, it is one of the more visible parts of these structures, and it suggests that when we publish and participate in/toward neoliberal metrics of success, we may be feeding or fighting a machine we want no part of yet are consistently reminded that we must participate in, whether it is accessible or not. Scholars situated outside the Anglophone world regularly have to work against gatekeeping and English-language shaming. Parents and those caring for intimate partners or elders feel the pressure of the grind in increasingly acute ways, as the 2019 pandemic laid bare. Many wrestle with the extractive character of data collection and dissemination and must navigate it each time community participants are approached, field sites are accessed, datasets purchased or collected, and so on. Many scholars see the invisibilization of their work, and BIPOC scholars find a normalization of the white gaze in addition to the frequent sidelining of their work.

However, what is different in this ongoing conversation, and which I see gaining greater momentum and traction, is the awareness brought on by a global pandemic and increased calls for change, collaboration, and more storytelling as part of an outward-facing geography (cf. Alderman 2019; Bawaka Country et al. 2016; Dufty-Jones and Gibson 2022; Harris 2024; Puāwai Collective 2019; Storying Geographies Collective et al. 2023). These are all things that feminist scholars had been writing about pre-pandemic (see Mountz et al. 2015; Puāwai Collective 2019).[13]

In writing about the "critical juncture" reached in academic publishing during the height of the COVID-19 pandemic, Dufty-Jones and Gibson argue strongly that "we must prioritize an ethic-of-care," suggesting "that scholarly excellence in our research writing is more productively achieved through the care-full cultivation of a range of interdependent relationships, times and spaces" (2022, 340). The recent vignettes published by the Storying Geographies Collective et al. (2023) are evidence of that argument. Writing collectively is a refusal to participate in the care-less academy. We are also encouraged to publish in nonacademic venues so that we can communicate geography to a wider audience, influence policy, and extend the production of knowledge beyond the academy. In practice, this attention to the care-lessness of neoliberal academic spaces may also ask us to consider how to change the very fibers of the academic fabric that weave us into rigid and universalizing spaces, and to reassess what work holds value.

This premise holds true across our forms of writing. It is a practice, and it is a shared space. We practice writing as a process, which includes publishing but also exists in the telling about our writing with other scholars, including at academic conferences.

Conferencing

We publish some of our writing, yes, but we also (theoretically) are in dialogue with one another through sharing our written/unwritten work at conferences and in other public forums. We have opportunities to network and to see mentors, colleagues, and friends in these spaces. Here, we can share ideas (and coffee, lots of coffee), generate excitement around our own and others' work, and be curious and learn and ask questions. However, opportunities to participate in these spaces can be inequitable; accessibility, affordability, and so on are factors. Scholars can be shut out of opportunities to present and have conversations about their work for many reasons.

The space of the academic conference can be enriching, but it can also be, as Martin writes, "a space of enclosure" (2022, 165). Harassment, bullying, unwanted advances, and the like can make the space toxic too (cf. Dowler, Cuomo, Dasgupta, et al. 2019). Geographers and the field of geography are not the first to recognize these issues and attempt to address them. Bias has not been uncommon if conference programs were scrutinized—who is giving keynotes, the lack of gender parity in panel discussions (a wider issue sometimes referred to as conferences having "manels"). When conferences take place in person, a pervasive homogenizing impact excludes those who do not identify as white, cisgender, able-bodied men—and changing this aspect of the academic conference remains a work in progress.

Moreover, the academic conference makes up part of the neoliberal institution that is the academy. We are expected to present our work at national conferences and give invited talks; this is part of how we are measured, how our research is valued, and how we are counted. And so there exists pushback against lingering exclusions that remain grounded in colonial/imperial logics.

The national Annual Meeting of the American Association of Geographers (AAG) allows anyone who can access the event to present—there is no abstract review for admittance. Recently, the organization adopted a hybrid model including recorded sessions that can be later accessed later (in part begun in response to the COVID-19 pandemic, but improved and maintained as part of the organization's response to climate change and the recommendations of its Climate Change Action Task Force; see Jepson, Martin, and Nevins 2022). This means that scholars who can present their work in English, or provide translation, or organize sessions in their native language, refusing the Anglocentric character of the meeting, have the possibility of participation.

However, anyone who has participated in these gatherings will be familiar with the way the conference population dwindles toward the end of the week, in some cases leaving presenters in a room without an audience. When graduate students name themselves as such when starting their presentations, you might have seen the simultaneous checking out of more established scholars, who turn their attention elsewhere. There is a privileging, somewhat divisive moment at conferences where scholars, in many cases without intention, make decisions about whose knowledge counts.

These practices are not exclusive to geography or the AAG annual scholarly meeting, of course. I am focusing on the AAG in particular, not because the organization has gotten it right and is a shining example that all should look to (see P. Martin 2022), but because its membership is global. The AAG is a place where we can and do build community around our geographic research (and other academic labor), and it is taking stock and actively trying to create a more care-full space to exchange our ideas—because the organization is a work in progress that is reflexive, working from the top down and the bottom up.

The very first annual meeting of what was until 2016 called the Association of American Geographers (the name changed by vote of the membership to the American Association of Geographers; see Bednarz 2016) was held in 1904 in Philadelphia. William Morris Davis, a geomorphologist who is also known for racist and environmental determinist stances in physical geography writings, was then the association's president (American Association of Geographers, n.d.). The conference program featured twenty-two papers on regional geographies, topographic qualities, and observations of physical changes in the landscape, all ostensibly presented by men (Annals of the Association of American Geographers 1911). Both the organization and the main event that is in large part why so many geographers maintain their memberships grew in tandem with a colonial/imperial, white, male discipline (see introduction and conclusion). Over one hundred AAG presidencies later, we are still working at making the conference a different space for geographers.

However, as I discuss in chapter 2, the AAG is more than just a meeting. As Martin notes, we may need to decenter the importance of the annual meeting (2022) and make visible the organization and its membership holistically. A decolonial, intersectional feminist praxis might then query what the meeting can be—what if, as Martin suggests, the meeting was a public good? "One path toward . . . reclaiming the AAG from neoliberal and neoconservative rationalities is to strongly reaffirm that the discipline of geography and the AAG Annual Meeting are public goods, anchored in and oriented toward a *strong engagement with the social* as a site of inclusion and active reckoning with multiple forms of inequalities and exclusions" (2022, 167, emphasis mine). This argument indicates that we can see the AAG and our participation in it not just as a conference to share our work, network, and see friends and colleagues. This can be a both/and situation—an opportunity to affirm our role as geographers and as members of a multifaceted international organization, and a chance to engage our organization in ways that help untether it from the neoliberal academy and long-standing exclusionary practices.

In the end, I suggest that Martin (2022) signals that we could share our research as something that is not separate from our other academic labor (see chapter 2), but is an extension of it and is braided through our work. This represents an offshoot of ongoing and conscientious work to change our organization and the annual meeting coming from multiple sites in geography. This continuation reminds us to reflect and adjust the ways we share our work outside of publishing and giving talks, and to mentor one another and a new generation of scholars to resist the grind (something I will address in greater depth in the final chapter of the book).

←◆→

In the introduction to a forum on feminist geographies, the authors note that "feminist ways of knowing are very much at the center of knowledge production in geography[,] pushing *all geographers* to incorporate critical liberatory goals as well as creative approaches to their work" (Hiemstra and Billo 2017, 288, emphasis mine). Imbuing an ethic of care through our research, including our writing—that is part of what feminist research looks like. Deconstructing universals and pluralizing difference offer a pathway to decolonial, intersectional feminism in geography.

What does scholarship produced at a different pace and from a feminist ethic of care (as discussed in chapter 1) mean for academic metrics? How are we to be evaluated for defenses, tenure, promotions, and academic and non-academic positions if, as a discipline, as a community of geographers, in being feminist we are on an island within the neoliberal university? If I actually had the answer to that second question, I would be joyfully shouting it from the rooftops. But one thing I will venture is that in our attempts to be the change, it must be done as a part of community of care. As Mountz et al. argue, to change the pace of our scholarship is not only a temporal act, it is a world-dismantling act. It is one that has to unmake the neoliberal university, and one that should be done collectively. I reemphasize the authors' claim that "slow scholarship cannot just be about making individual lives better, but must also be about re-making the university" (Mountz et al. 2015, 1238). Changing our pace (see Embodiment Lab et al. 2025) has to thrum at the core of our practices, reverberating out across the university and across our applications and letters of support to other institutions.

We can strive to model this pacing in our work at other levels of the university and in our extended scholarly spaces. In our publishing, as the ACME Editorial Collective argues, we can do our part through "exposing the structures, processes, and power practices of journals and our place within the academic publishing industry" (2023b, 751). The collective emphasizes that, in adopting such practices, "we can lay bare the production of academic knowledge itself, so that we can more carefully and critically create knowledge together" (2023b, 751). And we can ground this work in a feminist ethic of care, for, as Hiemstra and Billo urge, "[we] must not waiver in [our] critiques of oppressive and discriminatory structures" (2017, 287). This steadfastness means the unmaking of the neoliberal university—perhaps through restructuring rigid and patriarchal hierarchies such as the board of trustees, and by changing the ways that we value, appraise, and reward academic labor. We can start by being care-full and by steadily and collectively refusing the grind at the pace that we allow. Perhaps it means looking to the "unpause-ish framework" adopted by the ACME Editorial Collective to unearth and uplift a geography for the now (see also Kinkaid 2024).

Building an ethic of care in our research by threading decolonial, intersectional feminisms through our earth writing stands to make us all better geographers. The work of building these spaces can continue here. As generations of feminist scholars can attest, care-full and inclusive geographies will not simply appear if we wish them to. Therefore, patiently writing toward and waiting for an imagined future geography to arrive at our respective doorsteps on the heels of generations yet to come will not provide for all geographers (see Kinkaid 2024). However, we can imbue a geography for now (see conclusion) as part of our writing practice—something we work toward regularly throughout our processes of becoming, making it an affirming (Delyser 2022) and care-full part of who we are as scholars. We can write the earth with care and write ourselves into the multiplicity of geography.

CHAPTER 5

The Care-Full Classroom

Mapping Out an Ethic of Care in Geography Training

> Teaching is a radical act of hope. It is an assertion of faith in a better
> future in an increasingly uncertain and fraught present.
>
> —*Kevin M. Gannon* (2020, 5)

Equity in education is under attack in the United States as I write. The "Stop W.O.K.E Act" and Florida HB 999 under the current governor were brought to the floor of the state legislature respectively in 2023. The former measure prohibits the teaching of or hiring of staff trained in critical race theory in K-12 settings (in the United States: elementary, primary, middle [or junior], and high school [or secondary school] levels). Critical race theory is rarely taught in such settings and thus is likely to become a stand-in for any discussions of race or racism in the education system more broadly. The latter legislation bans courses or content on diversity, equity, and inclusion and prohibits the funding or other support for DEI initiatives at the university level; it also would take a strong administrative hand in faculty hiring and the tenure and promotion process at the state level. These are just a couple of examples from one state alone.

The very approaches I am suggesting in this book could soon be criminalized in some U.S. states. Indeed, in 2021–22, conservative lawmakers across the country introduced dozens of bills concerning so-called divisive concepts attending to race, privilege, and sexual and gender identity. These are the very points of discussion that must continue if we are to move toward equity and justice for those who have long fought for their very right to exist.

These efforts at the state and other levels not only undermine successes and ongoing work to create equitable spaces, but they also seek to maintain the very exclusionary and violent foundations of our educational institutions. How do we confront these legacies and ongoing violences and exclusions as part of how we teach and construct our classroom spaces? How do we teach with care? How can we map out a geographic education that allows and encourages students to face difference, and to try to understand and explain it? How can we inspire students to care for themselves, one another, and our non-human and earth others?

For a very long time (and with good reason) we have been talking about the importance of geography education in the United States (also outside the United States). We know that this training is essential for cultivating well-prepared students who will go out into the world and make change (something I discuss in greater depth in the conclusion). But we largely focus on curriculum and metrics as part of these discussions. While these more mundane conversations are important, I argue that we need to go beyond them and articulate a caring geography in all aspects of our teaching, from our curriculum and in-classroom settings to our teacher training and mentoring at all levels. Applying a feminist ethic of care and using a decolonial, intersectional feminist foundation in geographic education provide the scaffolding. And while this chapter comes later in the book, it provides a rather "dragon eating its own tail" moment, as the actualization of all geographers being feminist geographers can begin (continue) here. Making a world in which many worlds fit through Lawson's "caring geography" and Oswin's "an other geography" can start in our teachings both formal and informal.

In this chapter, I consider the ways we can reenvision teaching in all its forms as a site of care labor. While this chapter is more broadly focused on undergraduate teaching in the geography classroom and cultivating "citizens in the neoliberal university" (Naylor and Veron 2021), it is also a reflection of the pivot undertaken during COVID-19, and a meditation on the importance of mentoring as part of teaching practice.

The chapter begins with a discussion of the neoliberal university and the problematic character of historical and contemporary tuition as a form of exclusion, as well as the violence of the predominant whiteness of many university settings. I also present the issues with treating the student as a "customer." As an antidote to the commercial character of many discussions about education and the bottom line, I examine the importance of geographic education in creating care-full citizens and feminist geographers more broadly. The middle section of this chapter is a reflection on approaches to virtual and on-campus teaching undertaken during the pandemic in 2020. I address the competing efforts of instructors—some instituted draconian surveillance and policing measures, and others created sites of care—and what we can learn from this experience.

Shifting away from a COVID-tinted lens, I consider the ways in which we can adjust to create care-full classrooms, drawing on ideas that inspire inclusive, transgressive, abolitionist, and hopeful pedagogies (cf. Gannon 2020; Hogan and Sathy 2022; hooks 1994; Love 2019). Here I lay out some concrete actions, ideas, and resources, but I am not offering a full recipe, as the best ingredients will have to be tested in the context of the class/teaching. My suggestions include deconstructing the syllabus, as well as practicing care toward students by providing resources, sites of self-care, and a flexible course schedule with interactive or co-created syllabi. I also provide commentary on how we evaluate teaching and the ways it can be changed to be more care-full. Finally, I close out the chapter by thinking through the ways in which we care for and mentor scholars in the process of becoming.

At the Site of the Neoliberal Classroom

The neoliberal university is threaded through the contours of this book. In this chapter, I start with the question of whom education is for. Writing at the height of the COVID-19 pandemic, Taylor made the stark case for the depth of what Meyerhoff (2019) describes as the impasse in the broader neoliberal university system in the United States, discussing the "pre-existing conditions" brought on by centuries-old structural inequities driven by capitalism and racism in higher education (2020, 2). Structural racism was not introduced with the neoliberal turn at the university (as discussed in the introduction). However, the defunding of higher education and the ever-increasing cost of tuition unfolded with the introduction of racial-anxiety-induced privatization.

State-funded education in the civil rights era (1950s–60s) meant that free or affordable education was available to an increasingly diverse population through the public university system. Taylor offers up an example from when Ronald Reagan was governor of California. In 1966, amid protests against the Vietnam War, tuition was charged in the state's public university system for the first time. California public universities had the highest rate of Black college attendance in the country, and they were a crucible for antiwar protest (Taylor 2020, 10–13). If people of color were to use the university as a site of resistance to the state, higher education would have to be costly.

Let us be clear: higher education is still state subsidized, though perhaps not in the ways that we imagine. And, yes, most state budgets have budget lines dedicated to universities. But beyond those specific line items, rather than providing affordable or free tuition for students, for example, the state offers support in other budget appropriations. This funding is in the Supplemental Nutrition Assistance Program (SNAP) and other public benefits being drawn on by poorly remunerated graduate students and contingent faculty who are the main providers of classroom teaching in the United States (Kuimelis and Flannery 2023). *Public support for education indeed.*

As the undergraduate student body becomes more diverse (and indebted), so too does the graduate student population, and postdoctoral scholars and faculty in non-tenure-track and tenure-track positions. At the same time that higher education costs create barriers and opportunities to expanding the diversity in our classrooms, the ability to gain access to a living wage at the front of the classroom has diminished. The neoliberal university has created a diverse body of disposable workers. Education for whom?

To be a student in the neoliberal university is to be a number, a bill, a consumer, and to be driven to think that higher education is the best means to societally endorsed ends. Vocational attainment and monetary gain are emphasized over critical analytical thinking. Education becomes a way to purchase a credential, to pave a path forward by purchasing a most expensive piece of paper called a diploma. Meyerhoff (2019) argues that there is a simultaneous romanticization of education (you can do it—and society expects you to!) and crisis narrative (the various ills of the university—some of which I describe herein) maintaining neoliberalism's grip on institutions of higher education. Both positive and negative narratives are deeply steeped in neoliberal individualism and have the effect of reducing education to, as Gannon notes, "a frame of reference that sees higher education as primarily a skills-training venture, where we produce cogs in the machine, but those cogs have more polish" (2020, 15). To make legible our "value" as teachers, we adopt a neoliberal vocabulary of skill building, effectively commoditizing the work done in the classroom (Gannon 2020, 15–17). Suggesting that conversations around higher education, which fall into these neoliberal registers signal a need for a way out of this stalemate, Meyerhoff (2019) proffers different world-making strategies for building knowledge that moves "beyond education."

In symphony with the discussion undertaken regarding world making, I also pull through the thread of world dismantling. The neoliberal university will not be reformed in the classroom or otherwise. Thus, disrupting the idea of the student as a consumer, of education as a commodity or means to an end, and of the classroom as the starting point for the marketplace is an essential component of care-full pedagogies.

The continued monetization of higher education—and I am painting with broad brushstrokes here—is pervasive, present in textbook packages and online learning, as well as in third-party platforms and artificial intelligence (AI). ChatGPT appeared on the scene while I was still writing the first full draft of this book, and I watched as the academy had, well, thoughts about it. As an educator, I am committed to working with students to develop their critical thinking skills, and that dedication extends to my position on AI in the classroom.

There are so many tools and ingredients available to us, and AI is just another in a suite of technologies at our fingertips (although not without its problems). Many educators and upper administrators leaped to the conclusion that AI would result in widespread plagiarism and cheating. This belief feeds the neoliberal narrative that the student is the customer using the institution and any means necessary as a bottom-line device to become a successful wage earner. It makes me profoundly sad. Being stuck in a metric-bound institution where students have to check boxes (including on evaluations of teaching and learning, which I will address later in the chapter), maintain a certain GPA, and possibly be swimming in debt, not to mention having paid or unpaid work, including care work, in addition to school or confronting mental or physical health crises—all these possible circumstances never seem to be weighed against such negative assessments of students.

Putting the neoliberal character of the university aside briefly, I am reminded that geographic education is about cultivating well-informed citizens of the world. And so how do we create a care-full space in the classroom to help students develop their own critical earth writing? One way I suggest is through the world-dismantling and world-making practices I am attempting to thread through this book. I see hope and possibilities that we can use to disrupt the flow of neoliberal and white supremacist tendencies at the university in our classroom spaces.

Creating Citizens through Geographic Education

I do not need to underline too boldly the continuing importance of geographic education to anyone reading this book (see conclusion). What I do want to suggest is that in addition to a broader desire to increase the reach of geographic education, we might invite ourselves to also consider the depth of this training. By this point, I propose that we dismiss entirely the student-as-consumer mindset that the university impresses on us and instead embrace the student-as-citizen approach (see Bednarz 2019; Naylor and Veron 2021).

I can already see the shaking of heads, particularly from political geographers, at my use of the word "citizen" here. Let us be generous of this word as something on a spectrum of "showing up in the market as a paid laborer" and "giving of oneself to [insert country/cause]." I fully recognize that "citizen" is not a neutral word. But I use the term here as an entry point to moving away from the commodification of education and student as a capitalist "cog" model. I use it here toward seeing those people enrolled in our classes as full persons in all their complexity and their desires to be changemakers and problem solvers, to be civic minded and active in more than the marketplace. So small *c* citizen, if you will. As part of this work, I see a geographic education or training in geography as paramount.

Geography allows us to understand and explain differences across space and time. As discussed previously, geography and geographers must reckon with the who and the where that have long been held up as a singular apex (as discussed in the introduction), instead elevating geographies plural. Many geographers write about the importance of geography education and the need to maintain our relevance in the United States. I do not intend to repeat this well-trod ground. I do, however, want to reemphasize that teaching geography provides us with a twofold opportunity. First, as is well emphasized, it allows us to expand spatial thinking and encourage the examination of the nuances and complexities of human-environment relations; and, second, it establishes a role for what Bednarz terms "spatial citizens" (2019, 525).

Similarly, Bednarz uses "citizen" here as a placeholder for "member of society." Bednarz suggests, in considering how "geography can save the world," that "the idea of a spatial citizen acknowledges that citizenship is inherently spatial; recognizing that relationship enables productive and positive engagement with important societal issues such as equity, justice, and environmental stewardship. The goal is to prepare active, participatory, and emancipated members of society with an enhanced understanding of the world as seen through the key concepts of geography: space, place, scale, power, and human-environment relationships" (2019, 526). Even as we witness the "STEMification" (Seitz et al. 2024) and "geoscientization" (Cupples 2020) of our discipline, I encourage resistance to the neoliberal logics of the primacy of a "hard skills" classroom. This environment exists to provide students with tools that they can then use to present themselves in society at large as well as in the marketplace. Here we have an opportunity to take on world dismantling and world making that students can see themselves in.

That said, we should be care-full with how we construct the worlds we are engaging students in (see Newstead 2009). In tandem with discussions about what geographic education and training have looked like, we can also consider what a geographic education that is multiple (decolonial, intersectional, feminist) may prioritize and make possible. Again, d in this case is about knowledges plural—with those especially pushed to the margins being brought forward.[1] As a catalyst for critical thinking, I argue that this approach can bring us closer to what Lopez draws out as "geographic pedagogies of hope" where students find an "ethic of being in the world" (citizens!), not toward assimilation but toward transformation (2023, 796).

A critical component of the world dismantling and world making that can happen in the classroom, if we are to embed an ethic of care in our teaching based in a decolonial, intersectional feminist approach, is attending (in the United States in particular) to the settler-colonial, white, and patriarchal tendencies of PWIs. These tendencies seep into the classroom. As I discuss in previous chapters, the colonial character of geography remains problematic, and there are calls for a turn to the decolonial (cf. Daigle and Sundberg 2017; Jazeel 2017; Naylor et al. 2018; Naylor and Thayer 2022; Noxolo 2017; Radcliffe 2017, 2022). However, how we attend to that in the classroom is less clear. There are additional concerns about doing decolonizing work in neoliberal settings that might sideline discussions of colonial violence. These settings might also deradicalize decolonizing pedagogies by tying them to other diversity, equity, and inclusion initiatives that are so often diluted (see Cupples 2024).

As I indicate throughout the book, there is a *Decolonizing* that attends to Indigenous futurity and reparations (see Tuck and Yang 2012), and it is unlikely to be wholly achieved in the classroom. Simpson (2014) argues that many efforts to reconcile by pedagogical means maintain settler colonialism. Indeed, when discussing "decolonizing the university," conversations on "land back" are not so suspiciously absent (Bruno et al. 2024). There is also a *decolonizing* that I again speak to, and it is attentive to different ways of knowing and being that I suggest are essential to bringing a feminist ethic of care to the classroom. For Daigle and Sundberg, a decolonizing pedagogy in the geography classroom requires an embodied and accountable praxis that is attentive to both teaching and broader political commitments (2017, 338).

In the settler-colonial state of the United States, we can begin as Daigle and Sundberg (writing in a Canadian context) do: by asking how our institutions came to be established on Indigenous lands, and what colonial/imperial relations undergird the history of these places (2017, 339). Some students feel an overwhelming deservingness and unencumbered entitlement to be present in a university classroom. These feelings necessitate a discomfort geography (cf. Eaves et al. 2023) attentive to spatial relations of power that point to privilege, and to the imperative to recognize problematic histories of geography while being part of a geography for the now (which I address in more depth in the final chapter of the book). So, I suggest that if we are to underscore the geography classroom as one that can be decolonial, intersectional, and feminist—if we are to have a care ethic therein—it will ineludibly include discussions of entanglements of power and privilege, as well as reparations and repair (see also Bruno et al. 2024, 13).

This will mean fundamentally restructuring our teaching to have uncomfortable conversations. At the foundation, as Laing suggests, we have to radically rethink "how we teach" (2021). As Smith (with others) suggests in regard to remaking the university as a site of repair, "However we are situated, we go home to our institutions, and we consider, not a land acknowledgment, but repair, restoration, redistribution. . . . We take whatever resources are at our disposal: class assignments, service work, writing, and we reorient them *in the direction of repair, reparations, return.* This work is contextual, specific, and grounded" (in Bruno et al. 2024, 15, emphasis in original). In so doing, the geography classroom can become a space where we nurture and care for knowing citizens who can understand and explain the need for *Decolonization* and "land back" (perhaps in that first crucial moment with alumni relations postgraduation).

In my smaller classes, I ask students why they are here by asking them what problem they want to solve. In most cases, my classes are filled with people who want to address climate change and environmental injustice. These are students who found geography as a place to understand how to address the wrongs they see in the world. Yet how can we in good conscience send them out as potential changemakers without these critical foundations? If we truly care for our students and for geography, bringing the decolonial (plural) to the classroom is a crucial component of threading an ethic of care through our training.

What Is Feminist Training in Geography?

Chapter 1 does much of the work of describing where feminist geography sits in the discipline more broadly, and so I am not going to repeat the discussion of feminisms that I am urging here. This book is not intended to be prescriptive per se.[2] I am not providing a list of ingredients and recipe for the baking up of a care-full academy (cf. Hawkins and Kern 2024). But I do want to talk about a space where the training of all geographers as feminist geographers can be grounded, and that is in the classroom, which I have saved for discussion as the last substantive chapter of this book.

As discussed in earlier chapters, it is essential to bring decolonial, intersectional feminism to all facets of our academic labor, and to model it for our peers and for all of us who are in the process of becoming. Yet the classroom, the seminar, the way that we teach geography, I unsurprisingly argue, should be foundationally feminist for the other pieces we carve out in geography in order to keep the puzzle in place. Otherwise, how do we learn to be feminist? Mentoring and care in our research and purposeful academic labor are crucial, but threading them through our pedagogy as a discipline is essential.[3] Feminist training here must be care-fully combined with decolonial and intersectional thinking.

The graduate onboarding seminar I currently teach is not like the one I had. I am broadly trained. I had coursework in GIS and physical and human geographies and read Mackinder, Semple, Huntington, Davis, Hartshorne, Sauer, Tuan, Massey, Harvey, Golledge, and so on. I had the great gift of having fluvial geomorphologist Andrew Marcus and, occasionally, political geographer Alec Murphy (who was on sabbatical that year) tend to my incoming graduate class. I am well trained. But I am classically trained, and that is neither bad nor good. It just is. When I had the opportunity to teach our required graduate onboarding course as a faculty member in my home department, I was unable to reconcile my own graduate training with what I wanted to do to prepare our students. This inability was due to the reckoning facing geography that I discuss in the introduction and chapter 1 (see also Kinkaid and Fritzsche 2022; Oswin 2022).

How, then, to introduce new graduate students to the discipline in a way that problematized geography as a discipline but also argued that it mattered? I tried to deconstruct the syllabus—something I will discuss more in the latter section of this chapter. I wanted to introduce the importance of geography and then touch on important themes while drawing from a variety of thinkers and disciplinary approaches. Most of all, I wanted to prevent the siloing and subdisciplining (as it were) of the work being done in the department. Instead, I wanted to cultivate a space where all students believed that their work and approach were valued. This strategy is something that I think all of our classrooms (both undergraduate and graduate) could benefit from—showing that geography as a whole matters, not just the piece where our own expertise fits. Here, though, I suggest that one of the better places to start the deepest dive with this work is with first-year graduate students in our programs.

This example of foundational graduate education in geography, which ties back to the issues raised by Oswin (2022) and Kinkaid and Fritzsche (2022) concerning how we teach the history of the discipline, is intended to be a grounding example. How we talk about ourselves is an important place to start the work of training all geographers to be feminist. But what does it mean in practice to create a geography of belonging where at each educational level we all have some feminist training? Let us be clear: I am not arguing that everyone needs to take Feminist Geography 101 (but wow, would that be fabulous). I am suggesting that building decolonial, intersectional feminist foundations in our training at all levels will assist in threading these ideas through our classrooms. Undeniably, training sessions and one-time classes can be powerful experiences and provide much-needed skill building. However, for all geographers to be feminist geographers will require a long-term and ongoing (un)learning process, not a one-off event or a simplified box-checking exercise, as many of us have seen unfold, for example, with educational opportunities around diversity, equity, and inclusion at our institutions.

When we make deliberate choices about what is in the syllabus, what is on our course schedule, and what language and vocabulary we use in our assignments, lectures, and discussions (cf. Laing 2021), these decisions should be visible and be pointed out in real time so that we can regularly draw attention to them. For those of us who teach methods and methodology courses, our work is multiple in this regard. A feminist approach to research and data collection more broadly can be the foundation for teaching feminist geographies writ large. Not forgetting the decolonial and intersectional approaches that I argue are key to unsettling some of the more insidious problems of feminism, this means thinking about how to speak with and alongside those whose voices we are bringing into the classroom, rather than speaking for them (cf. Alcoff 1992).

It will therefore be essential to weave reflexivity through our geography training inside and outside our classes. Already existing feminist pedagogies suggest the need for reflexivity. Eaves notes, "Reflexivity signals that we are thoughtful about the varying and shifting power dynamics our embodiments produce, the impact of those power relations on students and other members of our educational communities, and, ideally, [the] work to mitigate power in ways that contribute to salutary pedagogical engagements" (2021a, 564). Everyone brings their experience to the classroom, yet there is often an authority in experience. One of the ways we can pursue change is by asking how we can both use our experience and be vulnerable and open to and appreciative of student expression (see hooks 1994). When we teach, we are enacting a politics (see also Reimer et al. 2023) around a very specific power dynamic. I bid teachers to practice care as a component of thinking through vulnerability, both our own and that of the students whom we cross paths with.

Virtual Realities—the Pandemic Classroom and a Crisis of Care

March 11, 2020. Take a moment here, because I am going to travel back to those first days of the declaration of the COVID-19 pandemic on U.S. campuses. On March 11, 2020, I received an email from the university president and, later, the provost explaining that the coronavirus had arrived on campus. Classes were canceled for two days, and spring break was moved up by one week to elongate our time away from campus beyond those two days. On March 15, 2020, we were informed that spring break would be two weeks long, campus would be closed for the duration of spring semester, we would be pivoting to virtual-only education, we would not be allowed to visit campus, and we could not undertake any research- or university-related travel. The students were emailed about moving out of their residence halls. We were told to distance, we were told what labor was considered essential, and we were otherwise expected to "keep calm and carry on."

As of April, faculty and students were expected to participate in classrooms in an entirely virtual atmosphere. This change had vastly different implications for the various impacted classes. For me, it meant canceling all field trips, as well as the semester-long community engagement project that made up the bulk of the undergraduate seminar I was teaching. I then dreamed up an entirely new research project assignment and mode of assessment. For some of my colleagues, the change to online education meant working tirelessly to ensure virtual access to the computer labs that housed our GIS programs. For still others, it meant gaining access to 3D scanning technologies to be able to bring specimens to our new virtual reality. It is well documented at this point that we made major shifts no matter what we were teaching (Corbera, Anguelovski, and Honey-Rosés 2021; Fuller et al. 2021; Fulweiler et al. 2021; Sparke and Anguelov 2020).

This moment contained an intensity that many had never been exposed to. Still, the neoliberal university carried on. Tuition had been collected; thus, education would be delivered. Yet what about the delivery? Yes, many of us who had never even considered teaching online were suddenly asked to excel on the new virtual platforms provided to us. And yes, the students were asked to find the right place to join at the appointed hour for class.[4] But these sudden expectations really told us nothing about how to care for one another in these virtual worlds. We encountered well-being resources and feel-good social media videos, but almost nothing about mutual care in the virtual classroom or what a care-full classroom might be.

At this point, it is well understood that we have not seen the last pandemic.

Human-environment relations are strained in this climate-changed world. Thus, the lessons learned during the COVID-19 pandemic—which, during the course of writing this book, saw lockdown, virtual everything, social/spatial distancing, vaccinations, return to campus, hybrid spaces, mask mandates, daily virus testing, a policy end point, maskless students, booster shots, and COVID absences—are lessons to be taken forward not just during periods of crisis, but as part of our everyday now. As I discuss in the introduction to the book, we might not have been expecting COVID-19, but we certainly have the tools at our disposal to address the intensities we face as educators in a global pandemic. I will stress here that this is not a book or a chapter about the pandemic. Even so, it is also very much a book and a chapter about the pandemic in that I am drawing from pandemic experiences. It was in this terrible and violent ordeal that many of us were faced with decisions about whether and how to support ourselves and one another to create an atmosphere of well-being.[5]

While I generally do not take a diagnostic approach in my writing, I am perhaps unpopularly going to suggest that some pandemic practices spurned the caring approach that so many of us are trying to make a case for. For example, increasing workload as an antidote to being online, requiring cameras to be on during class meetings, adopting surveillance technologies for anti-cheating measures, hiring third parties to proctor online tests (leading to harassment in some cases)—these and other practices that squeezed an already rather squished student population are not those I would merrily add to my best-practices grab bag (lessons learned, perhaps). A crisis of this scope . . . no, a crisis of any scope offers many of us an opportunity to show up for one another, to recognize the collective, to be vulnerable. It also suggests that we need to see our own position, recognize the differential experiences of others, and determine the forms of support that are best situated for addressing gaps created by those differences (see Neely and Lopez 2022). If we can look to the pandemic and take something from it, we might reconsider the possibility and affirm that we all need care (cf. Lawson 2007).

Care-Full Pedagogies

Teaching takes everything that we are, because it requires us to show up. Literally. We must see our students as full people. Period. End of sentence. Meaning that for those who are teaching *at* their students in their capacity as passive learners or as people paying for tuition, there is a good chance everyone involved might be missing something. So again, I ask for consideration of what it might be like if we imbued a feminist ethic of care throughout our teaching.

To reconsider what the university can do, what school is—for all of us. From the syllabus to the classroom and all those spaces in between.

In thinking about feminist praxis through discussion of the behaviors of marine mammals, Gumbs invites readers to consider the schools of striped dolphins: "These dolphin schools are organizational structures for learning, nurturance, and survival. . . . What if school, as we used it on a daily basis, signaled not the name of a process or institution through which we could be indoctrinated, not a structure through which social capital was grasped and policed, but something more organic like a scale of care, what if school was the scale at which we could care for each other and move together[?]" (2020, 55–56). To start from a space of care is to disrupt the consumer model of education, to learn in community with love at the center (Peña 2022, 81). We could treat our teaching not as a way of inputting information and instilling skills, but as a moment of care-full feminist praxis. If we did so, we might be part of world making that does indeed allow our school to face and possibly solve the most pressing issues faced globally.

Caring for students is not coddling them. It instead shows that we see them as complex and whole human beings—it is a form of the "engaged pedagogy" that hooks (1994, 13) welcomes us to embrace. Caring for students provides opportunities to build interactions that are meaningful, and that fly in the face of the neoliberal institutionalization we experience in many cases otherwise. To bring care into the classroom is not a non-zero-sum game; to care is not to jettison rigor or to lower expectations. A care-full approach may instead be recognized as a better pedagogical method or equated with excellence in teaching (cf. Anderson et al. 2020). Caring demands that we, at the most basic level, consider the multiple lived experiences and realities in our academic practices (Madge, Parvati, and Noxolo 2009). Pedagogy and practice centered on an ethic of care create distance between the idea of provisioning knowledge and the offering of possibilities for the co-creation of knowledges.

In seeking to distance ourselves from transactional modes of instruction, Gannon invites us to think of our teaching as a cooperative process, to remind students that they are not passive vessels waiting to be filled with knowledge, but are part of a "dynamic" space where they are "co-participants" (2020, 24). We might consider this approach by starting with our syllabi. The syllabus is a tool. It is a piece of technical writing that can be a tangible contract between student and instructor, and it is largely expected and required as part of instructional design in the university.

The syllabus, then, potentially becomes a foundational document for how the care-full classroom plays out. It might be the first contact point for students when they enroll in a class, setting a tone for what to expect. It can be a static or dynamic document; it can be interactive. It can be a place to uncover the hidden curriculum of the academy, provide resources, and set expectations. The syllabi that I develop for my courses tend to be on the longer side for these reasons. Returning to the admission that this is not a prescriptive book, I am not going to suggest what a care-full syllabus looks like. I do, though, want to emphasize one critical point here and draw out some provocations.[6] Our syllabi should be legible to our students.

Yes, legible—and by this statement I mean not that the syllabi should be simplified and readable, but that they should be understandable and relatable. As I discussed earlier, there is much discussion around decolonizing the geography curriculum. Simultaneously, there are calls across the academy to "decolonize the syllabus." At first glance, that demand might seem to fit neatly in a book about decolonial, intersectional feminist approaches to creating a care-full academy. However, for the reasons I noted earlier about capital *D* and lowercase *d* decolonizing, the syllabus is perhaps not an instrument of reparations. It might, however, be part of the process of repair that Bruno et al. (2024) urge geographers to consider. Instead, I encourage the practice of deconstructing the syllabus. Put differently, take the document apart piece by piece (world dismantling), and put it back together with equity, inclusivity, belonging, and care as the scaffolding (world making).

It is important that students not only find clear expectations in the syllabus, but that they also see themselves in it (Gannon 2020; see also Hogan and Sathy 2022). This practice extends beyond the politics of citation and into materials used in courses more broadly. It threads through our decision-making processes about content and materials and asks us to be holistic in imagining who our students are.[7] It also means considering where these materials live. How do our learning management systems (e.g., Canvas, Blackboard) assist or hinder our ability to be care-full in our teaching?

Returning to the earlier discussion of students as reluctant learners and the introduction of freely available artificial intelligence (AI) tools, I am reminded of a tweet (see figure 5.1) by news columnist Monica Hesse (2023), who shared the class AI policy written by Dr. Doug Hesse, an English professor at the University of Denver. I argue that this kind of policy is seeing students as learners, as curious individuals who are investing in themselves for whatever reason. This is a care-full approach to the introduction of new technology, and also to the use of technology more generally.

So many times, our neoliberal institutions ask us to police and surveil our students, to distrust them or to expect that they are deliberately misleading us

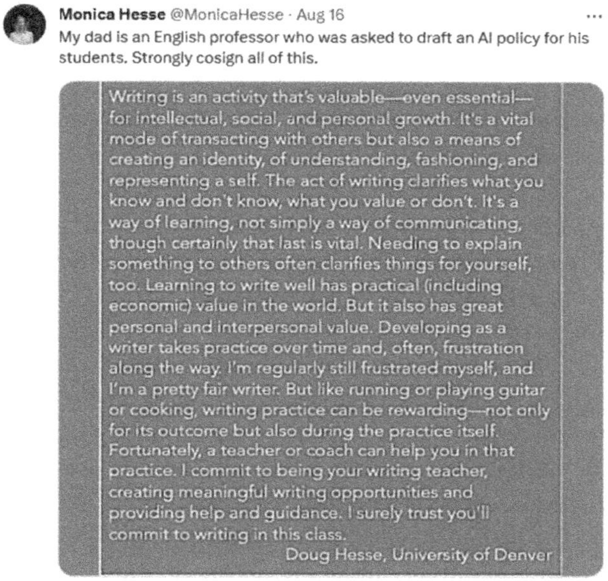

Monica Hesse @MonicaHesse · Aug 16   ...
My dad is an English professor who was asked to draft an AI policy for his
students. Strongly cosign all of this.

Writing is an activity that's valuable—even essential—
for intellectual, social, and personal growth. It's a vital
mode of transacting with others but also a means of
creating an identity, of understanding, fashioning, and
representing a self. The act of writing clarifies what you
know and don't know, what you value or don't. It's a
way of learning, not simply a way of communicating,
though certainly that last is vital. Needing to explain
something to others often clarifies things for yourself,
too. Learning to write well has practical (including
economic) value in the world. But it also has great
personal and interpersonal value. Developing as a
writer takes practice over time and, often, frustration
along the way. I'm regularly still frustrated myself, and
I'm a pretty fair writer. But like running or playing guitar
or cooking, writing practice can be rewarding—not only
for its outcome but also during the practice itself.
Fortunately, a teacher or coach can help you in that
practice. I commit to being your writing teacher,
creating meaningful writing opportunities and
providing help and guidance. I surely trust you'll
commit to writing in this class.
                              Doug Hesse, University of Denver

FIGURE 5.1. Screenshot of an AI policy from @MonicaHesse posted on the public forum previously known as Twitter.

concerning all manner of things associated with enrollment in our courses. I once was a teaching assistant for an instructor who asked that I continuously walk around the large lecture hall and make sure students were paying attention. I know you already know that some of them were not—but the point I want to make here is that I was extremely agitated after every class. I had to continuously redirect student attention away from online poker, skateboarding videos, dress shopping, etc., and so I was made into a surveillance system. Not a fan.

I do not mean to suggest that when we are at the front of the classroom, we are supposed to be interesting or entertaining enough to compete with Tony Hawk—let us be clear. What I am suggesting is that in many class settings we are not set up for success as related to the attention span of any person in a digital age (see, for example, instances of faculty checking their phones during chair remarks in faculty meetings).

At large research institutions and others, we are often thrown into big halls for those most important major-gaining introductory survey courses—human geography, physical geography, regional courses, geographic information systems. We are then asked to capture the attention of students who in large measure have never known everyday existence without the near omnipresence of digital technologies.[8] So, in tandem with many of the other wild things I am saying in this book, I think we need to reconsider how we approach these classes. The large lecture hall is not a product of the neoliberal university, but it certainly sits well within it. Moreover, the lecture hall sits within many tuition-based budget models, which actively encourage us to have increasing enrollments so that more university dollars flow to our units.[9] How, then, can we decenter the student as a consumer in this space and make room for the student as citizen?

There is value in reaching a large number of students at one time, just as there is value in a small seminar setting. We can approach both with a feminist grounding that allows for reflexivity and vulnerability (see chapter 3). This grounding also asks us to start with trust and care, rather than distrust and policing. It may require us to truly rethink what the learning objectives are in our classes, and how a care-full approach can help us get there. There is not one right way to create a care-full approach, and so this rethinking must be done collectively and be multiple; and we must give ourselves grace as we form these approaches, because we cannot ever be completely sure of how they will be received.

I often read teaching materials or hear scholars talk about creating a "safe space" in the classroom. To create such an imagined place oversimplifies the human experience to a spectacular degree. There is an apparent assumption that instructors at the front of the classroom are all knowing and all seeing. In reality, we do not have "perfect information" that could allow us to make a space where everyone in the room feels safe to be their full selves, to be vulnerable, to speak up/out, or to even know how to formulate a question that drives at the heart of what they want to know. Indeed, hooks challenged this idea decades ago, arguing that a "safe place" in the classroom often then translated "to mean that the professor lectures to a group of quiet students who respond only when they are called on" (1994, 30, 39). Understanding that the classroom can never be actualized as a "safe space" (a site of "mythical care" per Bartos 2021) returns us to the opening provided by recognizing differing positionalities and being reflexive in the classroom, just as we attempt to be in our research. It is an opportunity to acknowledge that all of us, no matter our background or training, bring our own lived experience to these spaces we inhabit and make meaning in. I invite those who tend to have the most power in the room to disrupt the hierarchy and consider that we are all scholars in the process of becoming, works in progress, who can learn from one another.

Recognizing difference and being reflexive also mean sitting again with the discomfort, returning to the hard collective work of building our decolonial, intersectional feminist lexicon and praxis. There may be no easier place to enact a feminist ethic of care in the academy than in the classroom, as so much power is given to those of us who teach. However, for many, instituting a feminist ethic of care means recognizing how some current systems of care maintain inequities that accrue benefits to the few in higher education. Per Bartos, "Those who are currently well cared for within the academy may be uncomfortable embracing those who are struggling and connecting them to their (comfortable) collective, but it is imperative" (2021, 318). And so, a care-full approach requires us to see and name the institution and those it was built to care for.

As noted in chapter 1, Gökariksel et al. remind geographers that "discomfort haunts feminist scholarship" and the ways in which it can be mobilized in the service of whiteness (2021, 7). At predominantly white institutions (PWIs), the classroom is an extension of the structural exclusions that the university was built on. Students of color arrive after enduring a K-12 education system that Love calls the "educational survival complex" (2019, 27).[10] This complex is built on the suffering of BIPOC students and is constructed out of a history in the United States that has at its core violent exclusionary and assimilationist measures. Love further argues that "Native American boarding schools, school segregation, English-only instruction, *Brown v. Board Education*, No Child Left Behind, school choice, charter schools, character education, Race to the Top . . . all have been components of an education system built on the suffering of students of color . . . in which students are left learning to merely survive, learning how schools mimic the world they live in, this making schools a training site for a life of exhaustion" (2019, 27). Love (2019, 27; see also 2023) advocates for abolitionist teaching as a way to tear down these educational structures. Ultimately, this method is about reinventing the education system wholeheartedly, with life and lifeways at the center. Teaching can be a site of "freedom" from white supremacy, the classroom a space of refusal and rebellion (Peña 2022, 63). This means sitting with the discomfort, as well as centering different worlds and voices in our teaching and in the shaping of our pedagogies.

Discomfort serves a purpose (cf. Chennault 2021, 60), within and beyond the classroom. As noted earlier, the classroom is not tabula rasa, and the world making we undertake in the classroom is always political. Thus, discomfort is always already present in the classroom (cf. Millner 2023). As part of undertaking a decolonial, intersectional feminist praxis in our pedagogy, it is important to draw attention to white supremacist and settler systems, violent exclusions, and cishet patriarchal and ableist norms as purposeful work. As Eaves notes,

"Feminist inquiry draws attention to uncomfortable spaces" (2021b, 253). Here, though, is another important site to thread through the ethic of care that I am suggesting throughout our work as geographers.

However, as Thayer (2023, 2025) argues, navigating the tensions between care and discomfort is a tricky affair. This tension ties back to the power we have as educators to shape classroom knowledge production, and to consider how we might balance subjects that might be uncomfortable for some with making care-full spaces. Zembylas argues for a pedagogy of discomfort, one where it is noted that "discomforting feelings are important in challenging dominant beliefs, social habits and normative practices that sustain social inequities and they create openings for individual and social transformation" (2015, 163). So, as we all face discomfort, a care-full classroom is intended to make room for sitting with, thinking through, and processing it.

An ethic of care in the classroom is not only about caring for the students; it also means caring for ourselves (Dufty-Jones and Gibson 2022). To teach with care at the center can be exhausting (see also Ahmed 2023). There are so many lived experiences, so many external influences, so much we cannot and should not be held responsible for bearing the weight of. So, per hooks (1994), we must be self-aware and reflexive about our own humanness too. Simultaneously, we need to be able to bring our "full selves" to the classroom (cf. Atkins 2022). To create a decolonial, intersectional feminist avenue toward a care-full academy, the work must be collective, and, as a result, that includes our students as coproducers of knowledge.[11]

At present, the leading way that students are included in providing feedback on the teaching process (not the day-to-day process, per se) is through end-of-term evaluations of classes and instructors. Indeed, here may be a moment to shout "abolish student evaluations of teaching!" We know that they are rife with inaccuracies and bias against faculty, particularly women and people of color (cf. Caretta and Bono 2022; Mengel, Sauermann, and Zölitz 2019; Neuhaus 2022), and we know that they are problematic. Yet they remain in most cases the single (or most important) documented evidentiary material around so-called excellence in teaching. Calling for new forms of faculty evaluation, Caretta and Bono (2022) argue that student feedback is a neoliberal measurement tool that actually reduces instructors' diversity and belonging. The authors further suggest peer review and student self-assessment (Caretta and Bono 127). Peer evaluation of teaching and teaching materials is part of making instruction and mentoring multiple. However, I want to focus here on the idea of student self-assessment as a site of care in the classroom.

If an aim of geography education is to co-create well-informed citizens who think critically, turning our attention to learning objectives and outcomes in cooperation with our students might help us understand how to achieve our aims. If we desire a coproduction of knowledge, an essential element will be framing expectations, assessment, and outcomes together. The classroom can be made into a space of knowledge exchange that is dialogic. Moreover, the classroom can be a space where feedback is bidirectional regarding course content and all parties' achievements in multiple ways, rather than unidirectional, where students assess courses and faculty members overall, and faculty assess a grade.[12] These forms of coproduction help decenter power in the classroom, and they can empower students to see themselves as active and responsible to themselves, to one another, and to the class more broadly (on antiracist co-teaching, see Wilson and Cook-Sather 2022). The classroom stands to be not only a site of care work, but also one where we might unravel how we teach and develop courses and course materials, where that training comes from, and where it can go.

Teaching to Teach

I discussed mentoring earlier in chapter 3, when talking about data collection and research training, and I will revisit it in greater depth in chapter 6. Again, mentoring deserves to be threaded through our academic practices as a whole. While we can discuss mentoring in our academic pursuits, here in the chapter on working toward care-full teaching praxis, the focus is twofold: teaching mentoring and mentoring teaching.

Teaching mentoring, whether through formal or informal channels, will remain an important practice as we move toward a feminist ethic of care, but in this space, I also want to return to the space of the classroom. I received no formal mentoring or training on being at the front of the classroom as an instructor. Zero. I expect my experience is not unusual for a graduate student, as I discuss subsequently (see also Eaves 2021a). Yet as a graduate student, I taught ten classes as the instructor of record and was the teaching assistant for several other courses. My teaching evaluations (an imperfect measure of success, as addressed earlier) show that I am "passionate" and "a force of energy," which may be why I was immediately and unceremoniously thrown into the front of the classroom at an R1 institution in the second year of my PhD.

I value my classroom encounters immensely, and I had an excellent overall experience in my department both as a student and a teacher. However, I share this memory in proposing that we have so much more potential when we have multiple opportunities to hone our craft in teaching geography. As an institution, the R1 university demonstrates a particular lack of care in treating students at all levels in this way. A sink-or-swim approach to teaching can have many ripple effects.

Again, there are formal and informal avenues for advancing our pedagogies and working toward praxis in the classroom. Adding mentoring to the mix provides new avenues to enhance the practices we might learn to adopt in the classroom. This guidance provides an opportunity to work care into the mix and create spaces to dialogue about what might be included in the carefull classroom I am emphasizing here. Mentoring on the practice of teaching can take many forms, ranging from instruction to suggested reading, practice, and informal critique. Thus there are many possibilities to enrich our understandings of how we might be in the classroom.

One of the core elements of teaching that is crucial to address here is how we approach students at all stages who may be on contract as teaching assistants (TAs). At the institutions where I received all of my degrees, (TAs) were on-contract graduate students or upper-level undergraduates—here, I will focus on the former. Various classes need varied levels of support. The ability to share workload, mentor, and provide opportunities for hands-on learning about teaching and for personal interfacing with students in the classroom or in student/office hours can be a central part of the graduate student experience. This experience also varies across TA appointments and institutions.

There is very little discussion of TAs when theorizing pedagogy or classroom techniques. TAs seem invisible or erased from the classroom landscape, yet they remain essential laborers. The interdisciplinary character of geography requires a number of different skillsets of support for the teaching in any one department. Even so, it seems that TA support is found to be transactional to the point of exploitation—especially as reported by international students (cf. Madden 2014)—rather than an experience in pedagogical training. I invite us to write TAs into our pedagogical considerations and to reflect on them as colleagues and partners in our teaching. How might our classes actually be different or made possible because of actual shared workload, not an uneven distribution of responsibilities? Here is another moment where our classrooms are made multiple, in that we are teaching our teachers as we are teaching our undergraduate students.

Mentoring on teaching at all levels remains important and holds a key role in bringing a feminist ethic of care to the forefront. To some degree, this may mean leading by example in the classroom. In addition, mentoring may include deeper discussions on pedagogical choices and making decisions about what will bring about effective learning outcomes. But it may also entail an invitation to step away from the grand ideas of teaching and enriching minds to dig into the mundane. Consider, for example, the details of university systems and structures—adopting books through the bookstore; getting training to develop grading rubrics; meeting expectations from the provost's office for grading and course documents and how to put them together; determining what goes in a syllabus, how long to keep student materials, and what the different levels of classes mean; and so on. Mentoring can involve peeling back the layers of things that may seem obvious, and just chatting through them. If the teaching of geography provides an example of how to enact care-full pedagogies at the site of the neoliberal university, mentoring can also be a world-dismantling and world-making process. Above all, we have the opportunity to strive to be mentors whom students wish to emulate.

←◆→

The classroom is a space where we make place and vice versa. Where we have a series of moments to make our way toward care-full geographies of belonging. We can use these spaces to expect more from ourselves and one another, and maybe, just maybe, we can inspire meaningful change.

CHAPTER 6

The Institution Will Never Love Us Back

> To hold us, to gently move us closer to a mirror in which our fire is collectively reflected back to us, unleashing our community as rebellion.
>
> —*Lorgia García Peña* (2022, xvii)

Geography is within and outside the academy. I write from within. I write from the site of the neoliberal university, where we are constantly being asked to do more with less and to make our institutions shine, to move them forward. We are inundated by contradictions here. We are told to do the work of diversity, equity, and inclusion but remain stymied by inaction by upper administrators and hostility from the state. Graduate students are important until they cost too much. Teaching must be excellent but is poorly remunerated. We are to strive for balance between work and life but do more and more and more. So it goes, on and on.

This noncomprehensive series of incongruities is not limited to geography. It is the academy. It is our academic selves, our academic lives. And so here, I continue to thread through the conversation the neoliberal university and the institutions academic geographers may find themselves in, and some of the struggles we may recognize in our academic lives. Again, as I note in the introduction, I am principally writing about larger, more research-focused, predominantly white institutions (PWIs) and from a U.S. perspective to ground this conversation. Much writing on these subjects suggests that these institutions are where the more negative issues we face in the academy are felt the most deeply.

But I do not want to imply that these are the only places such problems are encountered. I understand that there is nuance and that to be at a more teaching-focused institution, for example, does not mean that work and life are in balance, or that everyone feels included and like they belong. In part, this is a rationale for the book not being prescriptive—our experiences will necessarily be different.[1] However, in a book that begins by discussing the care-less academy, and one where I express hope that geography and geographers can be a site of change within the academy, these more pernicious aspects present in our academic spaces warrant discussion.

This chapter features a longer discussion about diversity, equity, inclusion, and belonging in geography and the academy more broadly. It then shifts to a series of vignettes centered on common conversations around an institution that will "never love us back" (Kelley 2018 in Peña 2022, 19), where I try to sprinkle in some different ways of addressing these pervasive issues. Finally, I turn to mentoring as a consideration for addressing sites of carelessness.

Equity, Belonging, and Care-Full Academic Lives

At the core of our communities of care must be a charge to create sites of belonging in the academy and in geography more generally. The surge in social justice organizing that occurred throughout 2020, largely in response to the murders of Breonna Taylor and George Floyd, was a continuation of years of organizing by Black-led social movements such as the more recent Black Lives Matter. Even so, the 2020 surge created a flurry of new diversity, equity, and inclusion (DEI) activity on campuses of higher education institutions. Simultaneously, many upper administrators made statements that demonstrated a seeming indifference, and they often used COVID-19 as a shield from dealing with the structural oppressions and assimilationist behaviors threaded through their institutions (see Naylor 2023). Indeed, despite an increased attention to DEI, Ahmed's (2017) discussions of diversity work as a brick wall remain relevant.

However, popular movements to expose the white cishetero-patriarchal character of the academy suggest that change making can and is happening. Consider the social media hashtags #BlackIntheIvory, #AcademicsforBlack-Lives, #WomenAlsoKnowStuff and #metoo, and the response in professional geography, including the work of the Black Geographies, Latinx, and Queer and Trans Specialty Groups. In addition, the American Association of Geographers is undertaking new justice, equity, diversity, and inclusion (JEDI) efforts.

We are surrounded by white men in geography and the academy more generally (Kinkaid, Parikh, and Ranjbar 2022). Colleagues, students, staff. Every day I am in my home department, I am confronted by the history and legacy of our programs. Geography was brought to the University of Delaware by Emma Charlotte Ehlers (1925) by way of the Women's College, where she was the first head of the department (1948) and taught for twenty-seven years at the rank of assistant professor (Mather 2003).[2] However, without an armchair history of the department Ehlers would be erased. Indeed, I walk past historic photos of white male (presenting) climatologists in the hall and look into Dr. Russ Mather's face (department chair for twenty-three years) when I enter our conference room (affectionately dubbed the Mather Room). On my campus, I once participated in a faculty writing support group that met in a faculty room lined with portraits of white male former department chairs. This atmosphere does not create a sense of belonging for many of us—and that is only thinking about race and gender, for diversity spans much more than those two categories.

There already exist volumes about the work of doing diversity, something Cox reminds us is an attempt that most only "play at."[3] So, while it is important, I am not going to repeat already existing excellent scholarship here. Instead, I will expand somewhat on what a decolonial, intersectional feminist approach to diversity work might look like as it relates to some of the discussion in this body of scholarship. Indeed, Ahmed suggests that feminist work is diversity work, *and* that we would be more willing to transform our institutions if we all had some feminist training (2017, 94).

Policies are in place across the academy, but they are frequently metric driven, underresourced, and unimplemented, or they are taken on by already exhausted and overcommitted people. Because as often happens (see chapter 2), the very people who make up those historically underrepresented and excluded groups are called on to do the work (Peña 2022). We know these things. They are well documented, and those of us who attempt to do the work see the many ways in which we are set up to fail. Because no matter the rhetoric of the university or the feel-good messages that abound on campus (see Thayer 2023), there is a violent and insidious disinterest in actual diversification, because it has at its foundation the dangerous assumption that "diversity sacrifices excellence" (Prescod-Weinstein 2021, 190). What, then, is the decolonial, intersectional feminist approach to creating equitable spaces of belonging that are care-full?

There is no single avenue toward equity and belonging in diversity and inclusion work. But I argue that there cannot be inclusive diversity without creating spaces that are equitable and provide opportunities for people to feel like they belong. Because the project of belonging is not a singular known (decolonial). It cannot be the same for every person or group (intersectional), and it should be imbued with an ethic of care—which allows for missteps and mistakes and learning (feminist). Prescod-Weinstein suggests, in discussing race and the academy, that BIPOC academics must create their own spaces of belonging because they may be the first ones in their program or even field (2021, 132). Nevertheless, as discussed in the introduction, the work of world dismantling and world making is collective work, and so we must reflect on how the collective creates belonging. This may mean that as people carve out spaces for themselves, we concurrently disrupt any measures that insist on assimilation.

As Ahmed notes, we must be willing to damage our institutions (2017, 140). World dismantling. As part of this work, we must refuse white supremacy and make every effort to tear it down at our institutions. We cannot undo past violences, but we can sit with them and learn about and from them. As part of the peer mentoring I discuss at the end of this chapter and the feminist training I discuss through the whole book, we must teach one another about racism, ableism, sexism, and other hateful projects that undergird exclusion and assimilationism. Through this teaching and mentoring, we may then be able to establish a much-needed vocabulary to communicate our world-dismantling and world-making processes. I once sat in a room with a number of physical scientists who came up blank when asked to describe diversity and inclusion. This suggests either that they are not participating in these conversations at other sites, or that they are not trained in concepts or contexts that would allow for meaningful participation. Again, I will turn to mentoring in the final section of this chapter as a strong focal point for where we can care-fully do this work.

Geography for a long time has looked much the same as the academy more broadly, but perhaps even less diverse by some measures (American Association of Geographers 2023a). Even a quick glance at the past presidents of the American Association of Geographers shows that very few women or people of color have held this leading role, which steers the mission of one of our oldest and largest member organizations.[4] As I discuss in the introduction, academic geography has long been a white, male-dominated discipline. Yet the work of making geography more diverse is underway—largely through the care-full crafting of spaces by and for historically underrepresented and excluded groups, and the emphasizing of some of the problematic legacies that we sit with in the discipline (cf. Gieseking 2023; Kinkaid and Fritzsche 2022; Kinkaid, Parikh, and Ranjbar 2022; Oberhauser and Caretta 2019).

The work that still needs to be done is in cultivating care-full communities of belonging beyond the already existing islands created by, for example, lab groups, society specialty groups, research teams, and mentoring networks. As geographers, we must see ourselves as a community and value not just work that promotes diversity, equity, and inclusion toward belonging. We must also value the work being done by geographers aside from research and teaching metrics alone (still topics of great importance, which I address in chapters 3–5). But we must undertake the work of *seeing*, of making visible, the collective work that is done, that makes our work as geographers possible and meaningful.

Returning to an earlier discussion in chapter 2, the matter of who does the work of diversity, equity, and inclusion and how that purposeful labor is valued and compensated (or not), we might consider rereading this labor as care work. We can change the way academic spaces are structured to be more inclusive, with a specific focus on geography and disciplinary approaches. As expressed throughout this book, the university was built and maintained on exclusionary behavior. As Gökariksel et al. note in a chapter that features multiple conversations with feminist geography collectives, the strategies we are taught for professional advancement and success in the academy are baked into the very structures that many of us are trying to resist (2021, 85). Moreover, I am not convinced that the hierarchies that exist in the academy, and that are intended to provide "academic freedom" such as tenure, are any less assimilationist than other practices in the neoliberal university. Instead, I have found in practice that the power of tenure is often only successfully wielded to uphold the institution, not work against it.

Diversity is a conversation in the university that we might easily historicize around affirmative action in university admissions—something that the U.S. Supreme Court effectively ended in 2023. Yet in higher education, diversity is a numbers game. It is adding those people who are excluded, and job done. Thus, conversations shifted to equity and inclusion and, later, justice and belonging.[5] And so we have these words and goals, and many of us who work with great dedication to bring about change can easily throw our hands into the air in exasperation for all the frustration we feel in doing this work.

It is clear, though, that this work must be done. It is not just about transforming our institutions, as most DEI efforts attempt to do. It can and should be threaded through every aspect of our academic pursuits, as I am attempting to argue throughout the book. A decolonial, intersectional feminist approach necessitates that we dismantle and construct anew with inclusion and belonging saturating our efforts. We must proceed in this manner because, as I discuss in shorter snippets in the next section, building from the introduction to this book, the academy can be an unwelcoming place.

The Academy Writ Large

In this section I am not speaking to geography specifically, although in some areas I rely on the work of geographers to guide my thinking. I am speaking here to the academy more generally. These perspectives are grounded in my experiences over the past fifteen or so years at research-intensive, predominantly white universities. As I explain in the introduction to the chapter, my experience may not map clearly onto other academic spaces and remains heavily biased toward U.S. institutions. But again, I offer here a series of shorter think pieces on sites where we, as geographers exercising a decolonial, intersectional feminist praxis, might work to dismantle the brick walls that are all too common in the academy. I should also point out that, for a book in which I claim there is no one right way, this section is not intended as a deviation. However, I do indicate some ways in which we might prevent ourselves from maintaining the carelessness in the academy more broadly by tempering these stated practices with some "do not" statements.

←◆→

Campuses are hostile built environments for some; in this case, campus itself is exclusionary. These inequitable or nonbelonging spaces include but are not limited to the following: inaccessible buildings and transportation for people with physical disabilities; university police presence and armed patrols; bathrooms that do not accommodate all genders; emergency blue lights; buildings, statues, or other memorializations of oppressors and enslavers; Anglocentric and nontactile or audio signage; and campus property sited on land stolen from or forcibly worked by ancestors. We have an opportunity, then, to rethink the very structures we situate ourselves in and ask questions about how to push back on these harms.

←◆→

Every year I see too many letters of recommendation, whether for graduate admissions, job candidates, or promotion files, that do a disservice to the applicant. The mix of extraordinary gender bias, lack of attention to detail, faint praise, inappropriate detail, or egregious self-promotion by the writers can be astounding. Even more astounding are the requested letters that never arrive. Writing recommendations is another of those unknown knowns; these letters are normalized and expected but rarely spoken about. Here is an area in which we can improve in our mentoring. Discussing what constitutes a letter of recommendation and how these documents change over time and career might start to address these errors in one of our most common practices.

←◆→

Perhaps we can do away with the phrase "two-body problem." What an abhorrent way to discuss another rather common aspect of our academic lives. Why not instead consider—as some universities already are—dual career possibilities? It should not come as a surprise that hiring for one position may offer an opportunity to hire the partner of the candidate. Rather than scramble for resources, universities should build this unexceptional experience into hiring budgets and plan for it. Also, perhaps celebrate it. Similarly, let's dispense with the phrase "trailing spouse"; the academic job market can already be unkind enough to the candidates ...

←◆→

In tandem with the previous banishment of bad turns of phrase around the academic job market, I will additionally suggest that the moniker of "terminal associate" should be done away with. What a demeaning way to essentialize mid- or late-career faculty who for whatever reason (it is their story, not yours) did not seek promotion to full professor, or were not successfully promoted. This also applies to ageism in the academy, the words "senior" and "junior" suggesting levels of expertise or ability to keep up with the latest literature or technology, and which have the potential to create hostile environments and become the subject of microaggressions. Related to the mentoring discussions throughout this book is the reminder that we are all in a process of becoming. No matter whether we are in the early years of our career or planning for retirement, assumptions about age and career stage tied to academic prowess have no place here.

←◆→

Reflecting on the cost of higher education and the diminishment of the university as a public good, we can also turn our attention to student debt. I carry debt from my first graduate degree. As a first-generation academic, I did not receive sufficient mentoring on the existence of fellowships and paid contracts/stipends in graduate education when applying for my MA. While I was writing this book, my payments were suspended, my debt forgiven by the sitting president, then made to be repaid by the Supreme Court of the United States, and my loan is in repayment once again as I write these words. I am one of many for whom this series of events played out. Taking on debt to finance

THE CHRONICLE OF HIGHER EDUCATION   SUBSCRIBE   Sign In

NEWS | ADVICE | THE REVIEW | TOPICS ∨ | CURRENT ISSUE | VIRTUAL EVENTS | STORE ∨ | JOBS ∨ | ⌕

ACADEMIC LABOR

FROM THE CHRONICLE STORE

Graduate Students Win Pay Raises as Union Efforts Surge

By Kate Marijolovic, Julian Roberts-Grmela, and Eva Surovell | JANUARY 11, 2023

The College Rankings Paradox

Winners, losers, and the race for prestige

Visit the Store

CHRISTINE PETERSON, TELEGRAM AND GAZETTE, USA TODAY NETWORK

A striking graduate student at Clark U. speaks to a crowd outside the Massachusetts university's main entrance in October.

FIGURE 6.1. Screenshot of the front page of the *Chronicle of Higher Education* (Marijolovic, Roberts-Grmela, and Surovell 2023) on January 11, 2023, after a successful strike led by unionized graduate students at Clark University.

higher education is a distinguishing feature of the neoliberalization of the university, becoming more widespread with the acceleration of student lending in the 1990s (Mbah 2023). Taking on debt is now an expectation, and the burdens that come with it are a lived experience for most university students and particularly those from low-income backgrounds. The expectation of a college education in the capitalist economy has led to crisis. This debt crisis is what some have called "catastrophic" (Mitchell 2021), as many are locked into cycles of payment that have no end in sight. While there are continuing calls to cancel student debt, we might simultaneously consider how to dismantle the university and remake it as a public good.

←◆→

UNIONIZE! (See figure 6.1.)

←◆→

Graduate students are in large measure underpaid and underresourced across the academy. Here, I am speaking specifically to graduate students on contract as research and teaching assistants. Students are employees or are students as the university deems necessary for the purposes of accounting for tuition and stipends. When students point to the need for a livable wage, I hear a number of arguments/excuses that suggest any number of ways that the stipend and tuition benefits combined add up to a living wage. These explanations ultimately amount to "graduate life is hard, deal with it." The uncaring academy. There is so much more we could do to support geographers at this stage, and I do think it may begin with remembering that graduate students are colleagues and we are all scholars in the process of becoming. The students are also humans (not sources of output), people with joys, needs, desires, and difficulties. Let us appropriately compensate people for their labor across this spectrum of scholarship. You cannot buy food with tuition benefits.

←◆→

I have been really rather quiet about university staff in this book, but that is not because they are not important to the decolonial, intersectional feminist praxis I am trying to convey. I am thinking of our administrative, IT, and custodial staff in particular, but I fully recognize "staff" is a much broader term in the academy. It encompasses those folks who do not have a tenure home and in many cases are not unionized and are often underpaid and underresourced. If the care-full labor of faculty in academic service roles makes research and teaching possible, we know that the staff make it *all* possible. Many things could be said here, but I will leave it with a simple idea: be kind.

←◆→

Which leads me to the power dynamics of the academy once again and how they need to be recognized. They exist, and if you are in a position of power, you are either deliberately or unwittingly exercising that power to one degree or another when interacting with someone who does not hold your role or title. I see these dynamics unfold in ways that show that people have largely forgotten what it was to not hold a position of power, or what they might have once been fighting for before they started rubbing shoulders with upper administration or the board of trustees. In some cases, the power dynamics show that these people have always held so much privilege that it never occurred to them to check it.

I very much doubt that most people in these positions are actively trying to do negative things or to intentionally hurt people or damage their careers, but I do posit that more could be done to wield power for good. Here are some additional thoughts for those in power to consider: listen; admit when you have made a mistake, and take responsibility for it; be transparent and accountable; do not assume inaction makes problems go away; do not pit people against one another; do not use your position only to advance yourself; do not take on a position of power you do not want or will not be willing to fulfill; do not promise things you cannot give; and do not ever attempt to control someone else's narrative to save face. It is crucial to see and name these power dynamics regularly.

For those who are not among the "most people" I earlier indicated, we require active intervention against harassment in all its forms: discrimination, bullying, racism, sexism, ableism, queer- and transphobia, ageism, and other forms of abuse and toxicity that some in the academy willingly perform. Per Mansfield et al., "We must make destructive power visible and refuse to celebrate abusive individuals" (2019, 85). Whisper networks (cf. Kelsky 2017) do some of this work, but if we are to create a care-full academy and a geography of belonging, we will need to loudly speak truth to power.[6]

←◆→

We are graduating people with PhDs at rates that are not commensurate with the availability of tenure-track academic positions. Many factors contribute to the low number of tenure lines in the U.S. academy—the neoliberalization of our institutions is one of many, in that there is an overreliance on precarious laborers rather than a maintenance or creation of tenure lines. Creating a care-full academy does suggest a move away from hiring people into contingent labor positions, but it likely necessitates a stronger embrace of jobs that are not based on tenure or in the university. For some areas of research, this has likely always been the case. However, in many areas it is a secondary consideration labeled "alt-ac." The use of the word "alternative" here signals the primacy of the academy as the endgame for scholarly work. It also signals that those PhD holders (or even master's students who do not pursue a PhD) are somehow doing less valuable work because it is outside the academy. As part of our care-full practice, I suggest distancing ourselves from a vocabulary that renders jobs outside the academy as "other."

←◆→

The academy demands much from us and gives little back. My partner is not an academic, and so when I started my PhD, like many (including those with academic partners), I had to very closely consider where work ended in my days/weeks/months. I remember saying that I was trying to find the work-life balance the neoliberal academy was whispering in my ear about. This is an unhelpful and unattainable binary. The neoliberal academy pats us on the head with well-being, self-care, and ways to take steps toward this mystical binary while slapping us across the face with the reality of the demands made on our time, our energy, our emotions, our intellect.

Hersey argues that "our drive and obsession to always be in a state of 'productivity' leads us to the path of exhaustion, guilt, and shame. We falsely believe we are not doing enough" (2022, 62). To the detriment of our work and lives, we feel an endless need to labor to move the dial on the metrics by which we are evaluated. For some this means being pushed to the brink, not being able to care even for themselves, let alone the collective. There is no such thing as work-life balance. I suggest the phrase be abolished from our vocabulary, because we are instead participating in more of a work-life triage. I hope that we can give ourselves some grace here and resist the grind as part of our care-full academic lives.

←◆→

Related to work-life considerations are those interventions centered on mental health. We are increasingly having conversations about mental and emotional well-being in the academy more generally and in geography specifically, something that was uncommon even ten years ago. A clear mental health crisis is rife within the academy, geography included (Mullings, Peake, and Parizeau 2016). As with many of the other issues I touch on in these snippets, work on burnout (cf. Laketa and Côte 2022; Nagoski and Nagoski 2019) and mental health and wellness in geography (cf. Mullings, Peake, and Parizeau 2016; Parizeau et al. 2016; Tucker and Horton 2019) already exists.[7] We are aware of the problem and reminded of it every day, especially as universities increasingly provide resources, programming, and reporting mechanisms for addressing the crisis among our undergraduate populations. The pandemic made many of us painfully aware of the mental health emergency. Many of us are not okay (see Pryal 2017).[8]

In reading for and writing this manuscript, I found that many of the conversations around mental health in the academy are ultimately conversations around care, feminist ethics, and mentoring (which I turn to in the final section of this chapter). As a result, much of what is being discussed already is important and needing to be read. I only offer here that continuing to talk about mental health, breaking down the taboo character of such discussions (especially for those coming from outside U.S. contexts, where these discussions are uncommon), and going beyond the neoliberal and superficial responses offered in our institutional settings will be necessary parts of the care-full work that needs to be done. As part of these considerations, we can look to the radical vulnerability that Nagar (2019) suggests and think about how we care for one another as well as ourselves, through and through.

←◆→

In this section of the chapter, I have accounted for just a few of the things that seem to most commonly come up in conversation among academics: precarity, overwork, underpaid or underappreciated labor, mental health, power dynamics. It is at times difficult to paint the academy in a favorable light. However, if we turn to an ethic of care, if we dismantle the more uncaring aspects of academic life, we may find more and better ways of interacting in these spaces. In the following section, I suggest that one of the ways we might approach a care-full academy is through our mentoring practices.

The Care and Mentoring of Geographers

If we consider mentoring as part of our feminist praxis (see Johnston-Anumonwo 2019; Moss et al. 1999), we should be immersed in mentoring all of the time. Perhaps an exaggeration. However, if all geographers were feminist geographers, that is what a caring geography could look like—an open invitation to support ourselves and one another in our academic journeys. This is not to suggest that we be available at all times of the night and day, nor that we demand others to be (see my earlier comments on getting away from grind culture). What I am suggesting is that we provide mentoring at all levels with care while receiving mentoring at all levels, as all of us are undergoing processes of becoming. I suggest that *everyone* can benefit from having official and informal advisers, that mentoring training provides opportunities to enrich our everyday lives as academic geographers (and otherwise). The consideration that everyone does not have the same background and experiences means that we will need multiple mentoring approaches.

Mentoring through an ethic of care is crucial work as we tend to our earth writing. How we are trained is important, which is why I suggest that we should be feminist, and that we all receive training grounded in decolonial and intersectional thinking that is imbued through all aspects of our processes of becoming geographers. I also want to suggest very firmly that we continue the work of breaking cycles of abuse in advising.

If all of us are feminist geographers in practice alongside our other training in the discipline (as geomorphologists, urban geographers, remote-sensing specialists, and so on), we can carry this work forth. We can also provide a space that allows opportunities to heal from the trauma of abusive, power-laden, and hierarchical relationships that some of us experience. Here, we can use our feminist training to strive for positive and supportive relationships that refuse neoliberal strictures (see Caretta and Faria 2020; Embodiment Lab et al. 2025; Oberhauser and Caretta 2019) and the "grind culture" (Hersey 2022) of academia, and that resolutely reject the myth of the autonomous academic. We are all in a process of becoming scholars (see Dufty-Jones and Gibson 2022). As Mountz et al. acknowledge, mentoring is "care work" that should be recognized and valued as part of our academic labor (2015, 1243), not an add-on that some provide and some receive, and certainly not something "extra" that does not count.

The long-standing structure of the academy makes the complexity of familiarity that may come with mentoring messier. As discussed earlier (see chapter 2), the education system in the United States puts BIPOC individuals into "perpetual survival mode" (Love 2019, 39). The academy and sites of higher education are institutions imbued with power and privilege. The character of success at the university is too often presented as benign meritocracy. In practice, women and members of underrepresented groups are often required to meet vastly different standards than our counterparts. There is a long history of exclusion and lack of support for these groups, and those who do have a measure of success in the academy are often forced through lack of mentoring or one-size-fits-all mentoring to adapt or assimilate to a structure that was not built for them.

Moreover, it may be difficult for scholars at PWIs to find a mentor who has the needed familiarity, experiences, or understandings, as the exclusion, alienation, and underrepresentation of scholars at all levels remains pervasive. This situation creates a twofold problem: First, scholars from historically underrepresented and excluded groups may not establish a strong mentoring relationship that allows them to feel integrated into their academic pursuits (see McCallum 2020). Second, scholars may end up merely surviving their program rather than thriving (see quote by Tiara Moore from chapter 2). We need to continue to name and make every effort to disrupt greater structural issues at all levels of the university, and multiple approaches will be necessary for this world-dismantling and world-making exercise (as discussed throughout the book). One approach that can be put into practice immediately is considering how we mentor scholars who are from groups that have been continuously excluded and are underrepresented in our discipline.[9]

As part of this practice, I invite readers to think beyond diversity and toward equitable inclusion and belonging. As noted earlier, diversity and inclusion without attention to equity and belonging are models for assimilation and adaptation. "Accepted to Assimilate," a presentation by BIPOC graduate students from UCLA, discusses the challenges of "racial mis-matches" in mentoring, suggesting that "care" must be paramount when entering a mentoring relationship (Baxter et al. 2021; see also Adams-Hutcheson and Johnston 2019; Goerisch et al. 2019). With historically excluded and underrepresented scholars in mind, we might take on mentoring roles that also fulfill the need for accompaniment and co-conspirators; those with power and privilege could literally and figuratively stand alongside those who remain otherized in the academy, presenting as allies in an ongoing struggle (see Queering Feminist Geography Collective, Eden Kinkaid, Christina Diamant, et al. forthcoming). We may also consider adopting practices of co-mentoring discussed by feminist collectives and those attempting to bring feminist praxis to their mentoring—a reflexive practice of how we shape our self-mentoring and dialogic mentoring (cf. Fem-Mentee Collective et al. 2017; Singh and Mathews 2019).

Everyone needs mentoring—so these ideas are not limited or bound to any one group of scholars. Moreover, there is no one right way to mentor. Again, the foundational thinking in a decolonial, intersectional approach asks that we consider multiple ways of knowing and being in these relationships through an ethic of care.[10] In this multiplicity we are provided with an opportunity to identify imbalanced power dynamics and less care-full practices and supplant them. The mutual relationships that are built through mentoring maintain the capacity to be life- or career-altering.

In my own experience, I have found that mentoring training is largely informal and led by example. This admission is not to suggest that what we see when we observe mentoring is best practice, but that it makes an impression. A door left open is no more visible than one kept shut. I led this section with the suggestion that we need mentors through every stage of our processes of becoming. Here, I want to point back to the myth of the autonomous academic that I addressed in chapter 2. *We are always in the process of becoming.* We are always learning. It is the character of the mentoring that necessarily changes, and our needs and career aspirations change over time. The expertise we seek out may need to adjust. We may need insiders and outsiders and friends to help us fill the gaps in our understandings, to give us feedback on ideas, and to answer potential questions yet unasked. Experience and care are paramount in establishing these relationships, which may be short or lifelong. The people we form these relationships with may be close peers. They may be varied in their experience, and they may be in the academy or outside it. They may be familiar or unfamiliar.

When I need guidance for a specific question, I think about who the best people might be to advise me, and I seek out what I call a "mentoring moment." Being unafraid of or willing to risk asking questions can be an important part of being mentored. Mentoring relationships of any kind may require vulnerability. Put simply, we have to care. Here, I invite readers to think about how we can care about ourselves, about one another, and about our academic practices. We should not just go through the motions—supervise a successful PhD, support a mentee through promotion and tenure, provide a recommendation for an application. Instead, we should undertake the dedicated labor of committing time and energy, and of recognizing our interdependence in our mentoring moments great and small. We talk a lot about interdependence in our conversations around space, place, and scale as geographers. Perhaps our lens needs to reflect back on us with more clarity as we seek to build care-full spaces of mentoring in the academy.

There is formal training on mentoring that focuses on communication, transparency, and accountability, as well as career building and networking. Formal training also addresses gaps in informal training, observation, and experience. There exist books, manuals, guides, and workshops for undertaking mentoring practice in academia. Again, this is not a prescriptive book, and so I have no intention of wading into the training arena and explaining how to mentor, as if there were one right way. In considering how to move away from a "resilience model" in PhD supervision, Hawkins raises a question: "What might it mean to develop spaces and practices of care that rather than seek to create tougher academic subjects up to the heroic task, enable acknowledgement of the challenges, and offer resistance and push-back against the logics of the neoliberal academy" (2019, 825)? What I hope to have underscored here is the importance of learning, practicing, and adjusting our mentoring, and why mentoring should have care at its core.

If we take this time for one another, it stands to enrich all of our experiences. If we widen our gaze and see what supportive structures make possible our scholarly pursuits (as discussed in depth in chapter 2), we might find ways to work together against some of these pervasive problems we face in the academy. We might rebel and persist.

CONCLUSION

An Entreaty to Geography and Geographers

> I do hereby pledge myself . . . to service in Geography . . . throughout my
> lifetime . . . in whatever capacity I may find . . . and to use Geography . . . to
> the service of humanity.
>
> —*Gamma Theta Upsilon International
> Geographical Honor Society Pledge*

The present *is* feminist plural. It *is* sustained by an ethic of care. It *deserves* to
be amplified. It deserves to be *valued. The present is now, and we should be able
to immerse ourselves in it (care)fully.* Let us be. We should not ever be again
asked to wait in the wings until our time has come.

If we can begin the work of maintaining and growing already existing
care-full spaces in academic geography, then we can also begin the process
of recruiting and maintaining a future generation of geographers toward an
inclusive, equitable, and diverse discipline with systems of support and retention that are attentive to peoples' lived experiences. If we can agree that we
want this geography for now, we can radically remake our institutions and our
capacities. We can remake geography as an archipelago of care radiating out
from our institutions in waves of possibility and hope.

I had originally considered this chapter as a periscope, a manifesto for the
future of geography. I wrote the last paragraph of this book before I even finished the introduction. However, in the process of writing and reading (in this
regard, specifically Kinkaid 2024 and Oswin 2022) and discussing the ideas in
the book, I keyed a full stop and asked myself why would it not be a demand,
an entreaty, for a geography for right now. To see what is right in front of us
and nurture those practices that could possibly flourish into the spaces many
of us are working in the now to build? How could I suggest to the early career
scholars working with me that they were the bright feminist future of the discipline instead of co-creating care-full spaces (beyond our department) for their
present? And so, perhaps radically, perhaps haphazardly, I suggest we cease the

project of waiting for our institutions to change (see chapter 6). We are already here. We are already speaking truth to power, participating in refusals, and writing our own damn narratives in place. It is joyous, and it is painful. We have shared our pain and anger toward changing the narrative (cf. Doan 2021, 183). It is all exhausting. But if we work collectively, we might see geography anew; we might be less exhausted (Ahmed 2010).

Asking all geographers to be trained in feminist geography is intended to help create a feminist ethic of care for "an other" geography (see Oswin 2020). It is above all asking for attention to equity and belonging through and through. In this chapter, I am asking geographers to envision a better now for academic geography by making training in feminist geographies a core part of geographic learning at all levels. If we want to engage in research, teaching, and other academic labor that is meaningful, we must be willing to train ourselves differently. This means turning our attention to an ethic of care in our pursuits in the field. I ask that in this feminist training we work to dismantle white feminism (see chapter 1), and we look to decolonial and intersectional ways that disrupt white supremacy, coloniality, and the patriarchy. In this brief conclusion, I return to the topics of the introduction to charge geographers to remake ourselves in the academy. And I repeat, *all geographers should be feminist geographers.*

This concluding entreaty starts with circling back to our discipline more generally. In the introduction to the book, I troubled geography and looked to the work of those calling for change. Here, I additionally want to celebrate geography and, taking a note from Bednarz (2019), consider the power of geography toward "saving the world." Following these remarks, I turn again to thinking through a caring geography, another geography, and the ways to embrace the here and now where we can see ourselves and support one another. In the last pages, I offer a final entreaty for a geography, for geographers, for now.

Geographers

While I am making the case that all geographers should receive some feminist training as part of their academic journey and that through this foundation, we will be able to understand and explain difference across space and place with an ethic of care; I simultaneously think *all students* should get some geography training, ideally throughout their educational experiences. Thus, no matter the academic program or career aspirations of our students, I urge that geography should be threaded throughout education.[1]

However, even as I offer this standpoint, I recognize that there are past conversations about the disappearance of geography programs from top institutions and ongoing conversations about the place of geography in STEM, or the "geoscientization" that many programs face.[2] As I discuss in earlier chapters, Cupples (2020) writes (from a New Zealand context) about the ongoing epistemic erasure geography faces. The long-standing struggle to make geography known is now combined with increased calls for emphasis on the hard sciences, which ignore the social science and humanities work in the discipline. Examples of ongoing disruptions at university geography programs include where the program is situated (e.g., in the College of Earth, Ocean and Environment, as my current program is), the demands made by administrators for department or major/minor name changes—ostensibly to attract STEM students, and other less visible differences in how we practice our craft (Cupples 2020).[3]

As many observe, these are not new concerns. However, calls to remake or regain ground in the discipline are increasing:

> Taken together, these different concerns not only illustrate what we already know—that the ground from which we might understand, talk about, collaborate, and alliance-build across global space is a highly uneven one—but provide resources to inform how we might collectively think and do Geography better together, with greater sensitivity to shared and distinct concerns. In a certain sense, what this amounts to is a particular kind of geography of Geography—one that identifies resonant shared concerns connected, for instance, to how geographers often have to "fight their corner" amid institutional change or political pressures, but that is also sensitive to the particularities of place and history. (McFarlane 2024, 1)[4]

A series of commentaries on the future of geography that heralded the launch of a new journal emphasizes a similar point. We are greater than the sum of our parts. Thus, by finding our "connective threads," we can make geography "matter more" (Castree et al. 2022, 4).[5]

Neoliberal moves within the university serve to divide us in a moment where Hay (2020), in reply to Cupples, suggests we need to collectively resist both top-down and bottom-up efforts to erase the interdisciplinary character of geography. Indeed, Henry (2020), also in response to Cupples, argues that we need to work together to solve the wicked problems that face the globe. Henry further suggests we must do this with care. Creating a foundational decolonial, intersectional, and feminist understanding of geography is one way that we may care for the collective and resist the erasure of our earth writing.

As a discipline, we place much value on geographic education. We know that geography training provides students with needed tools or ingredients to address some of the world's most pressing problems (Bednarz 2019). A strong example of the championing of geographic learning is the work done to get an Advanced Placement (AP) human geography course on the books with the U.S. College Board, and there have been increases in enrollment and the diversity of such programs. But we also know that we face challenges in teaching and learning in geography, even with these successes.

While it was good news that AP human geography programs began in the early 2000s (Murphy 2000), physical geography seems to have been displaced by AP environmental science. Murphy (2000) also notes that while "exciting," the actualization of AP human geography as a platform for enhancing the presence of geography at all levels of education has remained "challenging." The first twenty-five years of the AP program seems to have proved this observation true. First, while the curriculum itself grew in secondary schools in the United States, the movement into geography programs in higher education does not map onto those numbers (see Solem, Vander Weil, and Choi 2024). Second, even as some programs see success, there is still more that those of us in the academy can do at institutions outside our own, particularly at K-12 levels, to ensure the well-being of the subject area in higher education (Moseley, Lu, and Hill 2023). Finally, while we can point to increased access to geography education for students, and to an increase in the diversity of the population enrolled, there is still much work to do to create an accessible geography education (Seemann 2024) in AP curricula and beyond (as I discuss in chapter 6).

I do not intend to repeat the arguments made in chapter 5 around creating a care-full classroom. But I do want to reemphasize that strongly integrating an ethic of care into our teaching practices will provide much assistance in creating geographies of belonging. The ethic of care will also help get our students (and administrators) to care about geography, and to work together creatively to place value on the various geographies we practice.

Indeed, the geography classroom is but one place where we can dismantle disciplinary borders, making them more fluid and porous, by teaching more holistically, or in co-teaching. Sheppard notes that "courses that are co-taught by scholars from very different intellectual and personal backgrounds and philosophical and methodological inclinations could produce less narrow and specialized knowledge, arguably more relevant for students" (2022, 20).[6] Made more common, such a practice would require rethinking how workload is distributed, and it could be a world-dismantling process that changes the way labor is valued (as I discuss at length in chapter 2). It is also a vibrant way to include students in the richness of geography.

Our teaching of spatial thinking can be foundational in breaking the student-as-consumer model. It can achieve this end by encouraging students to be citizens, or to participate and learn about what Bednarz (2019) calls "spatial citizenship." The ability to understand the relationships between people and the environment is at the core of spatial thinking, as is the ability to understand the differences across space and place at multiple scales. The capacity to tell stories with map data and see interdependence is also central. As stated emphatically throughout this book, we know geography matters. It allows us to cultivate a sense of awareness where we can position ourselves in place and seek connections with phenomena occurring both internally or externally. Geography inspires an awe of the character of multiscalar difference and in asking the questions implied in the "why of where." Above all, it makes our presence and comprehension in and of society visible and invites us to participate as full citizens.

No one reading this will be surprised when I offer that most students and many administrators are generally stunned when they learn what geography is—'oh, it's not just making maps and locating countries?' (see also Dutta and McSweeny 2024). I am hopeful that we can stop calling geography a "discovery major" if we wave the flag for the subject, create better connections at all educational levels through events like Geography Awareness Week (see also Alderman 2017 on every week being about awareness, and for helpful how-to hints) and with articulation agreements that allow students to bring credits into geography major programs, and so on. What this means in practice is conducting our training in geography within and outside the classroom. I also suggest that we attend to ourselves as geographers as we train a new generation of spatial thinkers and move about our various worlds.

Seeing Geography Anew

As I discuss in chapter 5, there is no such thing as a safe space in the academy, but we can create spaces of belonging. That work is ongoing in the United States. Bruno and Faiver-Serna write about the specialty groups convened through the American Association of Geographers—specifically, Black Geographies, Latinx Geographies, Indigenous Geographies, and Queer and Trans Geographies—as "sacred spaces." The authors argue, "These sacred spaces are forged within a broader atmosphere of hostility toward marginalized geographers and geographies, and we recognize the efforts made to build *microclimates of survival*" (2022, 159, emphasis mine). These are some of the islands that I am making reference to. And here is the tricky and messy part. These islands must remain islands—these are sacred spaces built by and for people to withstand the toxicity of the academy, of geography.

Simultaneously, in crafting an archipelago of solidarity, interdependence, and mutual support, I invite us to uplift the practices of and provide resources to these islands in a way that allows for a dismantling of the idea that they must exist as a protective bubble. As Cahuas notes regarding whiteness in the discipline, we have an opportunity to "connect these practices to begin to address inequities in material ways," and, crucially, to center the knowledges and experiences of these groups (2023, 653). This work must be care-full and done in such a way that it is not appropriation or co-optation. Some geographers will have substantial discomfort to sit with as part of this process, if it is not to be one in which the hard work of others is expropriated or stolen. A process of unlearning, a development of common and shared vocabulary, a new lexicon for earth writing together will be necessary, but, again, it does not have to be exhausting if we are a collective.

If we train people in decolonial, intersectional feminist thinking, the academy—at least our corner of it—could become a caring space. We could imbue geography with a feminist ethic of care that not only recognizes the already existing collective of care, but also grows that collective, extending it throughout our academic spaces and lives. When we create these islands and work together, we are shedding the "norms of the neoliberal university," and we become a threat to it (Gökariksel 2021, 263–64). There will then be a need to stay angry for a little while, because, as Lorde (2018) reminds us, there is a deep urge to destroy those people who try to make change instead of staying in line. This is an opportunity, then, to remake our institutions.

Through understanding the work of decolonizing knowledge production and disrupting the idea that there is one right way to be in the academy, as geographers we can be a part of the much-needed world dismantling that is an imperative at the neoliberal university. There is not just the need to decolonize our discipline (cf. Jazeel 2017). Thus, we are being called on to decolonize our institutions and to disrupt the "cognitive dissonance" (McLean 2018) of an institution that provisions false care (Bartos 2021). From my comments in the introduction, I reiterate that the university was built through feeding on violent dispossession and exclusion; Bhambra, Nisancioglu, and Gebrial argue that "the foundations of universities remain unshakably colonial" (2018, 6). However, it is important to reiterate Tuck and Yang's caution: "Decolonization is not a swappable term for other things we want to do to improve our societies and schools. Decolonization doesn't have a synonym" (2012, 3). This is why I suggest that decolonization be world dismantling that results in world making. Again, it must be collectively done, and we should be finding ways to dismantle coloniality throughout our work. Barker and Pickerill (2024) intimate that place-based approaches are essential to the work of decolonizing universities. They further note that much work is emergent in decolonial geographies, but that our engagement as scholars within our institutions is falling behind.

If we are to cultivate a caring geography and work to decolonize our institutions, I argue that we must shift away from the "grind culture" that allows neoliberal capitalist structures to wear us down and dismantle where we derive our self-worth from (Hersey 2022). Being churned through this system has made us undervalue care and see justice as unattainable. Hersey (2022), whose work I draw on deeply to discuss this slow violence, suggests that we must decolonize knowledge production around productivity. Further, we must recognize that "rest" is our right and must be practiced: "We've been socialized from birth to ignore our deepest imaginings, to rush and to believe that our entire lives are built upon what we do for capitalism. It is a relentless attack happening daily and hourly. Rest exists to repair this trauma, fear, and misinformation" (2022, 12). Hersey suggests not just that we take up our right to rest, but that we do it collectively. That we do it through creating communities of care (2022). As Ahmed asserts, "Life requires that we give time to living" (2017, 243).

From where I sit, writing a book about creating care-full academic spaces that was drafted in its entirety between 2021 and 2023, I think geographers are hungry for change, desiring to emerge from the pandemic and not return to inhospitable spaces and practices. Yet would we have been spurred to demand a caring geography if there had not been a global pandemic? I will offer a strong yes, as geography was already in crisis, teetering on the edge of a knife of exclusionary practices. By themselves, the "sacred spaces" that Bruno and Faiver-Serna (2022) shed light on show that there is a deep desire from within geography for care-full spaces. However, that the number of papers published since 2020 alone accounts for much of the work I draw on to make a case for a care-full academic geography signals a heightened desire for change. Change that through grounding decolonial, intersectional feminisms we can nurture already existing practices while also making new spaces of equity and belonging. However, as important as this writing is, much of it falls into the trap of waiting for a future geography (see Rose-Redwood et al. 2024). Kinkaid pointedly asks whose future that will be (2024, 192). This is not to imply that these ideas do not have merit, but it is to return to the notion that *we are done waiting.*[7]

The challenge that I put to readers here is an ontological and epistemological one. The very ways that we inhabit and experience space and place are implicated therein, as well as the trajectory of thinking and data analysis within our various research and teaching programs. If we attend to both, we may indeed become the manifestation of our wildest dreams.

What if we were to underscore the mundane and everyday acts that make our work possible in geography? Lizotte (2024) offers kindness and care as a response to structural injustices faced in the academy. Pointing to places in the discipline where through our work we cultivated praxis and where through mutual aid we fostered solidarity, Lizotte notes that there is "change making kindness" in our interactions with one another (Lizotte 2024, 358). Similarly, Brice reminds us that "disciplinary practices of kindness, humility, and solidarity not only help to render many of us less vulnerable (to, for example, exploitation, abuse, neglect, or fatigue)," but they also require us to be vulnerable (2023, 593). Recognizing small, basic, and simple acts of kindness and care may very well set the stage for the large, complex, and difficult work needed for a geography of belonging for now. What this provocation suggests is that we need to inhabit space differently, which refers back to the core tenets of reflexivity and positionality that I address in chapters 1 and 3. Our experiences and what we bring to the world are paramount.

In addition to attending to our ways of being, I ask that we consider our ways of knowing. Critical geographies that extend from decolonial, intersectional feminist thinking can be at the heart of these considerations. Castree notes that while "all academic inquiry is critical, post-structural, decolonial, antiracist, and Indigenous approaches within geography raise core questions about situated knowledge and power" that can no longer be ignored from any corner of the discipline (2022, 9–10). So we can strive for expansiveness and multiplicity in our thinking. We are creators of knowledges. As a result, seeing what Jazeel signals as "frictions and fragments" (2019, 13) and turning over the messiness of human-environment relations are core considerations not just for our scholarship, but for the problem-solving and outward-facing character geography will increasingly need to take on. The epigraph that leads this chapter brings Gamma Theta Upsilon back to the conversation (see chapter 2), and I suggest that we can strive to be the best versions of ourselves so that we can use geography to benefit humanity and our earth others.

We all study difference, and here exists an opportunity to dive deep into what that means across academic geography and how it can be reorganized (cf.

McKittrick and Peake 2005) as a form of world dismantling and world making, perhaps. We have an opportunity to, as Raghuram suggests, "emplace care ethics" in geography (2016, 515). In writing about authorial voice in human geography, Brigstocke imagines a future in which geographic work published starting in the mid-2020s will reflect plurality, multiplicity, and difference, and suggests that what will make this possible is many authors "learning from feminist theory and postcolonial theory's calls to undo the discourse and practice of 'mastery.'" Suggesting that this will lead to epistemological trends in geography that are "more egalitarian and less tied to patriarchal and colonial poetics of knowledge," thus allowing geographic writing to reach "much wider audiences than it had previously" (2024, 363–64). I hear this speculative genealogy as an echo reverberating through the arguments I am making in this book, and I anxiously and hopefully look to it as realized.

In writing about collaborative research, Skop et al. (2021) offer a ten-point pledge that I suggest can be applied more broadly to the collective work it is imperative we undertake to create a geography of belonging. I include these points ahead of my final entreaty to readers:

> In our work together, we promise to:
>
> 1. Center our academic pursuits around a feminist ethic of knowledge production—one that recognizes the long-standing inequities and injustices of academe.
> 2. Embrace an explicitly antiracist, feminist approach that highlights the compounded academic pressures and hypervisibility/invisibility of BIPOC scholars.
> 3. Develop, promote and reward strategies to do academic work that centers social justice imperatives.
> 4. Make space to hear and learn from uncomfortable, innovative and transgressive ideas.
> 5. Create transparency and fairness by setting, communicating and respecting clear boundaries. Take time each year to reflect and revise these boundaries in recognition that over the course of our personal and professional lives those boundaries adapt and change.
> 6. Protect our mental, emotional and physical well-being and growth in the research process by supporting each other's professional and personal aspirations.
> 7. Share and rotate the labor of intellectually joyful and tedious tasks.
> 8. Mentor up, down and across professional and personal life—course stages to unsettle hierarchical relationships and promote an ethos of care.

9. Disrupt perfection: share insights and experiences overcoming challenges, failures and rejections as well as motivations, successes and ambitions.

10. Humanize our work by valuing the intellectual and ethical centrality of friendship, connection and responsibility.

← ◆ →

Here is my last entreaty to you, gentle reader: Let us make geography a caring place. Let us have the strength to defy business as usual. Let us break the cycles that perpetuate bad behaviors in the academy. Let us refuse the neoliberal tendencies of the academy. Let us be feminist. Let us encourage already existing practices of care and belonging and work to make them flourish right now through a decolonial and intersectional feminist praxis in geography.

In writing about the COVID-19 pandemic during its height, novelist Arundhati Roy suggested we might treat it as "a portal."[8]

> Historically, pandemics have forced humans to break with the past and imagine their world anew. This one is no different. It is a portal, a gateway between one world and the next. We can choose to walk through it, dragging the carcasses of our prejudice and hatred, our avarice, our data banks and dead ideas, our dead rivers and smoky skies behind us. Or we can walk through lightly, with little luggage, ready to imagine another world. And ready to fight for it. (2020, n.p.)

Let us imagine a portal for geography, one that allows us to break with the neoliberal and uncaring academy. Better still, let us amplify the world dismantling and world making already underway toward a caring geography, "an other" geography, an equitable geography, a diverse geography, a just geography. A geography for now, where we unapologetically belong. Let us write the earth anew together.

AFTERWORD

Imagine living in a world where there is no domination, where females and males are not alike or even always equal, but where a vision of mutuality is the ethos shaping our interaction. Imagine living in a world where we can all be who we are, a world of peace and possibility.

—bell hooks (2000, x)

There is a task we have before us of understanding this apparently new geopolitical constellation of power, this "new world order." What knowledges of it can we derive at this juncture, in this place?

—M. Jacqui Alexander (2006, 91)

Do you know what it means to write the earth?

This is a serious question. What does it mean?

To write the earth is the foundation of our discipline. How is it that we understand that none of our work is done without collaboration and the collective? When we ask the earth—its landforms, its climates, its plants, its animals, its humans—to give to us, to share stories with us.

Naylor has asked us to strip down our individual and collective practices all at once. In a post-COVID society, it seems that we would have thought more about this a half decade ago. Alas, we survived a global pandemic only to find accelerated and intensified expectations about every aspect of our academic careers. We are worn out, burned out, and confused, which only intensifies the urgency with which we must strip ourselves of professional geography as it has always been done. If we take apart every comfort-driven aspect of our professional lives, we see exactly where the concentration of power lies. And for some of us, we have to stop holding power. This takes place, of course, through the geopolitics of knowledge production. We are asked to trouble the historical fictions of equality. Attempts at equality in the discipline have a history of being care-less, as Naylor tells us, "mired in an exclusionary feminism that has at its heart white supremacy."

As this book invites us to take seriously, professional geography requires us to labor. And further, that labor—in the call for it to be feminist, antiracist, and decolonial work—is beyond urgent and, as Naylor characterizes it, "radical." For geography to be feminist or for all geographers to be feminist geographers, we call to task the myopic view of feminism. It brings Naylor in conversation with Black feminist scholars who are inspiring my work on feminist epistemologies and methodologies, in addition to broader disciplinary shifts. In thinking about Naylor with bell hooks, geographers are invited to manifest disciplinary futures through mutuality. Naylor, with M. Jacqui Alexander, urges us to take the nature of power seriously. Alexander's use of the word "constellation" should not be overlooked. Indigenous, decolonial, and Black feminist scholars and abolitionists have emphasized power as a means of organizing logics for (at least) two centuries. It really is past time to disrupt convention, the geography that represents the "just is" (McKittrick 2006).

On disruption, Naylor and I have built a relationship for nearly a decade now. Because of this shared history, I have witnessed the deep and long development of this book and been present as she has actively worked to enact the very practices she writes of here. She has given herself room to grow, to think deeply, to read broadly, and to develop new ideas. Such a scholarly practice lends itself to capaciousness and revolutionary thinking, and in doing so she is modeling how we write the earth anew.

LaToya E. Eaves

NOTES

1. See, for example, Askins and Blazek 2017; Bartos 2019; Dowler, Cuomo, Ranjbar, et al. 2019; Lawson 2007, 2009; Lopez 2019; Kim and Naylor 2022; McDowell 2004; Puāwai Collective 2019; Raghuram 2016, 2019; Smith 2005; Thayer 2025; Till 2012; Wood, Swanson, and Colley 2020.

2. The pandemic was the impetus for this book, and it is still ongoing as I write and revise.

3. Calarco, writing about U.S. systems of institutional caretaking, puts it aptly: "Other countries have social safety nets. The U.S. has women" (2024).

4. See, for example, Jackson in Carey et al. 2016; Kwan 2002; Lave et al. 2014.

5. Keighren (2017, 2018, 2020) and Ferretti (2020, 2021, 2022) have extensive bibliographies on geohistories.

6. We often have to write women back into geohistories (see Evans 2016 in Keighren 2018, 772).

7. Marston and de Leeuw note that disciplinary turns bring power dynamics too (2013 in Kinkaid 2019, 1787).

8. I do want to point out that these scholars were PhD candidates at the time of penning this paper (Kinkaid and Fritzsche 2022), which to me signals that a potential sea change for the now is already underway.

9. It is important as part of this work to speak to the land grab that is responsible for the U.S. land-grant university system, where Tribal land was stolen and distributed to create university private property (see Lee 2020; Palmer 2021). The University of Delaware (my home institution) is a land-grant university that received ninety thousand acres of land under the Morrill Act, displacing seventy Tribal nations. As of 2021, UD has a living land acknowledgement that also has action items that play at reparations but do not go far enough (see University of Delaware Anti-Racism Initiative 2021). The university is presently on the unceded lands of the Lenni-Lenape and Nanticoke tribes. UD is also an antebellum institution that benefited from exploited and enslaved Black labor (Lennon 2022).

10. The #ThanksForTyping hashtag that was trending in 2017 was a significant nod to the unpaid, undervalued, and otherwise uncited labor of many "wives" in their partners' scholarly work (see Mazanec 2017).

11. With their yearslong work on the harassment-free AAG initiative, Dowler, Cuomo, Dasgupta, et al. (2019) may be able to acknowledge firsthand what it means to do the work of transforming our institutions to be more care-full.

CHAPTER 1. FEMINISMS FOR THE TWENTY-FIRST CENTURY

1. To celebrate the twenty-fifth anniversary of *Gender, Place & Culture*, Blidon and Zaragocin (2019) curated a special issue on the state of feminist geography in a global context. It included 39 contributions from across the world: Asia (8), Africa (3), Europe (16), North America (3), Oceania (2), and South America and the Caribbean (7). See also Faria and Mollett (2020).

2. Lugones (2014) did critique Crenshaw's intersectionality argument as part of her decolonial theorizing, regarding it as in the service of "Western hegemony." However, as Thomas (2020) argues, this excludes Black women from decolonial theorizing.

3. It is because of the work of these feminist geographers that we have such a vibrant group of feminist thinkers in geography today. We stand with arms metaphorically interlinked, academic generation to academic generation.

4. Original: "El proceso vivo y múltiple de la experiencia de la descolonización debe tomar el espacio como dimensión de la multiplicidad. . . . Entonces la multiplicidad de varias posturas feministas utilizadas geopolíticamente desde el Abya Yala tiene que ver intrínsecamente con nociones de la interseccionalidad" (Zaragocin 2017, 21).

5. As discussed in the introduction, I am well aware of the potential for this book to reinforce the Anglocentricity of feminist geography (see Zaragocin 2021). However, by centering an ethic of care as a concept, we may start to do the work of embodying the praxis that is required.

CHAPTER 2. CARE-FULL GEOGRAPHIES OF PURPOSEFUL LABOR

1. For example, I am at a top-tier research university, often referred to as an R1 institution, and I started with an average assigned workload of 60 percent research, 30 percent teaching, and 10 percent service. When taking on a larger percentage in the service category, for me, that percentage comes out of my teaching—never my research. Each three-credit, one-semester course I teach is considered 12.5 percent of my workload at my institution.

2. This form of refusal/reward differs from the reward of benefiting from patriarchal gender binaries where men say no or do less service; this form of refusal is resistance on the part of people who would say yes to many things.

3. In contemporary language, "enslaved."

4. Anyone who lived through the COVID-19 pandemic in the United States will not gloss over my use of the word "essential" here. "Service" work is often viewed as demeaning or low-skilled work. During the pandemic, it was renamed "essential" in the nonacademic labor market so that nonservice workers could continue to enjoy key services, such as access to groceries, while they were locked down. I also point to the

way that conservative politicians demeaned the former service industry work of U.S. representative Alexandria Ocasio-Cortez, in response to which she reminded the U.S. public that *all work* is important.

5. Lavender groups were created as safe spaces for LGBTQIA+ folks on campuses across the United States.

6. One must only look at the laws and policies rolled out by the Florida governor in 2022–23 to identify the hostilities faced in the academy and the complete unwillingness to see white supremacy, ethnophobia, and the patriarchy at work (discussed in more depth in chapter 5). Likewise, see the countrywide negative response to the Pulitzer Prize–winning *1619 Project: A New Origin Story* (2021), led by Nikole Hannah-Jones.

7. Dr. Susan Hardwick, PhD (1945–2015). I miss her. She cared about people. She cared about graduate students. She was filled with just the right kind of hyperbole from here and to the moon that people could use to fill up their souls when they felt used and as though they were wasting away. I am so glad that the AAG has a mentoring award in her name.

8. Personal communication with fluvial geomorphologist Dr. Adriana Martinez, PhD (November 16, 2022).

9. If you question this statement or raise your eyebrows at it, I encourage you to consider the feedback garnered through the peer-review process for academic publishing as a starting point for rethinking the myth of the autonomous academic.

10. As I write, the AGS is in a revival period under the leadership of Dr. Marie Price, who has been an important mentor to me. However, when I was seeking membership in our professional spaces as a graduate student back in 2008, the AGS was experiencing controversy over the funding and research conducted through the Bowman Expeditions, and so it was not a particularly active space for sharing research and networking.

CHAPTER 3. FEMINIST CARE ETHICS IN GEOGRAPHIC RESEARCH

1. It was a jest, but a smart one. I did, in fact, end up publishing three papers a year on average. And I wrote an award-winning book. I also had the enormous luxury of a one-semester pretenure research leave in my third year; this is allotted to all pretenure faculty members at the University of Delaware. I tried to do my research work on my own terms and at my own pace—that does not mean I was successful and stayed out of the grind, though. I was hungry to prove myself as one of the few social scientists in my college, and as a human geographer in my department who would (ultimately) be the first to go up for tenure since 1994 and our move from the College of Arts and Sciences to the College of Earth, Ocean, and Environment. I felt enormous pressure that I kept trying and failing to shake off.

2. It should be noted that how we conduct and disseminate research is part of training ourselves and others to do geographic work, and so all research work is tied to mentoring, whether it is formal or informal. Thus, when I suggest a feminist ethic of care in all aspects of the research work we do, that includes the behaviors we model and how we train the folks who are at earlier stages in their processes of becoming scholars.

3. It may also signal opportunities to think about "just research" (see Herman and Inwood 2024).

4. The questions of how much of that physical space is taken up and by whom should

be addressed. A gender bias persists regarding who receives resources such as physical lab space (cf. Wadman 2023).

5. This is not to suggest social science labs are getting it right. As discussed in the introduction to the book, the academy is still a hostile place for many groups, and that trespasses scale. Everyone has heard stories about bad lab practices, but we have also heard stories about great lab practices (see the following note). What I am suggesting here is that if we work to bring a feminist ethic of care into lab spaces, we all benefit.

6. Related to creating welcoming spaces with supportive practices, a colleague who is a natural scientist has a refrigerator in her lab that is not for samples. She instead stocks it regularly with healthy snacks—and the freezer is stocked with ice cream. As another example, a portable crib can be made available for folks who have young children. I began this practice in our department in 2022 when three faculty members and four students brought babies into our geography community.

7. It should be noted here that accommodations are not "extra." Also, in the neoliberal university, accommodation is not synonymous with accessibility, as the institution puts the burden almost entirely on people with disabilities (see Pryal 2017).

8. See what I did there? That one is for you, Alec.

9. If we want to wade into the inequities in what counts as fundable, the arena of writing grant proposals and receiving funding is another entire chapter, or even book. I hint at it here, recognizing that it is another part of our research practice, but one that is beyond the scope of this book.

CHAPTER 4. WRITING THE EARTH WITH CARE

1. CRediT is a way of indicating transparently which author provided what labor in the production of the published work.

2. I used this emphatic language in the original draft, and I might have considered removing it if Wiley and Taylor & Francis had not just signed agreements to share academic content and other datasets with tech companies to improve the performance of artificial intelligence (AI) under development. Many are deeming this practice exploitative.

3. As an exception, I point to the role that the journal ACME: *An International Journal for Critical Geographies* plays in the geography publishing arena. ACME's "About the Journal" page explains, "We work to make radical scholarship accessible for free as a manifestation of our commitment to collective labor and mutual aid. We are fully open access. We set no subscription fees or article processing charges, we do not publish for profit, and ACME Editors do not receive compensation for their labour" (ACME Editorial Collective 2023a, n.p.). ACME now publishes in six languages and does not participate in neoliberal metrics for indexing and citing (ACME Editorial Collective 2023b). I will also note that other open-access and nonprofit publishing outlets (university presses, for example) are frequently outlets for academic work.

4. Indeed, as I note in chapter 3, not only was I told the rate at which I should be publishing in these spaces, but I was also actively discouraged from writing my first book with a university press, because it would only be "one more line" on my CV.

5. The h-index is a problematic metric calculated using citation rate of scholarly work and used as a stand-in for impact (see Gieseking 2020). The calculation is drawn

from the number of papers that have been cited, and how many times, compared with the papers that have been cited less often. For example, at the time of writing I have thirty-two scholarly entries posted to Google Scholar. Eleven of them have been cited ten or more times, making my h-index a ten. If you find this concept as befuddling as I do, you can thank physicist Jorge Hirsch, who developed it in 2005 as an "objective measure" of scholarly achievement. Hirsch has lately spoken about the index's unintended consequences and the utter failures that an overreliance on the h-index can produce (Conroy 2020).

6. In 2022, Utrecht University in the Netherlands abandoned impact factor as a part of hiring and promotion decisions, arguing that it contributed to a "'product-ification' of science that values sheer output over good research" (Woolston 2021, n.p.).

7. In general, anonymous peer review is termed "double-blind," but a vocabulary change is again needed—away from ableist language. Perhaps something akin to "anonymous and protected reviews" instead?

8. There is one thought I cannot entirely shake concerning these types of reviews. We might look to those people in positions of power—editors, for example—and suggest that a feminist ethic of care might begin by undertaking such acts as returning the kind of reviews we have all heard stories about and requesting an RR (revise and resubmit) *from the reviewer*. For writers at all stages, instituting an ethic of care in our writing also means pushing back, perhaps with the assistance of a mentor, against reviews that may indeed have substantive comments, but that may otherwise be prone to abusive behavior.

9. However, I do not intend to imply that these papers were solo efforts, as most of my work has been read and reviewed informally, whether in writing groups or by trusted peers. As disclosed in my acknowledgements, each chapter of this book was informally reviewed by peers ahead of formal review.

10. For example, we know that research about or by women was sidelined in geography for some time (Monk and Hanson 1982; McDowell 1999). Feminist geographers then carved out their own spaces to publish, leading to the codevelopment of the journal *Gender, Place & Culture* in the 1990s (Domosh and Bondi 2014).

11. I fully realize that by focusing primarily on publishing in this chapter, I am falling a little bit into my own trap, but this is an area of discussion that is ripe for future collective work among geographers with feminist training.

12. There is another branch on this tree with regard to the oft-maligned "reviewer two." In a care-full geography, that reviewer ceases to be. Be kind in your reviews, and be generous to yourself and others (see Derickson 2022). We can then begin to think about how to use our reviews to lift people up.

13. A quick glance at the references for this book will tell you that I was not the only one thinking about these topics starting in 2020—close to 50 percent or more of the citations in this work date from 2020 to 2024.

CHAPTER 5. THE CARE-FULL CLASSROOM

1. This work is already underway, and I see, particularly in conversations in queer, trans, and antiracist geographies after the height of the pandemic, a space for both radical vulnerability (cf. Nagar 2019) and moves toward healing and repair. See, for example, Brice 2023; DasGupta et al. 2021; Eaves 2021b; Gieseking 2023; Kinkaid, Parikh, and

Ranjbar 2022; Puttick 2023; Queering Feminist Geography Collective, Eden Kinkaid, Christina Diamant, et al. forthcoming; Rosenberg 2023; Thayer 2025.

2. Thanks to Dr. Shaul Cohen for reminding me early in my PhD studies that there is no such thing as a scholarly crystal ball.

3. For this idea, I owe an intellectual debt to Dr. Sarah Bednarz. While informally reviewing earlier chapters of this book, she effectively asked me, "How are you going to train everyone up as feminists?"

4. Some folks had to deal with unwanted visitors to their classes (sometimes called Zoom bombing). Then we were suddenly required to use authentication or some form of security to gain access to our classes. We also had to deal with inconsistent access to the internet in some cases, particularly for students who relied on the internet provided by the university and did not have paid subscriptions where they were living.

5. Let me be clear: I know not everyone had a choice or could choose.

6. Excellent models and suggestions for this work already exist, and so I point to the more recent ones: Cite Black Women 2017; Gannon 2020; Hogan and Sathy 2022; Love 2019; Naylor et al. 2021; Newstead 2009; Posselt 2020. Hogan and Sathy (2022) should be required reading for anyone involved in course design.

7. I started importing my syllabus into the survey software Qualtrics, where the students can interact with each piece of information it contains and provide me with immediate feedback within the first week of classes (Julie Klinger introduced me to this practice). Students reflect on the topics and assignments they are most excited about, acknowledge the course policies, read about the resources available, and note ones that are new to them. I also use this interaction as an opportunity for students to be vulnerable in an anonymized setting. One of the last questions I ask them to reflect on after engaging the syllabus is "what barriers have you had to overcome to be a student at UD?" Their answers contain multitudes.

8. While at the front of classrooms containing one hundred to three hundred people, I learned a lot of hard lessons about dealing with technology. I will not suggest I have a best practice, but I know that my attempts to control the use of technology in the classroom were definitely not setting anyone up for success. In the past, I have attempted to silence phones, restrict laptop usage to reserved front-row seats, shame students into not using technology so as not to be "cyberslackers" (Alsop 2015), ignore the phone under the desk while silently seething, and so on. I also came to realize that some of my approaches were ableist and actively hurt learning opportunities for some students. I now try to incorporate digital technology into my classes, and I hope to empower students to take responsibility for their education by asking that they use the technology they need to succeed in the classroom and find ways to limit distraction if needed.

9. There is perhaps a space here to talk about the introduction of MOOCs (massive open online courses), but this topic is somewhat tangential to the conversation I am attempting here.

10. Reflecting on the exclusionary experiences of being Black in a STEM discipline, Prescod-Weinstein points to the first *Black Panther* (Coogler 2018) movie and the science of one of the Black women characters in the fictional country of Wakanda as an example of the freedom of educational pursuit: "Shuri is what happens when indigenous intellect is not stifled" (2021, 111).

11. Beyond students, it also includes staff and those in the spaces between, such as

postdoctoral scholars. I have been largely quiet regarding staff at the university, a subject I briefly address in the chapter that follows.

12. There are excellent conversations happening around "ungrading" that provide a productive way to think about this practice (cf. Blum 2020); on inclusive teaching, see also Hogan and Sathy 2022.

CHAPTER 6. THE INSTITUTION WILL NEVER LOVE US BACK

1. For a curated set of suggestions for improving the academy, see Hawkins and Kern (2024).

2. The Women's College was merged with Delaware College in 1921 to create the University of Delaware. However, the board of trustees did not accept the merger until 1945.

3. Monica Cox, n.d., "Stop Playing Diversity," accessed November 20, 2023, https://www.drmonicacox.com/stop-playing-diversity.

4. This statement is also tempered by the new directions of the organization and the formation of a justice, equity, diversity, and inclusion (JEDI) committee that is well supported and well resourced. It also comes at a time of writing when the AAG and collaborators were awarded a grant to address inequities and uncaring in geography: "The National Science Foundation has awarded the American Association of Geographers (AAG) and the University of Colorado, Colorado Springs (UCCS) a collaborative grant to organize a convening around Strategies to Mitigate Implicit Bias and Promote an Ethos of Care in the Research Enterprise (NSF Awards #2324401 and #2324402)" (American Association of Geographers 2023b). It is clear I am not the only one thinking about and urging us toward caring geographies (see also Skop et al. 2021).

5. A result of this new vocabulary is the proliferation of committees and efforts with a staggering array of acronyms: DEI (diversity, equity, and inclusion) and JEDI (justice, equity, diversity, and inclusion) being those most commonly used. I presently sit on two such committees. One was originally (when helmed by a white, cis-male senior academic in my college) called the diversity and inclusion committee, or DIC, and it is now called the Inclusion, Diversity, Equity, and Accountability Committee (IDEA). The other, whose acronym was the result of a deep discussion among the founding members, sits in the Graduate College and is the Creating Accessible Realities and Equitable Spaces Working Group (CARES). And there are others as we continue this discussion and try to find or gain some ground in working to change our institutions.

6. Dr. Karen Kelsky (2017) created a crowdsourced anonymous survey about sexual harassment in the academy that accepted responses for eight months and garnered almost 2,500 responses. The database remains open for readers.

7. The Mental Health Task Force of the AAG Report: *Mental Health and Well-Being in Geography: Creating a Healthy Discipline* (Peake et al. 2018) and the robust membership of the Mental Health Affinity Group at the AAG are excellent examples.

8. Pryal estimates that 25 to 30 percent of academics have invisible psychiatric disabilities that are rarely disclosed (2017, 10).

9. In 2021, while in residence as a faculty fellow of the University of Delaware Anti-Racism Initiative, I worked on the "Anti-Assimilationist Mentoring Plan," a flexible guide to mentoring historically underrepresented and excluded graduate students (Naylor 2021).

10. *However*, there are problems with those who take on a so-called mentoring role and either ignore its responsibilities, or take negative approaches that may be overly demanding, construed as tough love, or outright extractive and abusive. Those are not mentoring relationships; they are bullying ones.

CONCLUSION. AN ENTREATY TO GEOGRAPHY AND GEOGRAPHERS

1. I say this as someone who had not taken a geography class until I started applying to PhD programs in geography. Appreciation to Drs. Hunter Shobe and Martin Lafrenz at Portland State University for introducing me to cultural and physical geography, respectively.

2. It would seem this topic has very little to do with geography and geographic inquiry, and more to do with the feminization and marginalization of the discipline and work not seen as mainstream (cf. Mountz and Williams 2023).

3. Cupples (2020) points specifically to publishing practices as a key site of difference within the discipline. Large research teams or labs often allow for more publishing opportunities in physical geography and GIS, while human geographers often do not have those same opportunities. I have mentioned throughout the book that I am one of a very few social scientists in my college, and that has led to a number of hurdles. But when my first papers from my dissertation were published—I was the solo author, as is much more common for human geographers—the dean at the time was deeply impressed at the sole authorship, which was uncommon for their field.

4. "As the editors of the Journal of Historical Geography write, we are in the midst of a 'shift in intellectual atmosphere, a metaphorical quake calling us to rethink and revise our intellectual foundations, scholarly orientations and ethical praxis,' a shift that pursues an ethos and practice of 'valuing scholarship and including scholarship from all corners of global historical geographical research'" (Tolia-Kelly et al. 2020, 1, 2 in McFarlane 2022, 6).

5. This launch did receive rightful critique on social media for having a table of contents populated almost entirely by male scholars (see also Kinkaid 2024, 195).

6. I have had the good fortune to collaborate on two classes that bridged specialty area divides. The geography course on climate change and food security that I co-taught with a colleague who is a climate scientist working in coastal and polar regions on wind, clouds, and precipitation was an enriching experience all around (see also Naylor and Veron 2021).

7. As an academic situated at a U.S. institution, I fully acknowledge that I have the privilege to dig in with my heels and make this case, while others outside the U.S. may yet be able to attend to these things. For example, as I make the last revisions to this manuscript pre-production in July 2024, Dhaka, Bangladesh, is under curfew. Police have orders to "shoot on sight," and communications are cut while university students protest for better job opportunities and an end to anachronistic government employment quotas (Ellis-Petersen and Parent 2024).

8. Natalie Oswin drew geographers' attention to Roy's ideas (2022, 390), and I take my cue here from this imperative.

REFERENCES

Abu-Lughod, Lila. 2002. "Do Muslim Women Really Need Saving? Anthropological Reflections on Cultural Relativism and Its Others." *American Anthropologist* 104, no. 3 (September): 783–90. https://doi.org/10.1525/aa.2002.104.3.783.

———. (2013) 2015. *Do Muslim Women Need Saving?* Reprint, Cambridge, Mass.: Harvard University Press.

ACME Editorial Collective. 2023a. "About the Journal." ACME: *An International E-journal for Critical Geographies.* 2023. https://acme-journal.org/index.php/acme/about.

———. 2023b. "An Unpause-Ish Statement: An ACME Editorial." ACME: *An International Journal for Critical Geographies* 22, no. 1 (March): 750–61.

Adams-Hutcheson, Gail, and Lynda Johnston. 2019. "Flourishing in Fragile Academic Work Spaces and Learning Environments: Feminist Geographies of Care and Mentoring." *Gender, Place & Culture* 26, no. 4 (April): 451–67. https://doi.org/10.1080/0966369X.2019.1596885.

Agnew, John. 2007. "Know-Where: Geographies of Knowledge of World Politics." *International Political Sociology* 1, no. 2 (May): 138–48. https://doi.org/10.1111/j.1749-5687.2007.00009.x.

Ahmed, Sara. 2006. "The Nonperformativity of Antiracism." *Meridians* 7, no. 1 (September): 104–26. https://doi.org/10.2979/MER.2006.7.1.104.

———. 2010. *The Promise of Happiness.* Durham, N.C.: Duke University Press.

———. 2017. *Living a Feminist Life.* Durham, N.C.: Duke University Press.

———. 2023. *The Feminist Killjoy Handbook: The Radical Potential of Getting in the Way.* New York: Basic Books.

Alcoff, Linda Martín. 1992. "The Problem of Speaking for Others." *Cultural Critique* no. 20 (Winter 1991–1992): 5–32.

Alderman, Derek. 2017. "Making Every Week about Geography Awareness and Advocacy." AAG *Newsletter*, November 1, 2017. President's Column. https://www.aag.org/making-every-week-about-geography-awareness-and-advocacy/.

———. 2019. "Keeping It REAL in a Post-Truth World: Geography as Reparative Storytelling." Past President's Address presented at the Annual Meeting of the American

Association of Geographers, Washington, D.C., April 6, 2019. https://aag.secure
-abstracts.com/AAG%20Annual%20Meeting%202019/sessions-gallery/24821.

Alexander-Floyd, Nikol G. 2012. "Disappearing Acts: Reclaiming Intersectionality in the
Social Sciences in a Post—Black Feminist Era." *Feminist Formations* 24, no. 1 (Spring):
1–25.

Alexander, M. Jacqui. 2006. *Pedagogies of Crossing: Meditations on Feminism, Sexual
Politics, Memory, and the Sacred.* 1st ed. Durham, N.C.: Duke University Press.

Alsop, Ronald. 2015. "A Generation of Cyberslackers." BBC News. April 9, 2015. Capital.
http://www.bbc.com/capital/story/20150408-a-generation-of-cyberslackers.

American Association of Geographers. 2023a. "National Science Foundation Provides
Grant to Promote Ethos of Care in Research." AAG: American Association of
Geographers. October 11, 2023. https://www.aag.org/national-science-foundation
-provides-grant-to-promote-ethos-of-care-in-research/.

———. 2023b. "The State of Geography: Patterns and Trends by Racial and Ethnic
Identity." AAG: American Association of Geographers. March 7, 2023. https://www
.aag.org/the-state-of-geography-patterns-and-trends-by-racial-and-ethnic-identity/.

———. n.d. "Presidents of the AAG." AAG: American Association of Geographers.
Accessed August 14, 2023. https://www.aag.org/presidents-of-the-aag/.

Anderson, Vivienne, Rafaela Rabello, Rob Wass, Clinton Golding, Ana Rangi, Esmay
Eteuati, Zoe Bristowe, and Arianna Waller. 2020. "Good Teaching as Care in Higher
Education." *Higher Education* 79, no. 1 (January): 1–19. https://doi.org/10.1007
/s10734-019-00392-6.

Annals of the Association of American Geographers. 1911. "Titles and Abstracts of Papers
Presented to the Association from 1904 to 1910, Inclusive." *Annals of the Association of
American Geographers* 1:101–50. https://doi.org/10.2307/2560847.

Anzaldúa, Gloria. 1987. *Borderlands: The New Mestiza = La Frontera.* 1st ed. Chicana
Studies. San Francisco: Aunt Lute.

Araujo, Erin. 2018. "Building an Alternative Economy as Decolonial Praxis." In *Indige-
nous Places and Colonial Spaces: The Politics of Intertwined Relations*, edited by Nicole
Gombay and Marcela Palomino-Schalscha, 1st ed., 211–25. Abingdon, Oxon ; New
York, NY: Routledge.

Askins, Kye, and Matej Blazek. 2017. "Feeling Our Way: Academia, Emotions and a
Politics of Care." *Social & Cultural Geography* 18, no. 8 (November): 1086–105. https:
//doi.org/10.1080/14649365.2016.1240224.

Atkins, Celeste. 2022. "Teaching Up: Bringing My Blackness into the Classroom." In *Picture a Professor: Interrupting Biases about Faculty and Increasing Student Learning*,
edited by Jessamyn Neuhaus, 1st ed., 271–84. Morgantown: West Virginia University
Press.

Bailey, Adrian J., Markus Breines, Phil Emmerson, James Esson, Sam Halvorsen, Jessica
Chloe Hope, Mikko Joronen, et al. 2023. "Care for Transactions." *Transactions of the
Institute of British Geographers* 48, no. 1 (January): 2–8. https://doi.org/10.1111
/tran.12592.

Barker, Adam Joseph, and Jenny Pickerill. 2024. "Geographies of Collective Responsibility: Decolonising Universities through Place-Based Praxis." *Journal of Geography in*

Higher Education 48, no. 4 (August): 1–22. https://doi.org/10.1080/03098265.2023.22 63741.

Bartos, Ann E. 2018. "The Uncomfortable Politics of Care and Conflict: Exploring Nontraditional Caring Agencies." *Geoforum* 88 (January): 66–73.

———. 2019. "Introduction: Stretching the Boundaries of Care." *Gender, Place & Culture* 26, no. 6 (June): 767–77. https://doi.org/10.1080/0966369X.2019.1635999.

———. 2021. "Troubling False Care: Towards a More Revolutionary 'Care Revolution' in the University." ACME: *An International E-journal for Critical Geographies* 20, no. 3 (July): 312–21.

Bawaka Country, Sarah Wright, Sandie Suchet-Pearson, Kate Lloyd, Laklak Burarr-wanga, Ritjilili Ganambarr, Merrkiyawuy Ganambarr-Stubbs, Banbapuy Ganambarr, Djawundil Maymuru, and Jill Sweeney. 2016. "Co-becoming Bawaka: Towards a Relational Understanding of Place/Space." *Progress in Human Geography* 40, no. 4 (August): 455–75. https://doi.org/10.1177/0309132515589437.

Baxter, Kaylan, James Bridgeforth, Jaymon Ortega, Isaiah Simmons, and Sarah Toutant. 2021. "Accepted to Assimilate: Implications for Racial Mismatch between Education PhD Students and Their Faculty." Presentation at NCORE: National Conference on Race and Ethnicity, University of Oklahoma Outreach, held virtually, March 3, 2021. YouTube video, 1:25:04. https://www.youtube.com/watch?v=-p4WophdT78.

Bednarz, Sarah. 2016. "New Year, New Name, New Proposal." AAG *Newsletter*, January 7, 2016. President's Column. https://www.aag.org/new-year-new-name-new-proposal/.

Bednarz, Sarah Witham. 2019. "Geography's Secret Powers to Save the World." *Canadian Geographies / Géographies canadiennes* 63, no. 4 (June): 520–29. https://doi.org/10.1111/cag.12539.

Bendels, Michael H. K., Ruth Müller, Doerthe Brueggmann, and David A. Groneberg. 2018. "Gender Disparities in High-Quality Research Revealed by Nature Index Journals." *PLOS One* 13, no. 1 (January): e0189136. https://doi.org/10.1371/journal.pone.0189136.

Bernard, Rachel E., and Emily H. G. Cooperdock. 2018. "No Progress on Diversity in 40 Years." *Nature Geoscience* 11, no. 5 (May): 292–95. https://doi.org/10.1038/s41561-018-0116-6.

Bhambra, Gurminder K., Kerem Nisancioglu, and Delia Gebrial, eds. 2018. *Decolonizing the University*. London: Pluto.

Blidon, Marianne, and Sofia Zaragocin. 2019. "Mapping Gender and Feminist Geographies in the Global Context." *Gender, Place & Culture* 26, nos. 7–9 (September): 915–25. https://doi.org/10.1080/0966369X.2019.1636000.

Blum, Susan D., ed. 2020. *Ungrading: Why Rating Students Undermines Learning*. 1st ed. Morgantown: West Virginia University Press.

Brice, Sage. 2023. "Making Space for a Radical Trans Imagination: Towards a Kinder, More Vulnerable, Geography." *Environment and Planning D: Society and Space* 41, no. 4 (August): 592–99. https://doi.org/10.1177/02637758231187449.

Brigstocke, Julian. 2024. "Form, Genre, Voice, and Authority in Human Geography: A Speculative Genealogy." *Dialogues in Human Geography* 14, no. 2 (July): 361–65. https://doi.org/10.1177/20438206231174634.

Bruno, Tianna, Andrew Curley, Mabel Denzin Gergan, and Sara Smith. 2024. "The Work of Repair: Land, Relation, and Pedagogy." *Cultural Geographies* 31, no. 1 (January): 5–19. https://doi.org/10.1177/14744740231203713.

Bruno, Tianna, and Cristina Faiver-Serna. 2022. "More Reflections on a White Discipline." *Professional Geographer* 74, no. 1 (January): 156–61. https://doi.org/10.1080/00330124.2021.1915822.

Butler, Judith. 1990. *Gender Trouble: Feminism and the Subversion of Identity.* 1st ed. New York: Routledge.

Cahuas, Madelaine C. 2023. "Building a Holistic Intersectional Feminist Praxis in Geography: Lessons from Community." *Professional Geographer* 75, no. 4 (July): 648–54. https://doi.org/10.1080/00330124.2022.2061536.

Calarco, Jessica. 2024. *Holding It Together: How Women Became America's Social Safety Net.* New York: Penguin.

Caretta, Martina Angela, and Federica Bono. 2022. "Students' Evaluation of Instruction: A Neoliberal Managerial Tool against Faculty Diversity." In *Bridging Worlds—Building Feminist Geographies: Essays in Honor of Jan Monk*, edited by Anindita Datta, Janet Momsen, and Ann M. Oberhauser, 121–32. New York: Routledge.

Caretta, Martina Angela, and Caroline V. Faria. 2020. "Time and Care in the 'Lab' and the 'Field': Slow Mentoring and Feminist Research in Geography." *Geographical Review* 110, nos. 1–2 (January): 172–82. https://doi.org/10.1111/gere.12369.

Carey, Mark, M. Jackson, Alessandro Antonello, and Jaclyn Rushing. 2016. "Glaciers, Gender, and Science: A Feminist Glaciology Framework for Global Environmental Change Research." *Progress in Human Geography* 40, no. 6 (December): 770–93. https://doi.org/10.1177/0309132515623368.

Castree, Noel. 2022. "Navigating Together without a Map: Metaphors for Making Geography's Future." *Environment and Planning F: Philosophy, Theory, Models, Methods and Practice* 1, no. 1 (March): 7–13. https://doi.org/10.1177/26349825221084177.

Castree, Noel, Louise Amoore, Alex Hughes, Nina Laurie, David Manley, and Susan Parnell. 2020. "Boundless Contamination and Progress in Geography." *Progress in Human Geography* 44, no. 3 (June): 411–14. https://doi.org/10.1177/0309132520920094.

Castree, Noel, Michael F. Goodchild, Audrey Kobayashi, Weidong Liu, and Richard A. Marston. 2017. *International Encyclopedia of Geography, 15 Volume Set: People, the Earth, Environment and Technology.* Hoboken, N.J.: Wiley.

Castree, Noel, Agnieszka Leszczynski, J. Anthony Stallins, Tim Schwanen, and Zarina Patel. 2022. "Reconstituting Geography for the 21st Century." *Environment and Planning F: Philosophy, Theory, Models, Methods and Practice* 1, no. 1 (March): 3–6. https://doi.org/10.1177/26349825211005376.

Chennault, Carrie. 2021. "The Path to Radical Vulnerability: Feminist Praxis and Community Food Collaborations." In *Feminist Geography Unbound: Discomfort, Bodies, and Prefigured Futures*, edited by Banu Gökariksel, Michael Hawkins, Christopher Neubert, and Sara Smith, 1st ed., 48–68. Morgantown: West Virginia University Press.

Cite Black Women. 2017. Cite Black Women website. 2017. https://www.citeblackwomencollective.org/.

Coddington, Kate. 2015. "Feminist Geographies 'beyond' Gender: De-coupling Feminist Research and the Gendered Subject." *Geography Compass* 9, no. 4 (April): 214–24. https://doi.org/10.1111/gec3.12207.

Collins, Patricia Hill. 2002. *Black Feminist Thought: Knowledge, Consciousness, and the Politics of Empowerment*. Oxfordshire, U.K.: Routledge.

———. 2015. "Intersectionality's Definitional Dilemmas." *Annual Review of Sociology* 41, no. 1 (August): 1–20.

Collins, Patricia Hill, and Sirma Bilge. 2016. *Intersectionality*. 1st ed. Malden, Mass.: Polity.

Combahee River Collective. 1986. *The Combahee River Collective Statement: Black Feminist Organizing in the Seventies and Eighties*. Latham, N.Y.: Kitchen Table Women of Color Press.

Connell, Raewyn. 2013. "The Neoliberal Cascade and Education: An Essay on the Market Agenda and Its Consequences." *Critical Studies in Education* 54, no. 2 (June): 99–112. https://doi.org/10.1080/17508487.2013.776990.

Conradson, David. 2003. "Geographies of Care: Spaces, Practices, Experiences." *Social & Cultural Geography* 4, no. 4 (December): 451–54. https://doi.org/10.1080/146493603 2000137894.

Conroy, Gemma. 2020. "What's Wrong with the h-Index, According to Its Inventor." Nature Index. March 24, 2020. https://www.nature.com/nature-index/news /whats-wrong-with-the-h-index-according-to-its-inventor.

Coogler, Ryan, dir. 2018. *Black Panther*. Burbank, Calif.: Marvel Studios.

Cook, Ian, et al. 2005. "Positionality / Situated Knowledge." In *Cultural Geography: A Critical Dictionary of Key Ideas*, edited by D. Sibley, Peter Jackson, D. Atkinson, and Neil Washbourne, 16–26. London: Tauris.

Coon, Jaime J., Nathan B. Alexander, Emmett M. Smith, Madeleine Spellman, Isaac M. Klimasmith, Lucas T. Allen-Custodio, Thea E. Clarkberg, et al. 2023. "Best Practices for LGBTQ+ Inclusion during Ecological Fieldwork: Considering Safety, Cis/Heteronormativity and Structural Barriers." *Journal of Applied Ecology* 60, no. 3 (March): 393–99. https://doi.org/10.1111/1365-2664.14339.

Cooper, Brittney. 2014. "Feminism's Ugly Internal Clash: Why Its Future Is Not up to White Women." Salon. September 24, 2014. https://www.salon.com/2014/09/24 /feminisms_ugly_internal_clash_why_its_future_is_not_up_to_white_women/.

Corbera, Esteve, Isabelle Anguelovski, and Jordi Honey-Rosés. 2021. "Academia in the Time of Covid-19: Towards an Ethics of Care." *Planning Theory & Practice* 21, no. 2 (May): 191–99. https://doi.org/10.1080/14649357.2020.1757891.

Cox, Monica. n.d. "Stop Playing Diversity." Dr. Monica Cox. Accessed November 20, 2023. https://www.drmonicacox.com/stop-playing-diversity.

Crenshaw, Kimberlé. 1989. "Demarginalizing the Intersection of Race and Sex: A Black Feminist Critique of Antidiscrimination Doctrine, Feminist Theory and Antiracist Politics." *Stanford Law Review* 43 (6): 1241–99.

Cupples, Julie. 2020. "No Sense of Place: Geoscientisation and the Epistemic Erasure of Geography." *New Zealand Geographer* 76, no. 1 (April): 3–13. https://doi.org/10.1111 /nzg.12231.

———. 2024. "The Decolonial Pedagogies of Colonial Violence: Curricular Decolonisation in the (Geo)Sciences." *Area* 56, no. 3 (September): e12941. https://doi.org/10.1111/area.12941.

Daigle, Michelle, and Margaret Marietta Ramírez. 2019. "Decolonial Geographies." In *Keywords in Radical Geography: Antipode at 50*, edited by the Antipode Editorial Collective, 78–84. New York: Wiley. https://doi.org/10.1002/9781119558071.ch14.

Daigle, Michelle, and Juanita Sundberg. 2017. "From Where We Stand: Unsettling Geographical Knowledges in the Classroom." *Transactions of the Institute of British Geographers* 42, no. 3 (September): 338–41. https://doi.org/10.1111/tran.12201.

DasGupta, Debanuj, Rae Rosenberg, John Paul Catungal, and Jen Jack Gieseking. 2021. "Pedagogies of Queer and Trans Repair: Letters from Queer Geographic Classrooms." ACME: *An International Journal for Critical Geographies* 20, no. 5 (November): 491–508.

Davies, Sarah, Hollie Putnam, Tracy Ainsworth, Julia Baum, Colleen Bove, Sarah Crosby, Isabelle Côté, et al. 2021. "Shifting Our Value System beyond Citations for a More Equitable Future." Preprints. February 2021. https://www.preprints.org/manuscript/202102.0493/v1.

Davis, Angela Y. 2016. *Freedom Is a Constant Struggle: Ferguson, Palestine, and the Foundations of a Movement.* Chicago: Haymarket Books.

Davis, Angela Y., Gina Dent, Erica R. Meiners, and Beth E. Richie. 2022. *Abolition. Feminism. Now.* Chicago: Haymarket Books.

de Jong, Sara, Rosalba Icaza, and Olivia Rutazibwa. 2019. *Decolonization and Feminisms in Global Teaching and Learning.* New York: Routledge.

de la Bellacasa, María Puig. 2017. *Matters of Care: Speculative Ethics in More than Human Worlds.* Vol. 41. Minneapolis: University of Minnesota Press.

de Leeuw, Sarah, and Sarah Hunt. 2018. "Unsettling Decolonizing Geographies." *Geography Compass* 12, no. 7 (July 2018): e12376. https://doi.org/10.1111/gec3.12376.

DeLyser, Dydia. 2022. "Writing's Intimate Spatialities: Drawing Ourselves to Our Writing in Self-Caring Practices of Love." *Environment and Planning A: Economy and Space* 54, no. 2 (March): 405–12. https://doi.org/10.1177/0308518X211068496.

DeLyser, Dydia, and Harriet Hawkins. 2014. "Introduction: Writing Creatively—Process, Practice, and Product." *Cultural Geographies* 21, no. 1 (January): 131–34. https://doi.org/10.1177/1474474012469006.

Demery, Amelia-Juliette Claire, and Monique Avery Pipkin. 2021. "Safe Fieldwork Strategies for At-Risk Individuals, Their Supervisors and Institutions." *Nature Ecology & Evolution* 5, no. 1 (January): 5–9.

Derickson, Kate. 2022. "The Case for Doing Less in Our Peer Reviews." *Environment and Planning D: Society and Space* 40, no. 6 (December): 963–66. https://doi.org/10.1177/02637758221142339.

Doan, Petra. 2021. "Interview with Petra Doan." In *Feminist Geography Unbound: Discomfort, Bodies, and Prefigured Futures*, edited by Banu Gökariksel, Michael Hawkins, Christopher Neubert, and Sara Smith, 1st ed., 180–90. Morgantown: West Virginia University Press.

Dombroski, Kelly. 2020. "Caring Labour: Redistributing Care Work." In *The Handbook of Diverse Economies*, edited by J. K. Gibson-Graham and Kelly Dombroski, 154–62. Cheltenham, U.K.: Edward Elgar.

Dombroski, Kelly, Stephen Healy, and Katharine McKinnon. 2019. "Care-Full Community Economies." In *Feminist Political Ecology and the Economics of Care: In Search of Economic Alternatives*, edited by Christine Bauhardt and Wendy Harcourt, 1st ed., 99–115. Routledge Studies in Ecological Economics. New York: Routledge.

Dombroski, Kelly, Alison F. Watkins, Helen Fitt, Jillian Frater, Karen Banwell, Kierin Mackenzie, Levi Mutambo, et al. 2018. "Journeying from 'I' to 'We': Assembling Hybrid Caring Collectives of Geography Doctoral Scholars." *Journal of Geography in Higher Education* 42, no. 1 (January 2): 80–93. https://doi.org/10.1080/03098265 .2017.1335295.

Domosh, Mona. 1991. "Toward a Feminist Historiography of Geography." *Transactions of the Institute of British Geographers* 16, no. 1 (January): 95–104.

Domosh, Mona, and Liz Bondi. 2014. "Remembering the Making of Gender, Place and Culture." *Gender, Place & Culture* 21, no. 9 (October 21): 1063–70.

Dowler, Lorraine. 2021. "Afterword." In *Feminist Geography Unbound: Discomfort, Bodies, and Prefigured Futures*, edited by Banu Gökariksel, Michael Hawkins, Christopher Neubert, and Sara Smith, 1st ed., 291–94. Morgantown: West Virginia University Press.

Dowler, Lorraine, and Jenna Christian. 2019. "Landscapes of Impunity and the Deaths of Americans LaVena Johnson and Sandra Bland." *Gender, Place & Culture* 26, no. 6 (June): 813–29. https://doi.org/10.1080/0966369X.2018.1553863.

Dowler, Lorraine, Dana Cuomo, Debanuj Dasgupta, Dydia DeLyser, LaToya Eaves, Candida Mannozzi, Beverley Mullings, et al. 2019. "AAG—Anti-Harassment Task Force Report." Washington, D.C.: American Association of Geographers.

Dowler, Lorraine, Dana Cuomo, and Nicole Laliberte. 2014. "Challenging 'The Penn State Way': A Feminist Response to Institutional Violence in Higher Education." *Gender, Place & Culture* 21, no. 3 (March): 387–94. https://doi.org/10.1080 /0966369X.2013.802676.

Dowler, Lorraine, Dana Cuomo, A. M. Ranjbar, Nicole Laliberte, and Jenna Christian. 2019. "Care." In *Keywords in Radical Geography: Antipode at 50*, edited by the Antipode Editorial Collective, 35–39. New York: Wiley. https://doi.org/10 .1002/9781119558071.ch6.

Dowtin, Asia L., and Delphis F. Levia. 2018. "The Power of Persistence." *Science* 360, no. 6393 (June): 1142. https://doi.org/10.1126/science.360.6393.1142.

Dufty-Jones, Rae, and Chris Gibson. 2022. "Making Space to Write 'Care-Fully': Engaged Responses to the Institutional Politics of Research Writing." *Progress in Human Geography* 46, no. 2 (April): 339–58. https://doi.org/10.1177/03091325211020807.

Dutta, Madhumita, and Kendra McSweeney. 2024. "Generative Tensions: Undergraduates' Experience of Geography in US Universities." *Transactions of the Institute of British Geographers* 49, no. 2 (June): e12623. https://doi.org/10.1111/tran.12623.

Eaves, LaToya E. 2021a. "The Controversy of the Twin Pandemics: Feminist Pedagogies and the Urgency of Revolutionary Praxis." ACME: *An International Journal for Critical Geographies* 20, no. 5 (November): 562–68.

———. 2021b. "Interview with LaToya Eaves." In *Feminist Geography Unbound: Discomfort, Bodies, and Prefigured Futures*, edited by Banu Gökariksel, Michael Hawkins, Christopher Neubert, and Sara Smith, 1st ed., 253–59. Morgantown: West Virginia University Press.

———. 2021c. "Power and the Paywall: A Black Feminist Reflection on the Socio-Spatial Formations of Publishing." *Geoforum* 118 (January): 207–9. https://doi.org/10.1016/j.geoforum.2020.04.002.

Eaves, LaToya, and Karen Falconer Al-Hindi. 2020. "Intersectional Geographies and COVID-19." *Dialogues in Human Geography* 10, no. 2 (July): 132–36. https://doi.org/10.1177/2043820620935247.

Eaves, LaToya, Banu Gökariksel, Mike Hawkins, Christopher Neubert, and Sara Smith. 2023. "Political Geographies of Discomfort Feminism: Introduction to the Themed Intervention." *Gender, Place & Culture* 30, no. 4 (April): 517–27. https://doi.org/10.1080/0966369X.2023.2169256.

Ellis-Petersen, Hannah, and Deepa Parent. 2024. "Bangladesh Police Given 'Shoot-on-Sight' Orders amid National Curfew." *Guardian* (*Observer* edition), July 20, 2024. World News. https://www.theguardian.com/world/article/2024/jul/20/bangladesh-police-given-shoot-on-sight-orders-amid-national-curfew.

Embodiment Lab. 2018. "Beginnings." Embodiment Lab: Human-Environment Relations at UDelaware. 2018. https://sites.udel.edu/geog-bodylab/beginnings/.

Embodiment Lab, Hanan Abou Ali, James Edward Bryan, Carrie Chennault, Dharni Grover, Mehrnaz Haghdadi, Faisal Bin Islam, et al. 2025. "Embodied Belonging in the Social Science Lab." *ACME: An International Journal for Critical Geographies* 24 (1): 1–25. https://doi.org/10.14288/acme.v24i1.2429.

England, Kim V. L. 1994. "Getting Personal: Reflexivity, Positionality, and Feminist Research." *Professional Geographer* 46, no. 1 (February): 80–89. https://doi.org/10.1111/j.0033-0124.1994.00080.x.

England, Kim, and Kevin Ward. 2011. *Neoliberalization: States, Networks, Peoples.* Hoboken, N.J.: John Wiley & Sons.

Evans, Sarah L. 2016. "Mapping Terra Incognita: Women's Participation in Royal Geographical Society–Supported Expeditions, 1913–1939." *Historical Geography* 44: 30–44.

Falconer Al-Hindi, Karen. 2000. "Women in Geography in the 21st Century: Introductory Remarks; Structure, Agency, and Women Geographers in Academia at the End of the Long Twentieth Century." *Professional Geographer* 52, no. 4 (November): 697–702. https://doi.org/10.1080/00330124.2000.9628415.

———. 2019. "Vibrant Mentoring Landscapes in Feminist Geography." *Gender, Place & Culture* 26, no. 12 (December): 1657–63. https://doi.org/10.1080/0966369X.2019.1681372.

Falconer Al-Hindi, Karen, and LaToya E. Eaves. 2022. "For an Intersectional Sensibility: Feminisms in Geography." In *The Routledge Handbook of Methodologies in Human Geography*, edited by Sarah A. Lovell, Stephanie E. Coen, and Mark W. Rosenberg, 72–80. New York: Taylor & Francis.

Faria, Caroline Veronica. 2020. "Call for Papers." ACME: *An International Journal for Critical Geographies* 19, no. 2 (September): 413–23.

Faria, Caroline, Bisola Falola, Jane Henderson, and Rebecca Maria Torres. 2019. "A Long

Way to Go: Collective Paths to Racial Justice in Geography." *Professional Geographer* 71, no. 2 (April): 364–76. https://doi.org/10.1080/00330124.2018.1547977.

Faria, Caroline, and Sharlene Mollett. 2016. "Critical Feminist Reflexivity and the Politics of Whiteness in the 'Field.'" *Gender, Place & Culture* 23, no. 1 (January): 79–93. https://doi.org/10.1080/0966369X.2014.958065.

———. 2020. "'We Didn't Have Time to Sit Still and Be Scared': A Postcolonial Feminist Geographic Reading of 'An Other Geography.'" *Dialogues in Human Geography* 10, no. 1 (March): 23–29. https://doi.org/10.1177/2043820619898895.

Farris, Emily M., Julia Marin Hellwege, and Andrea Malji. 2021. "Supporting Junior Women: Strategies for Men Colleagues." *PS: Political Science & Politics* 54, no. 3 (July): 506–7. https://doi.org/10.1017/S1049096521000068.

Farrow, Heather, Pamela Moss, and Barbara Shaw. 1995. "Symposium on Feminist Participatory Research." *Antipode* 27, no. 1 (January): 71–74.

Fem-Mentee Collective, Alison L. Bain, Rachael Baker, Nicole Laliberté, Alison Milan, William J. Payne, Léa Ravensbergen, and Dima Saad. 2017. "Emotional Masking and Spill-Outs in the Neoliberalized University: A Feminist Geographic Perspective on Mentorship." *Journal of Geography in Higher Education* 41, no. 4 (October): 590–607. https://doi.org/10.1080/03098265.2017.1331424.

Ferretti, Federico. 2020. "History and Philosophy of Geography I: Decolonising the Discipline, Diversifying Archives and Historicising Radicalism." *Progress in Human Geography* 44, no. 6 (December): 1161–71. https://doi.org/10.1177/0309132519893442.

———. 2021. "History and Philosophy of Geography II: Rediscovering Individuals, Fostering Interdisciplinarity and Renegotiating the 'Margins.'" *Progress in Human Geography* 45, no. 4 (August): 890–901. https://doi.org/10.1177/0309132520973750.

———. 2022. "History and Philosophy of Geography III: Global Histories of Geography, Statues That Must Fall and a Radical and Multilingual Turn." *Progress in Human Geography* 46, no. 2 (April): 716–25. https://doi.org/10.1177/0309132521106270.

Fisher, B., and J. Tronto. 1991. "Toward a Feminist Theory of Care." In *Circles of Care: Work and Identity in Women's Lives*, edited by Emily K. Abel and Margaret K. Nelson, 35–62. Albany: State University of New York Press.

Fuller, Sara, Kristian Ruming, Andrew Burridge, Richard Carter-White, Donna Houston, Linda Kelly, Kate Lloyd, et al. 2021. "Delivering the Discipline: Teaching Geography and Planning during COVID-19." *Geographical Research* 59, no. 3 (August): 331–40. https://doi.org/10.1111/1745-5871.12472.

Fulweiler, Robinson W., Sarah W. Davies, Jennifer F. Biddle, Amy J. Burgin, Emily H. G. Cooperdock, Torrance C. Hanley, Carly D. Kenkel, et al. 2021. "Rebuild the Academy: Supporting Academic Mothers during COVID-19 and Beyond." *PLOS Biology* 19, no. 3 (March): e3001100. https://doi.org/10.1371/journal.pbio.3001100.

Gamma Theta Upsilon. n.d. "Initiation Ceremony." Gamma Theta Upsilon International Geographical Honor Society. Accessed November 16, 2022. https://www .gammathetaupsilon.org/initiation-ceremony.html.

Gannon, Kevin M. 2020. *Radical Hope: A Teaching Manifesto.* 1st ed. Morgantown: West Virginia University Press.

Garcia-Ramon, Maria-Dolors. 2003. "Globalization and International Geography: The Questions of Languages and Scholarly Traditions." *Progress in Human Geography* 27, no. 1 (February): 1–5.

Gibert, Sophie Holland (@sophiehollandart), and Leah Pierson (@leah_pierson). 2022. "Saying No to Things Punch Card." Instagram. January 30, 2022. https://www .instagram.com/p/CZW1e2xr4A7/.

Gibson-Graham, J. K. (1996) 2006. *The End of Capitalism (as We Knew It): A Feminist Critique of Political Economy*. Reprint, Minneapolis: University of Minnesota Press.

———. 2006. *A Postcapitalist Politics*. Minneapolis: University of Minnesota Press.

———. 2008. "Diverse Economies: Performative Practices for 'Other Worlds.'" *Progress in Human Geography* 32, no. 5 (October): 613–32.

———. 2011. "A Feminist Project of Belonging for the Anthropocene." *Gender, Place & Culture* 18, no. 1 (January): 1–21. https://doi.org/10.1080/0966369X.2011.535295.

Gibson-Graham, J. K., Jenny Cameron, and Stephen Healy. 2013. *Take Back the Economy: An Ethical Guide for Transforming Our Communities*. Minneapolis: University of Minnesota Press.

Gibson, Katherine, Deborah Bird Rose, and Ruth Fincher, eds. 2015. *Manifesto for Living in the Anthropocene*. Santa Barbara, Calif.: Punctum Books.

Gieseking, Jack Jen. 2023. "Reflections on a Cis Discipline." *Environment and Planning D: Society and Space* 41, no. 4 (August): 571–91. https://doi.org/10.1177 /02637758231191656.

Gieseking, Jen Jack. 2020. "Citing You on Behalf of an Other Digital Geographical Imagination." *Dialogues in Human Geography* 10, no. 1 (March): 41–45. https://doi .org/10.1177/2043820619898896.

Goerisch, Denise, Jae Basiliere, Ashley Rosener, Kimberly McKee, Jodee Hunt, and Tonya M. Parker. 2019. "Mentoring With: Reimagining Mentoring across the University." *Gender, Place & Culture* 26, no. 12 (December): 1740–58. https://doi.org/10.1080 /0966369X.2019.1668752.

Gökariksel, Banu, Michael Hawkins, Christopher Neubert, and Sara Smith, eds. 2021. *Feminist Geography Unbound: Discomfort, Bodies, and Prefigured Futures*. 1st ed. Morgantown: West Virginia University Press.

Gökariksel, Banu, and Sara Smith. 2017. "Intersectional Feminism beyond US Flag Hijab and Pussy Hats in Trump's America." *Gender, Place & Culture* 24, no. 5 (May): 628–44.

Grosfoguel, Ramón. 2002. "Colonial Difference, Geopolitics of Knowledge, and Global Coloniality in the Modern/Colonial Capitalist World-System." *Review (Fernand Braudel Center for the Study of Economies, Historical Systems, and Civilizations)* 25 (3): 203–24.

Grove, Kevin, Kimberley Peters, Caroline Nagel, Tor A. Benjaminsen, Stefano Costalli, Filippo Menga, and Antonis Vradis. 2021. "Making Time in 2020." *Political Geography* 84 (January): 102332. https://doi.org/10.1016/j.polgeo.2020.102332.

Gumbs, Alexis Pauline. 2020. *Undrowned: Black Feminist Lessons from Marine Mammals*. Stirling, U.K.: AK Press.

Gutiérrez y Muhs, Gabriella, Yolanda Flores Niemann, Carmen G. González, and Angela P. Harris. 2012. *Presumed Incompetent: The Intersections of Race and Class for Women in Academia*. Denver: University Press of Colorado.

Hagy, Jessica. 2022. "Caretaking of Everyone and Everything, for Example." Indexed. May 9, 2022. https://thisisindexed.com/2022/05/caretaking-of-everyone-and-everything -for-example/.

Hall, Sarah Marie. 2021. "Care, COVID-19 and Crisis: Area as a Space for Critical Contributions." *Area* 53, no. 1 (March): 2–3. https://doi.org/10.1111/area.12702.

Hamilton, Aretina R. 2020. "The White Unseen: On White Supremacy and Dangerous Entanglements in Geography." *Dialogues in Human Geography* 10, no. 3 (November): 299–303. https://doi.org/10.1177/2043820620966489.

Hannah-Jones, Nikole, Caitlin Roper, Ilena Silverman, and Jake Silverstein, eds. 2021. *The 1619 Project: A New Origin Story*. New York: One World.

Hanrahan, Kelsey B., Ann M. Oberhauser, and Darcy Besch. 2020. "Redefining Our Identity, Recognizing Our Challenges: GPOW Becomes the Feminist Geographies Specialty Group." *Professional Geographer* 72, no. 4 (October): 535–46. https://doi.org /10.1080/00330124.2020.1750438.

Hanrahan, Kelsey B., and Christine E. Smith. 2020. "Interstices of Care: Re-imagining the Geographies of Care." *Area* 52, no. 2 (June): 230–34. https://doi.org/10.1111/area.12502.

Hanson, Susan. 2007. "Service as a Subversive Activity: On the Centrality of Service to an Academic Career." *Gender, Place & Culture* 14, no. 1 (February): 29–34. https://doi .org/10.1080/09663690601122176.

Haraway, Donna. 1988. "Situated Knowledges: The Science Question in Feminism and the Privilege of Partial Perspective." *Feminist Studies* 14 (3): 575–99.

———. 1991. *Simians, Cyborgs, and Women: The Reinvention of Nature*. New York: Routledge.

Harris, Dylan M. 2024. "Stories, Crisis, and Meaning-Making: Storying Possibility and Community in the Terrain of Cultural Struggle." *Cultural Geographies* 31, no. 1 (January): 33–46. https://doi.org/10.1177/14744740221147550.

Hawkins, Harriet. 2019. "Creating Care-Full Academic Spaces? The Dilemmas of Caring in the 'Anxiety Machine.'" ACME: *An International Journal for Critical Geographies* 18, no. 4 (September): 816–34.

Hawkins, Roberta, and Leslie Kern. 2024. *Higher Expectations: How to Survive Academia, Make It Better for Others, and Transform the University*. Toronto: Between the Lines.

Hay, Iain. 2020. "On Geoscientisation: A Response to Cupples." *New Zealand Geographer* 76, no. 1 (April): 14–17. https://doi.org/10.1111/nzg.12247.

Henry, Matthew. 2020. "Geoscientisation: Genealogies, Assemblage and Our Duty of Care." *New Zealand Geographer* 76, no. 1 (April): 21–23. https://doi.org/10.1111 /nzg.12258.

Herman, Agatha, and Joshua Inwood, eds. 2024. *Researching Justice: Engaging with Questions and Spaces of (In)justice through Social Research*. Bristol, U.K: Bristol University Press. https://orca.cardiff.ac.uk/id/eprint/169789/.

Hersey, Tricia. 2022. *Rest Is Resistance: A Manifesto*. New York: Little, Brown.

Hesse, Monica (@MonicaHesse). 2023. "My dad is an English professor who was asked to draft an AI policy for his students. Strongly cosign all of this." Twitter [X], August 16, 2023, 12.58 p.m. https://twitter.com/MonicaHesse/status /1691856964714725826.

Hiemstra, Nancy, and Emily Billo. 2017. "Introduction to Focus Section: Feminist

Research and Knowledge Production in Geography." *Professional Geographer* 69, no. 2 (April): 284–90. https://doi.org/10.1080/00330124.2016.1208103.

Hogan, Kelly A., and Viji Sathy. 2022. *Inclusive Teaching: Strategies for Promoting Equity in the College Classroom*. Morgantown: West Virginia University Press.

hooks, bell. (1984) 2015. *Feminist Theory: From Margin to Center*. New ed. Cambridge, Mass.: South End.

———. 1994. *Teaching to Transgress: Education as the Practice of Freedom*. New York: Routledge.

———. 2000. *Feminism Is for Everybody: Passionate Politics*. Cambridge, Mass.: South End.

Housel, Jacqueline, Patrick Shabram, and Marissa Isaak Wald. 2022. "Geography for All: The Community College Geographer." *Professional Geographer* 74, no. 4 (October): 589–601. https://doi.org/10.1080/00330124.2022.2048869.

Howitt, Richard. 2022. "Ethics as First Method: Reframing Geographies at an(other) Ending-of-the-World as Co-motion." *Environment and Planning F: Philosophy, Theory, Models, Methods and Practice* 1, no. 1 (March): 82–92. https://doi.org/10.1177/26349825221082167.

Islam, Faisal Bin, Lindsay Naylor, James Edward Bryan, and Dennis J. Coker. 2024. "Climate Coloniality and Settler Colonialism: Adaptation and Indigenous Futurities." *Political Geography* 114 (October):103164. https://doi.org/10.1016/j.polgeo.2024.103164.

Jackson, M. 2019. *The Secret Lives of Glaciers*. West Brattleboro, VT: Green Writers Press.

Jadallah, Christopher C. 2025. "Positionality, Relationality, Place, and Land: Considerations for Ethical Research with Communities." *Qualitative Research* 25 (1): 227–42. https://doi.org/10.1177/14687941241246174.

Jazeel, Tariq. 2017. "Mainstreaming Geography's Decolonial Imperative." *Transactions of the Institute of British Geographers* 42, no. 3 (September): 334–37. https://doi.org/10.1111/tran.12200.

———. 2019. "Singularity. A Manifesto for Incomparable Geographies." *Singapore Journal of Tropical Geography* 40, no. 1 (January): 5–21. https://doi.org/10.1111/sjtg.12265.

Jemisin, N. K. 2020. *The City We Became*. London: Orbit.

Jepson, Wendy, Patricia Martin, and Joseph Nevins. 2022. "Sorry to Bother You: The AAG Climate Action Task Force as a Necessary Inconvenience." *Professional Geographer* 74, no. 1 (January): 147–49.

Johnston-Anumonwo, Ibipo. 2019. "Mentoring across Difference: Success and Struggle in an Academic Geography Career." *Gender, Place & Culture* 26, no. 12 (December): 1683–700. https://doi.org/10.1080/0966369X.2019.1681369.

Johnston, R. J., and James D. Sidaway. 2016. *Geography and Geographers: Anglo-American Human Geography since 1945*. 7th ed. London: Routledge.

Katz, Cindi. 1994. "Playing the Field: Questions of Fieldwork in Geography." *Professional Geographer* 46, no. 1 (February): 67–72.

Kaufman, Emily C. 2021. "Staying with the Trouble of Collegiality, Professionalism and Care: Fertilities in Academia." *Environment and Planning C: Politics and Space* 39, no. 8 (December): 1737–54. https://doi.org/10.1177/23996544211014198.

Keighren, Innes M. 2017. "History and Philosophy of Geography I: The Slow, the Turbulent, and the Dissenting." *Progress in Human Geography* 41, no. 5 (October): 638–47. https://doi.org/10.1177/0309132516653285.

———. 2018. "History and Philosophy of Geography II: The Excluded, the Evil, and the Anarchic." *Progress in Human Geography* 42, no. 5 (October): 770–78. https://doi .org/10.1177/0309132517730939.

———. 2020. "History and Philosophy of Geography III: The Haunted, the Reviled, and the Plural." *Progress in Human Geography* 44, no. 1 (February): 160–67. https://doi .org/10.1177/0309132518818725.

Keighren, Innes M., Jeremy W. Crampton, Franklin Ginn, Scott Kirsch, Audrey Kobayashi, Simon N. Naylor, and Jörn Seemann. 2017. "Teaching the History of Geography: Current Challenges and Future Directions." *Progress in Human Geography* 41, no. 2 (April): 245–62. https://doi.org/10.1177/0309132515575940.

Kelley, Robin D. G. 2018. "Black Study, Black Struggle." *Ufahamu: A Journal of African Studies* 40, no. 2 (Summer): 153–68. https://doi.org/10.5070/F7402040947.

Kelsky, Karen. 2017. "A Crowdsourced Survey of Sexual Harassment in the Academy." The Professor Is In. December 1, 2017. https://theprofessorisin.com/2017/12/01 /a-crowdsourced-survey-of-sexual-harassment-in-the-academy/.

Kendall, Mikki. 2021. *Hood Feminism: Notes from the Women White Feminists Forgot.* New York: Bloomsbury.

Kimmerer, Robin Wall. 2015. *Braiding Sweetgrass: Indigenous Wisdom, Scientific Knowledge and the Teachings of Plants.* Minneapolis: Milkweed.

Kim, Nari, and Lindsay Naylor. 2022. "COVID-19, Social Distancing, and an Ethic of Care." ACME: *An International Journal for Critical Geographies* 21, no. 1 (February): 65–80.

King, Gabrielle. 2023. "Towards a Culture of Care for Ethical Review: Connections and Frictions in Institutional and Individual Practices of Social Research Ethics." *Social & Cultural Geography* 24, no. 1 (January): 104–20. https://doi.org/10.1080/14649365 .2021.1939122.

King, Leonora, and Marc Tadaki. 2018. "A Framework for Understanding the Politics of Science (Core Tenet #2)." In *The Palgrave Handbook of Critical Physical Geography*, edited by Rebecca Lave, Christine Biermann, and Stuart N. Lane, 67–88. Cham, Switz.: Springer International. https://doi.org/10.1007/978 -3-319-71461-5_4.

Kinkaid, Eden. 2019. "At the Limits of Critical Geography: Creative Interventions into the Exclusionary Spaces of U.S. Geography." *Gender, Place & Culture* 26, no. 12 (December): 1784–811. https://doi.org/10.1080/0966369X.2019.1639633.

———. 2020. "Can Assemblage Think Difference? A Feminist Critique of Assemblage Geographies." *Progress in Human Geography* 44, no. 3 (June): 457–72. https://doi .org/10.1177/0309132519836162.e

———. 2024. "Whose Geography, Whose Future? Queering Geography's Disciplinary Reproduction." *Dialogues in Human Geography* 14 (2): 192–96. https://doi.org /10.1177/20438206221144839.

Kinkaid, Eden, and Lauren Fritzsche. 2022. "The Stories We Tell: Challenging Exclusionary Histories of Geography in U.S. Graduate Curriculum." *Annals of the American Association of Geographers* 112, no. 8 (November): 2469–85. https://doi.org /10.1080/24694452.2022.2072805.

Kinkaid, Eden, Aparna Parikh, and A. Marie Ranjbar. 2022. "Coming of Age in a Straight White Man's Geography: Reflections on Positionality and Relationality as Feminist

Anti-oppressive Praxis." *Gender, Place & Culture* 29, no. 11 (November): 1556–71. https://doi.org/10.1080/0966369X.2021.2020733.

Kitchener, Caroline. 2020. "Women Academics Seem to Be Submitting Fewer Papers during Coronavirus. 'Never Seen Anything like It,' Says One Editor." The Lily. April 30, 2020. https://www.thelily.com/women-academics-seem-to-be-submitting-fewer -papers-during-coronavirus-never-seen-anything-like-it-says-one-editor/.

Kobayashi, Audrey. 1994. "Coloring the Field: Gender, 'Race,' and the Politics of Field-work." *Professional Geographer* 46, no. 1 (February): 73–80.

——. 2009. "Situated Knowledge, Reflexivity." In *International Encyclopedia of Human Geography: A 12-Volume Set*, edited by Nigel Thrift and Rob Kitchin, 1st ed., 138–43. Amsterdam: Elsevier Science.

Kobayashi, Audrey, and Linda Peake. 1994. "Unnatural Discourse. 'Race' and Gender in Geography." *Gender, Place & Culture* 1, no. 2 (September): 225–43. https://doi .org/10.1080/09663699408721211.

——. 2000. "Racism Out of Place: Thoughts on Whiteness and an Antiracist Geogra-phy in the New Millennium." *Annals of the Association of American Geographers* 90 (2): 392–403.

——. 2008. "Racism in Place: Another Look at Shock, Horror, and Racialization." In *Feminisms in Geography: Rethinking Space, Place, and Knowledges*, edited by Pamela Moss and Karen Falconer Al-Hindi, 171–78. Lanham, Md.: Rowman & Littlefield.

Koopman, Sara. 2016. "Beware: Your Research May Be Weaponized." *Annals of the American Association of Geographers* 106, no. 3 (May): 530–35. https://doi.org/10 .1080/24694452.2016.1145511.

Kuimelis, Carolyn, and Mary Ellen Flannery. 2023. "Life as a Contingent Faculty Mem-ber." *NEA Today*, May 23, 2023. https://www.nea.org/nea-today/all-news-articles /life-contingent-faculty-member.

Kwan, Mei-Po. 2002. "Feminist Visualization: Re-envisioning GIS as a Method in Feminist Geographic Research." *Annals of the Association of American Geographers* 92, no. 4 (December): 645–61.

——. 2004. "Beyond Difference: From Canonical Geography to Hybrid Geographies." *Annals of the Association of American Geographers* 94, no. 4 (December): 756–63.

Laing, Anna F. 2021. "Decolonising Pedagogies in Undergraduate Geography: Student Perspectives on a Decolonial Movements Module." *Journal of Geography in Higher Education* 45, no. 1 (January): 1–19. https://doi.org/10.1080/03098265.2020.1815180.

Laketa, Sunčana, and Muriel Côte. 2023. "Discomforts in the Academy: From 'Academic Burnout' to Collective Mobilisation." *Gender, Place & Culture* 30, no. 4 (April): 574–87. https://doi.org/10.1080/0966369X.2021.2014405.

Lave, Rebecca, Matthew W. Wilson, Elizabeth S. Barron, Christine Biermann, Mark A. Carey, Chris S. Duvall, Leigh Johnson, K. Maria Lane, Nathan McClintock, and Darla Munroe. 2014. "Intervention: Critical Physical Geography." *Canadian Geogra-pher /Le Géographe Canadien* 58, no. 1 (March): 1–10.

Lawson, Victoria. 2007. "Geographies of Care and Responsibility." *Annals of the Associa-tion of American Geographers* 97, no. 1 (March): 1–11. https://doi.org/10.1111/j .1467-8306.2007.00520.x.

―――. 2009. "Instead of Radical Geography, How about Caring Geography?" *Antipode* 41, no. 1 (January): 210–13. https://doi.org/10.1111/j.1467-8330.2008.00665.x.

Lee, Robert. 2020. "Land-Grab Universities." *High Country News*, March 2020. https://www.hcn.org/issues/52.4/indigenous-affairs-education-land-grab-universities.

Lennon, Tara. 2022. "Students, Delaware College, and the Exploited Labor of Black People: Legacies of Enslavement and Dispossession at UD." University of Delaware Anti-Racism Initiative. July 7, 2022. https://sites.udel.edu/udari-legacies/2022/06/23/students-delaware-college-and-the-exploited-labor-of-black-people/.

Lerback, J. C., B. Hanson, and P. Wooden. 2020. "Association between Author Diversity and Acceptance Rates and Citations in Peer-Reviewed Earth Science Manuscripts." *Earth and Space Science* 7, no. 5 (May): e2019EA000930. https://doi.org/10.1029/2019EA000946.

Liboiron, Max. 2021a. "Decolonizing Geoscience Requires More than Equity and Inclusion." *Nature Geoscience* 14 (December): 876–77. https://doi.org/10.1038/s41561-021-00861-7.

―――. 2021b. *Pollution Is Colonialism*. Durham, N.C.: Duke University Press.

Lizotte, Chris. 2024. "For Ordinary Kindness in Human Geography." *Dialogues in Human Geography* 14 (2): 357–60. https://doi.org/10.1177/20438206231177077.

Lopez, Patricia J. 2019. "Toward a Care Ethical Approach to Access to Health Care in Neoliberal Times." *Gender, Place & Culture* 26, no. 6 (June): 830–46. https://doi.org/10.1080/0966369X.2019.1619523.

―――. 2023. "For a Pedagogy of Hope: Imagining Worlds Otherwise." *Journal of Geography in Higher Education* 47, no. 5 (October): 792–804. https://doi.org/10.1080/03098265.2022.2155803.

Lopez, Patricia J., and Kathryn Gillespie. 2016. "A Love Story: For 'Buddy System' Research in the Academy." *Gender, Place & Culture* 23 (12) (December 2016): 1689–700.

Lorde, Audre. 1984. "The Master's Tools Will Never Dismantle the Master's House." In *Sister Outsider*, 110–13. Berkeley: Crossing.

―――. 2018. *The Master's Tools Will Never Dismantle the Master's House*. London: Penguin.

Love, Bettina L. 2019. *We Want to Do More Than Survive: Abolitionist Teaching and the Pursuit of Educational Freedom*. Boston: Beacon.

―――. 2023. *Punished for Dreaming: How School Reform Harms Black Children and How We Heal*. New York: St. Martin's.

Lugones, María. 2007. "Heterosexualism and the Colonial/Modern Gender System." *Hypatia* 22, no. 1 (January): 186–209.

―――. 2010. "Toward a Decolonial Feminism." *Hypatia* 25, no. 4 (October): 742–59. https://doi.org/10.1111/j.1527-2001.2010.01137.x.

―――. 2014. "Radical Multiculturalism and Women of Color Feminisms." *Journal for Cultural and Religious Theory* 13, no. 1 (January): 68–80.

Madden, Meredith. 2014. "Pedagogical Encounters, Graduate Teaching Assistants, and Decolonial Feminist Commitments." *Feminist Teacher* 25 (1): 55–74. https://doi.org/10.5406/femteacher.25.1.0055.

Madge, Clare, Parvati Raghuram, and Patricia Noxolo. 2009. "Engaged Pedagogy and Responsibility: A Postcolonial Analysis of International Students." *In* "Postcoloniality,

Responsibility and Care." Themed issue, *Geoforum* 40, no. 1 (January): 34–45. https://doi.org/10.1016/j.geoforum.2008.01.008.

Mahtani, Minelle. 2002. "Women Graduate Students of Colour in Geography: Increased Ethnic and Racial Diversity, or Maintenance of the Status Quo?" *Great Lakes Geographer* 9 (1): 11–18.

———. 2004. "Mapping Race and Gender in the Academy: The Experiences of Women of Colour Faculty and Graduate Students in Britain, the US and Canada." *Journal of Geography in Higher Education* 28, no. 1 (March): 91–99.

———. 2006. "Challenging the Ivory Tower: Proposing Anti-Racist Geographies within the Academy." *Gender, Place & Culture* 13, no. 1 (February): 21–25.

———. 2014. "Toxic Geographies: Absences in Critical Race Thought and Practice in Social and Cultural Geography." *Social & Cultural Geography* 15, no. 4 (May): 359–67.

Mansfield, Becky, Rebecca Lave, Kendra McSweeney, Anne Bonds, Jaclyn Cockburn, Mona Domosh, Trina Hamilton, et al. 2019. "It's Time to Recognize How Men's Careers Benefit from Sexually Harassing Women in Academia." *Human Geography* 12, no. 1 (March): 82–87. https://doi.org/10.1177/1942778619o1200110.

Marijolovic, Kate, Julian Roberts-Grmela, and Eva Surovell. 2023. "Graduate Students Win Pay Raises as Union Efforts Surge." *Chronicle of Higher Education*, January 12, 2023. https://www.chronicle.com/article/graduate-students-win-pay-raises-as -union-efforts-surge.

Marston, Sallie A., and Sarah de Leeuw. 2013. "Creativity and Geography: Toward a Politicized Intervention." *Geographical Review* 103, no. 2 (April): iii–xxvi.

Martin, Geoffrey J. 2015. *American Geography and Geographers: Toward Geographical Science*. New York: Oxford University Press.

Martin, Patricia M. 2022. "The Contemporary Academic Conference: A Space of Enclosure." *Professional Geographer* 74, no. 1 (January): 165–68. https://doi.org/10 .1080/00330124.2021.1915821.

Massey, Doreen. 2012. "Learning from Latin America." *Soundings*, no. 50 (April) 131–41.

Massey, Doreen B. 1994. *Space, Place, and Gender*. Minneapolis: University of Minnesota Press.

Massey, Doreen B., John Allen, James Anderson, Susan Cunningham, Christopher Hamnett, and Philip Sarre. 1984. *Geography Matters! A Reader*. Cambridge: Cambridge University Press.

Matallana-Peláez, Susana E. 2020. "From Gender to Omeotlization: Toward a Decolonial Ontology." *Hypatia* 35, no. 3 (July): 373–92.

Mather, Russ. 2003. "75 Years of Geography at the University of Delaware." Unpublished manuscript. Newark: University of Delaware, Department of Geography and Spatial Sciences.

Mathie, Alison, Jenny Cameron, and Katherine Gibson. 2017. "Asset-Based and Citizen-Led Development: Using a Diffracted Power Lens to Analyze the Possibilities and Challenges." *Progress in Development Studies* 17, no. 1 (January): 54–66. https://doi .org/10.1177/1464993416674302.

Mayes, Renae (@DrRDMayes). 2022. "When minoritized folk talk about invisible labor, the solution isn't for us to learn how to say no. It's to understand that this labor is for love, resistance & survival for ourselves and other minoritized faculty & students. It's a cultural ethic." *Twitter* [X], February 4, 2022, 8:21 a.m. https://twitter.com /DrRDMayes/status/1489589963863863301.

May, Vivian M. 2014. "'Speaking into the Void'? Intersectionality Critiques and Epistemic Backlash." *Hypatia* 29, no. 1 (January): 94–112. https://doi.org/10.1111/hypa.12060.

Mazanec, Cecilia. 2017. "#ThanksForTyping Spotlights Unnamed Women in Literary Acknowledgments." National Public Radio. March 30, 2017. History. https://www .npr.org/2017/03/30/521931310/-thanksfortyping-spotlights-unnamed-women-in -literary-acknowledgements.

Mbah, Ruth Endam. 2023. "Financing American Higher Education: Reviewing the Trend in Student's Perceptions of Their Student Debt." *Advances in Social Sciences Research Journal* 10, no. 4 (April): 99–110. https://doi.org/10.14738/assrj.104.14404.

McArdle, Rachel. 2022. "Flexible Methodologies: A Case for Approaching Research with Fluidity." *Professional Geographer* 74, no. 4 (October): 620–27. https://doi.org/10.1080 /00330124.2021.2023593.

McCallum, Carmen M. 2020. "Othermothering: Exploring African American Graduate Students' Decision to Pursue the Doctorate." *Journal of Higher Education* 91, no. 6 (September): 953–76. https://doi.org/10.1080/00221546.2020.1731262.

McDowell, Linda. 1999. *Gender, Identity and Place: Understanding Feminist Geographies.* Minneapolis: University of Minnesota Press.

———. 2004. "Work, Workfare, Work/Life Balance and an Ethic of Care." *Progress in Human Geography* 28, no. 2 (April): 145–63. https://doi.org/10.1191 /0309132504ph478oa.

———. 2016. "Reflections on Feminist Economic Geography: Talking to Ourselves?" *Environment and Planning A: Economy and Space* 48, no. 10 (October): 2093–99.

McDowell, Linda, Kathryn Ray, Diane Perrons, Colette Fagan, and Kevin Ward. 2005. "Women's Paid Work and Moral Economies of Care." *Social & Cultural Geography* 6, no. 2 (April): 219–35.

McEwan, Cheryl, and Michael K. Goodman. 2010. "Place Geography and the Ethics of Care: Introductory Remarks on the Geographies of Ethics, Responsibility and Care." *Ethics, Place & Environment* 13, no. 2 (June): 103–12. https://doi.org/10.1080 /13668791003778602.

McFarlane, Colin. 2022. "Editorial: Geography in the World." *Transactions of the Institute of British Geographers* 47, no. 1 (March): 2–8. https://doi.org/10.1111/tran.12497.

———. 2024. "Geography in the World Part 2: Editorial." *Transactions of the Institute of British Geographers* 49, no. 2 (June): e12655. https://doi.org/10.1111/tran.12655.

McKinnon, Katharine. 2020. "Framing Essay: The Diversity of Labour." In *The Handbook of Diverse Economies*, edited by J. K. Gibson-Graham and Kelly Dombroski, 116–28. Cheltenham, U.K.: Edward Elgar.

McKittrick, Katherine. 2006. *Demonic Grounds: Black Women and the Cartographies of Struggle.* Minneapolis: University of Minnesota Press.

———. 2016. "Diachronic Loops/Deadweight Tonnage/Bad Made Measure." *Cultural Geographies* 23, no. 1 (January): 3–18. https://doi.org/10.1177/1474474015612716.

McKittrick, Katherine, and Linda Peake. 2005. "What Difference Does Difference Make to Geography?" In *Questioning Geography: Fundamental Debates*, edited by Noel Castree, Alisdair Rogers, and Douglas Sherman, 39–54. Oxford: Blackwell.

McLean, Heather. 2018. "It's Time Universities Walk Their Decolonial Talk." Times
    Higher Education (THE). October 16, 2018. https://www.timeshighereducation.com
    /blog/its-time-universities-walk-their-decolonial-talk.
Mendos, Lucas Ramon, Kellyn Botha, Rafael Carrano Lelis, Enrique López de la Peña,
    Ilia Savelev, and Daron Tan. 2020. State-Sponsored Homophobia Report. Geneva:
    International Lesbian, Gay, Bisexual, Trans and Intersex Association. https://ilga.org
    /state-sponsored-homophobia-report.
Mendoza, Breny. 2015. "Coloniality of Gender and Power: From Postcoloniality to
    Decoloniality." In The Oxford Handbook of Feminist Theory, edited by Lisa Disch and
    Mary Hawkesworth, 100–121. Oxford: Oxford University Press.
Mengel, Friederike, Jan Sauermann, and Ulf Zölitz. 2019. "Gender Bias in Teaching
    Evaluations." Journal of the European Economic Association 17, no. 2 (April): 535–66.
    https://doi.org/10.1093/jeea/jvx057.
Meyerhoff, Eli. 2019. Beyond Education: Radical Studying for Another World. 1st ed.
    Minneapolis: University of Minnesota Press.
Mignolo, Walter. 2002. "The Geopolitics of Knowledge and the Colonial Difference."
    South Atlantic Quarterly 101, no. 1 (January): 57–96.
Mignolo, Walter, and Catherine E. Walsh. 2018. On Decoloniality: Concepts, Analytics,
    Praxis. Durham, N.C.: Duke University Press.
Millner, Naomi. 2023. "Unsettling Feelings in the Classroom: Scaffolding Pedagogies
    of Discomfort as Part of Decolonising Human Geography in Higher Education."
    Journal of Geography in Higher Education 47, no. 5 (October): 805–24. https://doi
    .org/10.1080/03098265.2021.2004391.
Mitchell, Josh. 2021. The Debt Trap: How Student Loans Became a National Catastrophe.
    New York: Simon & Schuster.
Mohammad, Robina. 2017. "Feminist Geography." In International Encyclopedia of
    Geography, 15 Volume Set: People, the Earth, Environment and Technology, edited by
    Noel Castree, Michael F. Goodchild, Audrey Kobayashi, Weidong Liu, and Richard
    A. Marston. Hoboken, N.J.: Wiley.
Mohanty, Chandra Talpade. 1984. "Under Western Eyes: Feminist Scholarship and
    Colonial Discourses." Boundary 2 12/13 (Spring/Autumn 1984):333–58. https://doi
    .org/10.2307/302821.
Mollett, Sharlene. 2017. "Irreconcilable Differences? A Postcolonial Intersectional
    Reading of Gender, Development and Human Rights in Latin America." Gen-
    der, Place & Culture 24, no. 1 (January): 1–17. https://doi.org/10.1080/09663
    69X.2017.1277292.
Mollett, Sharlene, and Caroline Faria. 2013. "Messing with Gender in Feminist Political
    Ecology." Geoforum, Risky Natures, Natures of Risk 45 (March): 116–25. https://doi
    .org/10.1016/j.geoforum.2012.10.009.
———. 2018. "The Spatialities of Intersectional Thinking: Fashioning Feminist Geo-
    graphic Futures." Gender, Place & Culture 25, no. 4 (April): 565–77. https://doi.org/10
    .1080/0966369X.2018.1454404.
Monk, Janice. 1999. "Editorial: Valuing Service [1]." Journal of Geography in Higher
    Education 23, no. 3 (November): 285–89.

———. 2012. "Canons, Classics, and Inclusion in the Histories of Geography." *Dialogues in Human Geography* 2, no. 3 (November): 328–31.

Monk, Janice, and Susan Hanson. 1982. "On Not Excluding Half of the Human in Human Geography." *Professional Geographer* 34, no. 1 (January): 11–23. https://doi .org/10.1111/j.0033-0124.1982.00011.x.

Moore, Tiara. 2022. "Are You Ready?" Presentation at the American Geophysical Union (AGU) Second National Conference: Justice in Geoscience, Washington, D.C., August 16, 2022. https://agu.confex.com/agu/22chapman2/meetingapp.cgi/ Home/0.

Moraga, Cherríe, and Gloria Anzaldúa, eds. (1981). 2015. *This Bridge Called My Back: Writings by Radical Women of Color.* 4th ed. Albany: State University of New York Press.

Moseley, William G., Max Lu, and Greg Hill. 2023. "A Bridge between Two Worlds: Why Advanced Placement Human Geography Is Good for the Discipline of Geography." *Professional Geographer* 75, no. 6 (November): 871–81. https://doi.org/10.1080 /00330124.2023.2215840.

Moss, Pamela. 1993. "Focus: Feminism as Method." *Canadian Geographer / Le Géographe Canadien* 37, no. 1 (January): 48–49.

Moss, Pamela, and Karen Falconer Al-Hindi. 2008. *Feminisms in Geography: Rethinking Space, Place, and Knowledges.* Lanham, Md.: Rowman & Littlefield.

Moss, Pamela, Karen Falconer Al-Hindi, and Hope Kawabata. 2002. *Feminist Geography in Practice: Research and Methods.* Hoboken, N.J.: Wiley-Blackwell.

Moss, Pamela, Karen J. Debres, Altha Cravey, Jennifer Hyndman, Katherine K. Hirschboeck, and Michele Masucci. 1999. "Toward Mentoring as Feminist Praxis: Strategies for Ourselves and Others." *Journal of Geography in Higher Education* 23, no. 3 (November): 413–27. https://doi.org/10.1080/03098269985371.

Mott, Carrie, and Daniel Cockayne. 2017. "Citation Matters: Mobilizing the Politics of Citation toward a Practice of 'Conscientious Engagement.'" *Gender, Place & Culture* 24, no. 7 (July): 954–73. https://doi.org/10.1080/0966369X.2017.1339022.

Mountz, Alison, Anne Bonds, Becky Mansfield, Jenna Loyd, Jennifer Hyndman, Margaret Walton-Roberts, Ranu Basu, et al. 2015. "For Slow Scholarship: A Feminist Politics of Resistance through Collective Action in the Neoliberal University." *ACME: An International Journal for Critical Geographies* 14, no. 4 (August): 1235–59.

Mountz, Alison, and Kira Williams. 2023. "Let Geography Die: The Rise, Fall, and 'Unfinished Business' of Geography at Harvard." *Annals of the American Association of Geographers* 113, no. 8 (September): 1977–2002. https://doi.org/10.1080/24694452 .2023.2208645.

Müller, Martin. 2021. "Worlding Geography: From Linguistic Privilege to Decolonial Anywheres." *Progress in Human Geography* 45, no. 6 (December): 1440–66. https: //doi.org/10.1177/0309132520979356.

Mullings, Beverley, Linda Peake, and Kate Parizeau. 2016. "Cultivating an Ethic of Wellness in Geography." *Canadian Geographer / Le Géographe Canadien* 60, no. 2 (Summer): 161–67. https://doi.org/10.1111/cag.12275.

Murphy, Alexander B. 2000. "Teaching Advanced Placement Human Geography."

Journal of Geography 99, nos. 3–4 (May): 93–97. https://doi.org/10.1080
/00221340008978904.

———. 2018. *Geography: Why It Matters*. Cambridge, U.K.: Polity.

Nagar, Richa. 2019. *Hungry Translations: Relearning the World through Radical Vulnerability*. Chicago: University of Illinois Press.

Nagoski, Emily, and Amelia Nagoski. 2019. *Burnout: The Secret to Unlocking the Stress Cycle*. Illustrated ed. New York: Ballantine Books.

Nancy, Jean-Luc. 1991. "Of Being-in-Common." In *Community at Loose Ends*, edited by Miami Theory Collective, translated by James Creech, 1–12. Minneapolis: University of Minnesota Press.

Narayan, U. 1995. "Colonialism and Its Others: Considerations on Rights and Care Discourses." *Hypatia* 10, no. 2 (Spring): 133–40. https://doi.org/10.1111/j.1527-2001.1995.tb01375.x.

Nash, Jennifer C. 2008. "Re-thinking Intersectionality." *Feminist Review* 89, no. 1 (June): 1–15. https://doi.org/10.1057/fr.2008.4.

Nast, Heidi J. 1994. "Women in the Field: Critical Feminist Methodologies and Theoretical Perspectives." *Professional Geographer* 46, no. 1 (February): 54–66.

Naylor, Lindsay. 2019. *Fair Trade Rebels: Coffee Production and Struggles for Autonomy in Chiapas*. Minneapolis: University of Minnesota Press.

———. 2021. "Lindsay Naylor, UDARI Faculty Fellow Project Update: Anti-Assimilationist Mentoring Plan." University of Delaware Anti-Racism Initiative. July 22, 2021. https://sites.udel.edu/antiracism-initiative/2021/07/22/lindsay-naylor-udari-faculty-fellow-project-update/.

———. 2023. "A Feminist Ethic of Care in the Neoliberal University." *Society & Space*, October 2, 2023. https://www.societyandspace.org/articles/a-feminist-ethic-of-care-in-the-neoliberal-university.

Naylor, Lindsay, Abigail Clarke-Sather, and Michael Weber. 2020. "Troubling Care in the Neonatal Intensive Care Unit." *Geoforum* 114 (August): 107–16. https://doi.org/10.1016/j.geoforum.2020.05.015.

Naylor, Lindsay, Michelle Daigle, Sofia Zaragocin, Margaret Marietta Ramírez, and Mary Gilmartin. 2018. "Interventions: Bringing the Decolonial to Political Geography." *Political Geography* 66 (September): 199–209. https://doi.org/10.1016/j.polgeo.2017.11.002.

Naylor, Lindsay, Adam Foley, Carla Guerrón Montero, Georgina Ramsay, Claire Rasmussen, Nicholas Russell, Nathan Thayer, and Luisa Turbino Torres. 2021. "Deconstructing Syllabi: Best Practices Training Guide." University of Delaware Anti Racism Initiative. https://bpb-us-w2.wpmucdn.com/sites.udel.edu/dist/1/11314/files/2021/06/Deconstructing-Syllabi-Best-Practices-Training-Guide_final-for-distribution.pdf.

Naylor, Lindsay, and Nathan Thayer. 2022. "Between Paranoia and Possibility: Diverse Economies and the Decolonial Imperative." *Transactions of the Institute of British Geographers* 47, no. 3 (September): 791–805. https://doi.org/10.1111/tran.12534.

Naylor, Lindsay, and Dana Veron. 2021. "Geographic Education in the Anthropocene: Cultivating Citizens at the Neoliberal University." *Annals of the American Association of Geographers* 111, no. 3 (April): 958–69. https://doi.org/10.1080/24694452.2020.1785834.

Neely, Abigail H., and Patrica J. Lopez. 2020. "Care in the Time of Covid-19." *Antipode Online* (blog). April 4, 2020. https://antipodeonline.org/2020/04/04/care-in-the-time-of-covid-19/.

Neely, Abigail H., and Patricia J. Lopez. 2022. "Toward Healthier Futures in Post-Pandemic Times: Political Ecology, Racial Capitalism, and Black Feminist Approaches to Care." *Geography Compass* 16, no. 2 (February): e12609. https://doi.org/10.1111/gec3.12609.

Nelson, Ingrid L. 2013. "The Allure and Privileging of Danger over Everyday Practice in Field Research." *Area* 45, no. 4 (December): 419–25. https://doi.org/10.1111/area.12036.

Nelson, Lise, and Joni Seager. 2005. *A Companion to Feminist Geography*. Malden, Mass.: Blackwell.

Neuhaus, Jessamyn, ed. 2022. *Picture a Professor: Interrupting Biases about Faculty and Increasing Student Learning*. 1st ed. Morgantown: West Virginia University Press.

Newstead, Clare. 2009. "Pedagogy, Post-Coloniality and Care-Full Encounters in the Classroom." In "Postcoloniality, Responsibility, and Care," Themed issue, *Geoforum* 40, no. 1 (January): 80–90. https://doi.org/10.1016/j.geoforum.2008.04.003.

Noxolo, Patricia. 2009. "'My Paper, My Paper': Reflections on the Embodied Production of Postcolonial Geographical Responsibility in Academic Writing." In "Postcoloniality, Responsibility, and Care," Themed issue, *Geoforum*, 40, no. 1 (January): 55–65. https://doi.org/10.1016/j.geoforum.2008.06.008.

———. 2017. "Introduction: Decolonising Geographical Knowledge in a Colonised and Re-colonising Postcolonial World." *Area* 49, no. 3 (September): 317–19. https://doi.org/10.1111/area.12370.

Oberhauser, Ann M., and Martina Angela Caretta. 2019. "A Space for Feminist Mentoring: The Role of Geographic Perspectives on Women (GPOW) Specialty Group in Higher Education." *Gender, Place & Culture* 26, no. 12 (December): 1664–82. https://doi.org/10.1080/0966369X.2019.1660310.

O'Meara, Kerryann. 2016. "Whose Problem Is It? Gender Differences in Faculty Thinking about Campus Service." *Teachers College Record* 118, no. 8 (August): 1–38.

Ortega, Mariana. 2017. "Decolonial Woes and Practices of Un-knowing." *Journal of Speculative Philosophy* 31, no. 3 (July): 504–16. https://doi.org/10.5325/jspecphil.31.3.0504.

Oswin, Natalie. 2020. "An Other Geography." *Dialogues in Human Geography* 10, no. 1 (March): 9–18. https://doi.org/10.1177/2043820619890433.

———. 2022. "The View from Here." *Environment and Planning D: Society and Space* 40, no. 3 (June): 389–92. https://doi.org/10.1177/02637758221103197.

Palmer, Meredith Alberta. 2021. "Debts, Ethics, and Redress: Moving Land Grab University Work Forward." *Cornell University and Indigenous Dispossession Project* (blog). October 1, 2021. https://blogs.cornell.edu/cornelluniversityindigenousdispossession/2021/10/01/debts-ethics-and-redress-moving-land-grab-university-work-forward/.

Parizeau, Kate, Laura Shillington, Roberta Hawkins, Farhana Sultana, Alison Mountz, Beverley Mullings, and Linda Peake. 2016. "Breaking the Silence: A Feminist Call to Action." *Canadian Geographies / Géographies Canadiennes* 60, no. 2 (Summer/été): 192–204. https://doi.org/10.1111/cag.12265.

Peake, Linda, and Audrey Kobayashi. 2002. "Policies and Practices for an Antiracist Geography at the Millennium." *Professional Geographer* 54, no. 1 (February): 50–61.

Peake, Linda, Beverley Mullings, Kate Parizeau, Gina K. Thornburg, Jon Magee, Deborah Metzel, Vandana Wadhwa, et al. 2018. *Mental Health and Well-Being in Geography: Creating a Healthy Discipline.* Washington, D.C.: American Association of Geographers Task Force on Mental Health.

Pedersen, Daphne E., and Krista Lynn Minnotte. 2018. "University Service Work in STEM Departments: Gender, Perceived Injustice, and Consequences for Faculty." *Sociological Focus* 51, no. 3 (July): 217–37. https://doi.org/10.1080/00380237.2018 .1393607.

Peña, Lorgia García. 2022. *Community as Rebellion: A Syllabus for Surviving Academia as a Woman of Color.* New York: Haymarket Books.

Pérez, Emma. 1999. *The Decolonial Imaginary: Writing Chicanas into History.* Bloomington: Indiana University Press.

Phipps, Alison. 2020. *Me, Not You: The Trouble with Mainstream Feminism.* 1st ed. Manchester: Manchester University Press.

Pile, Steve. 2010. "Emotions and Affect in Recent Human Geography." *Transactions of the Institute of British Geographers* 35, no. 1 (January): 5–20. https://doi.org/10 .1111/j.1475-5661.2009.00368.x.

Popke, Jeff. 2006. "Geography and Ethics: Everyday Mediations through Care and Consumption." *Progress in Human Geography* 30, no. 4 (August): 504–12.

Porter, Stephen R. 2007. "A Closer Look at Faculty Service: What Affects Participation on Committees?" *Journal of Higher Education* 78, no. 5 (September/October): 523–41. https://doi.org/10.1353/jhe.2007.0027.

Posselt, Julie R. 2020. *Equity in Science: Representation, Culture, and the Dynamics of Change in Graduate Education.* Stanford, Calif.: Stanford University Press.

Prescod-Weinstein, Chanda. 2021. *The Disordered Cosmos: A Journey into Dark Matter, Spacetime, and Dreams Deferred.* New York: Bold Type.

Pryal, Katie Rose Guest. 2017. *Life of the Mind Interrupted: Essays on Mental Health and Disability in Higher Education.* Chapel Hill: Blue Crow.

Puāwai Collective. 2019. "Assembling Disruptive Practice in the Neoliberal University: An Ethics of Care." *Geografiska Annaler Series B, Human Geography* 101, no. 1 (January 2019): 33–43. https://doi.org/10.1080/04353684.2019.1568201.

Pulido, Laura. 2002. "Reflections on a White Discipline." *Professional Geographer* 54, no. 1 (February): 42–49. https://doi.org/10.1111/0033-0124.00313.

Puttick, Steve. 2023. "Geographical Education II: Anti-Racist, Decolonial Futures." *Progress in Human Geography* 47, no. 6 (December): 850–58. https://doi.org/10 .1177/03091325231202248.

Pyke, Karen. 2011. "Service and Gender Inequity among Faculty." *PS: Political Science & Politics* 44, no. 1 (January): 85–87. https://doi.org/10.1017/S1049096510001927.

———. 2014. "Faculty Gender Inequity and the 'Just Say No to Service' Fairytale." In *Disrupting the Culture of Silence,* edited by Kristine de Welde and Andi Stepnick, 1st ed., 83–95. New York: Routledge.

Queering Feminist Geography Collective, Eden Kinkaid, Cristina Diamant, Nick Koenig, Aila Bandagi Kandlakunta, Rowan Rush-Morgan, Kelsey Emard, LaToya E.

Eaves, Colleen C. Myles-Baltzly, Wiley Sharp, Julia Wagner, Markia Silverman-Rodríguez, Jennifer Langill, A. Marie Ranjbar, Thien-Kim Bui, Alicia Danze, Heather Davis, Ingrid Nelson, and Lindsay Naylor. forthcoming. "Queering Feminist Geography III: Calling All Allies and Accomplices." *Gender, Place & Culture.*

Queering Feminist Geography Collective, Eden Kinkaid, Wiley Sharp, Sarah Fogel, Aila Bandagi Kandlakunta, Gabi Kirk, Lindsay Naylor, LaToya E. Eaves, Nick Koenig, and Ingrid Nelson. forthcoming. "Queering Feminist Geography II: Trans-Exclusionary Feminisms." *Gender, Place & Culture.*

Quijano, Aníbal. 1999. "Colonialidad del Poder, Cultura y Conocimiento en América Latina." *Dispositio* 24, no. 51: 137–48.

———. 2008. "Coloniality of Power, Eurocentrism and Social Classification." In *Coloniality at Large: Latin America and the Postcolonial Debate*, edited by Mabel Moraña, Enrique D. Dussel, and Carlos A. Jáuregui, 181–224. Durham, N.C.: Duke University Press.

Radcliffe, Sarah A. 2017. "Decolonising Geographical Knowledges." *Transactions of the Institute of British Geographers* 42, no. 3 (September): 329–33. https://doi.org/10.1111/tran.12195.

———. 2022. *Decolonizing Geography: An Introduction.* New York: John Wiley & Sons.

Raghuram, Parvati. 2016. "Locating Care Ethics beyond the Global North." *ACME: An International Journal for Critical Geographies* 15, no. 3 (September): 511–33.

———. 2019. "Race and Feminist Care Ethics: Intersectionality as Method." *Gender, Place & Culture* 26, no. 5 (May): 613–37. https://doi.org/10.1080/0966369X.2019.1567471.

Raghuram, Parvati, Clare Madge, and Pat Noxolo. 2009. "Rethinking Responsibility and Care for a Postcolonial World." In "Postcoloniality, Responsibility and Care." Themed issue, *Geoforum* 40, no. 1 (January): 5–13. https://doi.org/10.1016/j.geoforum.2008.07.007.

Raphael, Marilyn. 2022. "Toward More Just Geographies." AAG *Newsletter*, December 14, 2022. President's Column. https://www.aag.org/toward-more-just-geographies/.

———. 2023. "Reflections on the State of Geography." AAG *Newsletter*, February 1, 2023. President's Column. https://www.aag.org/reflections-on-the-state-of-geography/.

Reimer, Christopher, Sarah-Louise Ruder, Michele Koppes, and Juanita Sundberg. 2023. "A Pedagogy of Unbecoming for Geoscience Otherwise." *Annals of the American Association of Geographers* 113, no. 7 (August): 1711–27. https://doi.org/10.1080/24694452.2022.2151406.

Reyes, Victoria. 2022. *Academic Outsider.* Stanford, Calif.: Stanford University Press.

Rhoads, Bruce L. 2004. "Whither Physical Geography?" *Annals of the Association of American Geographers* 94, no. 4 (December): 748–55.

———. 2022. "Whither Physical Geography Redux: Revisiting the Place of Physical Geography in the United States." *Environment and Planning F: Philosophy, Theory, Models, Methods and Practice* 1, no. 1 (March): 52–65. https://doi.org/10.1177/26349825221082171.

Ribarovska, Alana K., Mark R. Hutchinson, Quentin J. Pittman, Carmine Pariante, and Sarah J. Spencer. 2021. "Gender Inequality in Publishing during the COVID-19

Pandemic." *Brain, Behavior, and Immunity* 91 (January): 1–3. https://doi.org/10.1016/j
.bbi.2020.11.022.

Robinson, Fiona. 1999. *Globalizing Care: Ethics, Feminist Theory, and International
Relations.* Boulder, Colo.: Westview.

Rodó-Zárate, Maria. 2023. "Intersectionality and the Spatiality of Emotions in Feminist
Research." *Professional Geographer* 75, no. 4 (July): 676–81. https://doi.org/10.1080
/00330124.2022.2075406.

Roelvink, Gerda, Kevin St. Martin, and J. K. Gibson-Graham. 2015. *Making Other Worlds
Possible: Performing Diverse Economies.* Minneapolis: University of Minnesota Press.

Rose, Gillian. 1993. *Feminism and Geography: The Limits of Geographical Knowledge.*
Minneapolis: University of Minnesota Press.

———. 1995. "Tradition and Paternity: Same Difference?" *Transactions of the Institute of
British Geographers* 20, no. 4 (January): 414–16.

———. 1997. "Situating Knowledges: Positionality, Reflexivities and Other Tactics."
Progress in Human Geography 21, no. 3 (June): 305–20.

Rosenberg, Rae. 2023. "On Surviving a Cis Discipline." *Environment and Planning D:
Society and Space* 41, no. 4 (August): 600–605. https://doi.org/10.1177
/02637758231185228.

Rose-Redwood, Reuben, CindyAnn Rose-Redwood, Elia Apostolopoulou, Tyler
Blackman, Han Cheng, Anindita Datta, Sharon Dias, et al. 2024. "Re-imagining the
Futures of Geographical Thought and Praxis." *Dialogues in Human Geography* 14, no.
2 (July): 177–91. https://doi.org/10.1177/20438206241264631.

Roy, Ananya. 2016. "Divesting from Whiteness: The University in the Age of Trumpism."
Society & Space, November 28, 2016. https://societyandspace.org/2016/11/28
/divesting-from-whiteness-the-university-in-the-age-of-trumpism/.

Roy, Arundhati. 2020. "Arundhati Roy: 'The Pandemic Is a Portal.'" *Financial Times*,
April 3, 2020. Life & Arts. https://www.ft.com/content/10d8f5e8-74eb-11ea
-95fe-fcd274e920ca.

Salmond, Anne, Gary Brierley, and Dan Hikuroa. 2019. "Let the Rivers Speak: Thinking
about Waterways in Aotearoa New Zealand." *Policy Quarterly* 15, no. 3 (August):
45–54. https://doi.org/10.26686/pq.v15i3.5687.

Santos, Milton. (1978) 2021. *For a New Geography.* Translated and with an introduction
by Archie Davies. Minneapolis: University of Minnesota Press.

Schuller, Kyla. 2021. *The Trouble with White Women: A Counterhistory of Feminism.* New
York: Bold Type Books.

Schurr, Carolin, Martin Müller, and Nadja Imhof. 2020. "Who Makes Geographical
Knowledge? The Gender of Geography's Gatekeepers." *Professional Geographer* 72,
no. 3 (July): 317–31. https://doi.org/10.1080/00330124.2020.1744169.

Seemann, Jörn. 2024. "How Inclusive, Diverse, and Equitable Is Advanced Placement
Human Geography? A Comparison of Participation and Performance by Ethnicity
and Race." *Professional Geographer* 76, no. 1 (January): 97–107. https://doi.org/10
.1080/00330124.2023.2223259.

Seitz, David K., Daniel Cockayne, Ryan Z. Good, Kathryn L. Hannum, Adrianne C.
Kroepsch, Mark Alan Rhodes II, Jack Swab, and Nancy Worth. 2024. "Navigating
STEMification for Critical Geography Educators: Finding Leverage in Classroom and

Institutional Pedagogies." *Journal of Geography in Higher Education* 48, no. 3 (May): 501–17. https://doi.org/10.1080/03098265.2023.2261863.

Sharp, Emma L., Gary J. Brierley, Jennifer Salmond, and Nicolas Lewis. 2022. "Geoethical Futures: A Call for More-Than-Human Physical Geography." *Environment and Planning F: Philosophy, Theory, Models, Methods and Practice* 1, no. 1 (March): 66–81. https://doi.org/10.1177/26349825221082168.

Sharp, Joanne. 2009. "Geography and Gender: What Belongs to Feminist Geography? Emotion, Power and Change." *Progress in Human Geography* 33, no. 1 (February): 74–80. https://doi.org/10.1177/0309132508090440.

Sharp, Joanne P. 2013. "Geopolitics at the Margins? Reconsidering Genealogies of Critical Geopolitics." *Political Geography* 37 (November): 20–29. https://doi.org/10.1016/j.polgeo.2013.04.006.

Sharp, Joanne, and Lorraine Dowler. 2011. "Framing the Field." In *A Companion to Social Geography*, 146–60. New York: John Wiley & Sons. https://doi.org/10.1002/9781444395211.ch9.

Sheppard, Eric. 2022. "Geography and the Present Conjuncture." *Environment and Planning F: Philosophy, Theory, Models, Methods and Practice* 1, no. 1 (March): 14–25. https://doi.org/10.1177/26349825221082164.

Simpson, Leanne Betasamosake. 2014. "Land as Pedagogy: Nishnaabeg Intelligence and Rebellious Transformation." *Decolonization: Indigeneity, Education & Society* 3, no. 3 (November): 1–25.

Singh, Taveeshi, and Tayler J. Mathews. 2019. "Facilitating Queer of Color Feminist Co-mentorship: Reflections on an Online Archive of Scholar-Activism." *Gender, Place & Culture* 26, no. 12 (December): 1701–20. https://doi.org/10.1080/0966369X.2019.1636768.

Sismondo, Sergio. 2010. *An Introduction to Science and Technology Studies.* New York: John Wiley and Sons.

Skop, Emily, Martina Angela Caretta, Caroline Faria, and Jessie Smith. 2021. "An Ethos of Care." *Inside Higher Ed*, October 14, 2021. Opinion. https://www.insidehighered.com/advice/2021/10/15/pledge-foster-more-equitable-research-collaborations-opinion.

Slaughter, Sheila, and Gary Rhoades. 2000. "The Neo-liberal University." *New Labor Forum* 18, no. 6 (Spring–Summer 2000): 73–79.

Smith, Susan J. 2005. "States, Markets and an Ethic of Care," Political Geography Plenary Lecture. *Political Geography* 24, no. 1 (January): 1–20. https://doi.org/10.1016/j.polgeo.2004.10.006.

Smyth, Araby. 2023. "Proceeding through Colonial Past-Presents in Fieldwork: Methodological Lessons on Accountability, Refusal, and Autonomy." *Antipode* 55, no. 1 (January): 268–85. https://doi.org/10.1111/anti.12885.

Smyth, Araby, Jess Linz, and Lauren Hudson. 2020. "A Feminist Coven in the University." *Gender, Place & Culture* 27, no. 6 (June): 854–80. https://doi.org/10.1080/0966369X.2019.1681367.

Smythe, SA. 2022. "Can I Get a Witness? Black Feminism, Trans Embodiment, and Thriving Past the Fault Lines of Care." *Palimpsest: A Journal on Women, Gender, and the Black International* 11 (1): 85–107. https://doi.org/10.1353/pal.2022.0003.

Solem, Michael, and Ken Foote. 2022. "Valuing Mentoring." In *Bridging Worlds*—

Building Feminist Geographies: Essays in Honor of Jan Monk, edited by Anindita Datta, Janet Momsen, and Ann M. Oberhauser, 1st ed., 111–20. London: Routledge. https://doi.org/10.4324/9781032275611-13.

Solem, Michael, Brendan P. Vander Weil, and Yusik Choi. 2024. "Advanced Placement Human Geography: Program Access and Effectiveness by Grade Level, 2001–2020." *Professional Geographer* 76, no. 1 (January): 66–76. https://doi.org/10.1080/00330124.2023.2228870.

Sparke, Matthew, and Dimitar Anguelov. 2020. "Contextualising Coronavirus Geographically." *Transactions of the Institute of British Geographers* 45, no. 3 (September): 498–508. https://doi.org/10.1111/tran.12389.

Spivak, Gayatri Chakravorty. 1988. "Can the Subaltern Speak?" In *Marxism and the Interpretation of Culture*, edited by Lawrence Grossberg and Cary Nelson, 271–316. Chicago: University of Illinois Press.

Staeheli, Lynn A., and Michael Brown. 2003. "Where Has Welfare Gone? Introductory Remarks on the Geographies of Care and Welfare." *Environment and Planning A: Economy and Space* 35, no. 5 (May): 771–77.

Staeheli, Lynn A., and Patricia M. Martin. 2000. "Spaces for Feminism in Geography." *Annals of the American Academy of Political and Social Science* 571, no. 1 (September): 135–50. https://doi.org/10.1177/000271620057100110.

Staeheli, Lynn A., and Don Mitchell. 2005. "The Complex Politics of Relevance in Geography." *Annals of the Association of American Geographers* 95, no. 2 (June): 357–72. https://doi.org/10.1111/j.1467-8306.2005.00464.x.

Starks, Brian Chad. 2022. "Question Session K." Presentation at the American Geophysical Union (AGU) Second National Conference: Justice in Geoscience, Washington, D.C., August 16, 2022.

Storying Geographies Collective, Sarah Wright, Joseph Palis, Natalie Osborne, Fiona Miller, Uma Kothari, Karen Paiva Henrique, Phoebe Everingham, and Maria Borovnik. 2023. "Storying Pandemia Collectively: Sharing Plural Experiences of Interruption, Dislocation, Care, and Connection." *GeoHumanities* 9, no. 1 (January): 1–23. https://doi.org/10.1080/2373566X.2022.2147445.

TallBear, Kim. 2019. "Caretaking Relations, Not American Dreaming." *Kalfou* 6 (1) (April 2019): 24–41.

Taylor, Astra. 2020. "The End of the University." *New Republic*, September 8, 2020. https://newrepublic.com/article/159233/coronavirus-pandemic-collapse-college-universities.

Thayer, Nathan. 2023. "Care and Uncaring: White Supremacy, Diversity Work, and Antiracist Pedagogies." PhD diss., University of Delaware.

———. 2025. "Caring for White Supremacy: The Case of Kyle Rittenhouse." *Annals of the American Association of Geographers* 115 (2): 441–55. https://doi.org/10.1080/24694452.2024.2428307.

Thomas, David S. G. 2022. "Geography Needs Science, Science Needs Geography." *Environment and Planning F: Philosophy, Theory, Models, Methods and Practice* 1 (1) (March 1, 2022): 41–51. https://doi.org/10.1177/26349825221082161.

Thomas, K. Bailey. 2020. "Intersectionality and Epistemic Erasure: A Caution to Decolonial Feminism." *Hypatia* 35 (3) (June 2020): 509–23. https://doi.org/10.1017 /hyp.2020.22.

Thompson, Samantha. 2024. "Caring Housing Futures: A Radical Care Framework for Understanding Rent Control Politics in Seattle, USA." *Antipode* 56, no. 3 (September): 779–800. https://doi.org/10.1111/anti.12874.

Till, K. 2012. "Wounded Cities: Memory-Work and a Place-Based Ethics of Care." *Political Geography* 31, no. 1 (January): 3–14. https://doi.org/10.1016/j.polgeo.2011.10.008.

Titus, Steve, and Patrick Sanaghan. 2021. "The Case for Good Followership on Campuses." *Inside Higher Ed*, August 5, 2021. Opinion. https://www.insidehighered.com /advice/2021/08/05/importance-not-only-good-leaders-also-good-followers-opinion.

Tolia-Kelly, Divya, Diogo de Carvalho Cabral, Stephen Legg, Maria Land, and Nicola Thomas. 2020. "Historical Geographies of the 21st Century: Challenging Our Praxis." *Journal of Historical Geography* 69 (July): 1–4. https://doi.org/10.1016/j.jhg.2020 .08.002.

Tronto, Joan. 1993. *Moral Boundaries: A Political Argument for an Ethic of Care*. New York: Routledge.

Tucker, Faith, and John Horton. 2019. "'The Show Must Go On!' Fieldwork, Mental Health and Wellbeing in Geography, Earth and Environmental Sciences." *Area* 51 (1) (March 1, 2019): 84–93. https://doi.org/10.1111/area.12437.

Tuck, Eve, and K. Wayne Yang. 2012. "Decolonization Is Not a Metaphor." *Decolonization: Indigeneity, Education & Society* 1 (1) (August 9, 2012): 1–40.

Tuhiwai-Smith, Linda. 1999. *Decolonizing Methodologies: Research and Indigenous Peoples*. Dunedin, N.Z.: Zed Books; University of Otago Press; St. Martin's.

Ugarte, Rodrigo. 2020. "Research in Times of Crisis: Caring for Researchers' Mental Health in the Covid-19 Era." *Items* (blog). Social Science Research Council. December 12, 2020. https://items.ssrc.org/covid-19-and-the-social-sciences/social-research-and-insecurity/research-in-times-of-crisis-caring-for-researchers-mental -health-in-the-covid-19-era/.

University of Delaware Anti-Racism Initiative. 2021. "Living Land Acknowledgement." University of Delaware Anti-Racism Initiative. 2021. https://sites.udel.edu/anti-racism-initiative/committees/indigenous-programming/living-land -acknowledgement/.

U.S. National Science Foundation. 2023. "Summary of Changes to the PAPPG (NSF 23-1)." NSF: U.S. National Science Foundation. 2023. https://beta.nsf.gov/policies /pappg/23-1/summary-changes.

Valentine, Gill. 2007. "Theorizing and Researching Intersectionality: A Challenge for Feminist Geography." *Professional Geographer* 59, no. 1 (February): 10–21. https: //doi.org/10.1111/j.1467-9272.2007.00587.x.

Vallega, Alejandro A. 2020. "The Aisthetic-Cosmological Dimension of María Lugones's Decolonial Feminism." *Critical Philosophy of Race* 8, nos. 1–2 (January): 61–83. https://doi.org/10.5325/critphilrace.8.1-2.0061.

Velez, Emma D., and Nancy Tuana. 2020. "Toward Decolonial Feminisms: Tracing the Lineages of Decolonial Thinking through Latin American / Latinx Feminist Philosophy." *Hypatia* 35, no. 3 (July): 366–72. https://doi.org/10.1017/hyp.2020.26.

Vergès, Françoise. 2021. *A Decolonial Feminism*. Translated by Ashley J. Bohrer. London: Pluto.

Viglione, Giuliana. 2020. "Are Women Publishing Less during the Pandemic? Here's What the Data Say." *Nature* 581, no. 7809 (May): 365–66. https://doi.org/10.1038 /d41586-020-01294-9.

Wadman, Meredith. 2023. "Women Scientists at Famed Oceanography Institute Have Half the Lab Space of Men." *Science*, January 23, 2023. https://www.science.org/content/article/women-scientists-famed-oceanography-institute-have-half-lab -space-men.

Ware, Cellestine. 1970. *Woman Power: The Movement for Women's Liberation*. Cleveland, Ohio: Tower.

Watts, Vanessa. 2013. "Indigenous Place-Thought and Agency amongst Humans and Non Humans (First Woman and Sky Woman Go on a European World Tour!)." *Decolonization: Indigeneity, Education & Society* 2, no. 1 (May): 20–34.

Whyte, Kyle. 2017. "Indigenous Climate Change Studies: Indigenizing Futures, Decolonizing the Anthropocene." *English Language Notes* 55, no. 1 (Spring/Fall): 153–62.

Wilmer, Hailey, Alison M. Meadow, Amanda Bentley Brymer, Stephanie Russo Carroll, Daniel B. Ferguson, Ibrahim Garba, Christina Greene, Gigi Owen, and Dannele E. Peck. 2021. "Expanded Ethical Principles for Research Partnership and Transdisciplinary Natural Resource Management Science." *Environmental Management* 68, no. 4 (October): 453–67. https://doi.org/10.1007/s00267-021-01508-4.

Wilson, Chanelle, and Alison Cook-Sather. 2022. "Enacting Anti-Racist Pedagogy with Students as Co-teachers." In *Picture a Professor: Interrupting Biases about Faculty and Increasing Student Learning*, edited by Jessamyn Neuhaus, 1st ed., 201–18. Morgantown: West Virginia University Press.

Wölfle Hazard, Cleo. 2022. *Underflows: Queer Trans Ecologies and River Justice*. Seattle: University of Washington Press.

Wood, Lydia, Kate Swanson, and Donald E. Colley III. 2020. "Tenets for a Radical Care Ethics in Geography." *ACME: An International Journal for Critical Geographies* 19, no. 2 (September): 424–47.

Woolston, Chris. 2021. "Impact Factor Abandoned by Dutch University in Hiring and Promotion Decisions." *Nature*, June 25, 2021. Career News. https://doi.org/10.1038 /d41586-021-01759-5.

Wynter, Sylvia. 2003. "Unsettling the Coloniality of Being/Power/Truth/Freedom: Towards the Human, after Man, Its Overrepresentation—an Argument." *CR: The New Centennial Review* 3, no. 3 (Fall): 257–337.

Yusoff, Kathryn. 2018. *A Billion Black Anthropocenes or None*. Forerunners: Ideas First from the University of Minnesota Press. Minneapolis: University of Minnesota Press.

Zakaria, Rafia. 2021. *Against White Feminism: Notes on Disruption*. New York: Norton.

Zaragocin, Sofia. 2017. "Feminismo Decolonial y Buen Vivir." In *Feminismo y Buen Vivir: Utopías Decoloniales*, edited by Soledad Varea and Sofia Zaragocin, 17–25. Cuenca, Ecua.: PYDLOS Ediciones—Universidad de Cuenca. http://dspace.ucuenca.edu.ec /jspui/bitstream/123456789/27831/1/feminismo%20y%20buen%20vivir%20pdf %20PARA%20IMPRESION%20%281%29.pdf#page=19.

———. 2018. "Geopolitica del Utero, Hacia Una Geografia Feminista Decolonial." In *Cuerpos, Territorios y Feminismos*, edited by D. Cruz and M. Bayon, 83–100. Quito, Ecua.: AbyaYala y Estudios Ecologistas del Tercer Mundo.

———. 2019. "Gendered Geographies of Elimination: Decolonial Feminist Geographies in Latin American Settler Contexts." *Antipode* 51, no. 1 (January): 373–92. https://doi .org/10.1111/anti.12454.

———. 2021. "Challenging Anglocentric Feminist Geography from Latin American Feminist Debates on Territoriality." In *Feminist Geography Unbound: Discomfort, Bodies, and Prefigured Futures*, edited by Banu Gökariksel, Michael Hawkins, Christopher Neubert, and Sara Smith, 1st ed., 235–52. Morgantown: West Virginia University Press.

———. 2023. "Feminist Futurities: LatinX Geographies and Latin American Decolonial Feminist Geographies." *Gender, Place & Culture* 30, no. 4 (April): 588–95. https://doi .org/10.1080/0966369X.2021.1994930.

Zaragocin, Sofia, and Martina Angela Caretta. 2021. "Cuerpo-Territorio: A Decolonial Feminist Geographical Method for the Study of Embodiment." *Annals of the American Association of Geographers* 111, no. 5 (July): 1503–18. https://doi.org/10.1080 /24694452.2020.1812370.

Zebracki, Martin, and Aydan Greatrick. 2022. "Inclusive LGBTQ+ Fieldwork: Advancing Spaces of Belonging and Safety." *Area* 54, no. 4 (December): 551–57. https://doi .org/10.1111/area.12828.

Zembylas, Michalinos. 2015. "'Pedagogy of Discomfort' and Its Ethical Implications: The Tensions of Ethical Violence in Social Justice Education." *Ethics and Education* 10, no. 2 (May): 163–74.

INDEX

ableism, 113n8, 115
abusive behavior, 129, 133n10
accessibility, 112, 112n6,138
accommodations, 57n7
affirmative action, 124
American Association of Geographers: 41n7, 45; annual meeting, 46, 69, 95–97; Antiharassment Initiative of, 15n11, 46; JEDI, 121, 123n4; Mental Health Affinity Group of, 130n7; name change, 96; presidents of, 96, 123; specialty groups within, 29, 121
anastomosing, 42
Anthropocene, 64
anxiety: 1, 66; research and, 65–66. *See also* mental health
artificial intelligence, 87n2, 103, 112–13
assimilation, 3, 9, 10, 20, 43, 44, 105, 115, 121, 124, 133
autonomous academic, 5–6, 37, 45, 67, 85, 132

being in common, 61, 86
belonging, 29, 116, 119, 121, 122, 123, 132–33, 139, 142, 144
BIPOC: 3, 44, 85, 94, 123, 143; decolonial, 23; education, 44, 101, 115, 115n10, 132; feminism, 18, 20, 21; geography, 8, 9; service, 32, 33, 34, 35
Black Lives Matter, 121

campus, as hostile space, 125
capitalism, 18
care, 1, 13–15, 26, 108, 109, 114, 115, 116, 133; archipelago of, 135, 140; care work, 37–39, 70–71, 124; carelessness, 1, 2, 5, 62, 128;

caring for, caring with, caring about 36; false or mythical care, 14, 26, 39–40, 114; self-care, 5, 40. *See also* ethic of care
citation practices, 87, 89, 90–91, 94n3
citizens, students as, 103–4, 139
classes, large lecture, 113–14
climate change, 66, 96,
collective, xix, xx, 5, 12–15, 18, 30, 35, 36, 38, 41, 45, 87, 98, 116, 122, 137
community colleges, 52–53
conferences, 95–96
contingent faculty, 102
course evaluations, 116–17
COVID-19: 4–5, 4n2, 38, 38n4, 39, 45, 65, 69–77, 88, 89, 93, 96, 99, 105n1, 109–10, 121, 141, 144; post-pandemic, xix, 144, 145; teaching and, 4, 75

debt, 103, 126–27
decolonial: 22–24; feminism, 23–24, 49; feminist geographies, 29, 74; geography, 24–27, 140–41; intersectionality, 23n2, 24, 133
decolonial intersectional feminisms, 29, 30–31, 37, 38, 40, 42, 50, 52, 57, 106, 108, 115, 122, 124
decolonizing, 22, 56, 105–6, 112, 140–41
discomfort, 26, 29–30, 105, 114, 115–16, 140
diversity, 60, 102, 116, 122, 138
diversity, equity, inclusion programs, 121, 124, 124n5
dual careers, 125

early career scholars, 34, 38, 87
emotions, 65–66

185

GEOGRAPHIES OF JUSTICE AND SOCIAL TRANSFORMATION